TYING THE KNOT

Kate Gunn

About the Author

Kate Gunn is from the seaside town of Greystones, Wicklow. She had an idyllic childhood chasing waves and building friendships before moving to Maynooth University to study English and Sociology. She worked in the technology industry before leaving the corporate life in her 20s to go travelling solo. She met Kristian at the very first hostel she stayed in. Her 30s saw her return to Ireland, get married, settle down and have three wonderful children – Kaya, Marley and Baxter. Just weeks after turning 40 she and her family moved to Spain to try a new life, but returned separately the next year.

Kate has always used writing as a way to make sense of her life and work out the complexity of thoughts and emotions. She is a well-known blogger and features writer in both the UK and Irish parenting realms, and has written regularly for the *Irish Independent,* as well as featuring on Irish, UK and US parenting sites such as *eumom, everymum, netmums, Scarymommy* and many more. She has also appeared on BBC radio, RTE's *Today with Seán O'Rourke*, RTE's *Today with Maura and Daithi,* and numerous regional radio shows.

Kate is now back living in Greystones, surrounded by old school friends and close family.

Untying the Knot

How to Consciously Uncouple in the Real World

Kate Gunn

ORPEN PRESS

Published by
Orpen Press
Upper Floor, Unit K9
Greenogue Business Park
Rathcoole
Co. Dublin
Ireland

email: info@orpenpress.com
www.orpenpress.com

Paperback ISBN 978-1-78605-068-7
ePub ISBN 978-1-78605-069-4

Printed in Dublin by SPRINTprint Ltd

To my sisters, who picked me up and carried me.

Acknowledgements

First and foremost, I would like to thank Kristian. When I first came up with the concept of this book I thought it was something that could help others. In the early days of my own separation I had desperately trawled bookshops and websites searching for personal stories like mine – someone else who had felt this way before, someone who could show me that there was hope, that I wouldn't always feel this bad, and that, yes, everything would be ok.

I never found it.

Four years down the line I knew that if *I* could write that book it might ease someone else through the process. But to tell my story I had to tell Kristian's story too. I am so grateful to him that he was open-minded enough to listen to the idea, trusted me enough to do it, and even agreed to help. Thank you. I know it can't have been easy.

My children, Kaya, Marley and Baxter, never cease to surprise. When I spoke to them about writing the book they didn't react with horror, in fact they couldn't have been prouder. I hope they still feel that way when they are old enough to actually read it.

My partner, Aodhán, who let me share our tale of meeting and falling in love. How embarrassing. You cheered me on from the sidelines daily and I am so grateful to have you in my life.

To my sisters, Maria and Siobhán, my 'family over the wall', Liam and Christine, my brother Donal, my mum, Catherine, and my in-laws, Tony and Sandra – thank you all for your unending, judgement-free support. And to my dad, who, although not with us anymore, made me the person I am. 'Never judge another until you have walked in their shoes' he always told us – a tiny part of his compassion and understanding is instilled deep in my bones.

To my friends who poured cups of tea and glasses of red wine when I needed them.

To Anya, who was my lifeline in those first awful weeks – you'll never truly understand how much you helped me.

To my wonderful social media community – who rallied and supported at every turn, especially my Red ladies who are always a source of comfort, support and wise advice.

As everyone told me, it takes a whole team to write a book. I now know this to be true. Thanks firstly to Gerry, Ailbhe and Eileen at Orpen Press, who took a chance on me and calmly guided me through the process.

To Christine Doran, author and editor extraordinaire – the first reader of the book, whose feedback and insights were gold dust.

To all those who let me quote them, especially Regina and Eva, who gave me their personal tales to tell.

Massive thanks of course to all the experts in these pages, who gave their time and expertise freely, with the sole purpose of helping others who are hurting. Dr Sara O'Byrne, Deirdre Burke, Mary Miles, Shane Martin, Emma Kenny, Stella O'Malley, Erica McKinney and Peadar Maxwell – thank you. Also to Marie Murray, who so kindly offered to write the foreword. Thanks to Design for Writers for the wonderful cover and Paula Costa Photography for the profile photo.

Writing this book helped me realise just how many good people surround me. Family comes in all shapes and sizes these days. I'm so very proud to have mine.

'Rock bottom became the solid foundation on which I rebuilt my life.'

J.K. Rowling

It is through sharing stories that we share our humanity.

Contents

Foreword

'Nobody wants to go through separation and divorce, but unfortunately it happens' writes Kate Gunn in her beautifully told tale of exactly what happens, step by painful step, to everyone in the family when a marriage ends. For the end of a marriage is not a single event. It is a process. One of such painful, prolonged proportions that the story is rarely told in the startling way that this story is told. That makes this book special. It provides insight into the lived reality of the lives of everyone in a family when marriage breaks down.

Untying the Knot: How to Consciously Uncouple in the Real World is an exceptional book. It is written with forensic excavation of the personal trauma and turmoil for Kate, Kristian and their three children when Kate and Kristian realise that their marriage is over. The reader is brought up close and personal through the many complex, practical and psychological stages of the subsequent separation process that 'untying the knot' entails.

Knots are easily tied but untying them is a difficult task, because the tighter they are tied the more difficult they are to unpick. Couples who have lived together, loved each other, had children together and tied their lives tightly to each other do not part without pain. Untying tightly tied knots means that fingers are bruised, nails get torn, and the rope becomes broken, bloodied and frayed. In this unravelling, everybody gets hurt in their own individual way.

Kate guides us through each painful unpicking, even as she weaves a new future in which the family, though separated, are not driven apart. This is an amazing feat, not just because of how she does it but how successfully she achieves it. She acts decisively while threading gently; she takes advice while trusting her intuitive self; she adjusts to financial realities, as does Kristian; she does not deny the past but recognises and reinvents a future. Most of all, Kate does not shy away from, dismiss or deny the enormous impact of this on her children and that 'the damage being done may be irreparable'. She understands their questions, their confusion, their fears, their stress and that all that children want 'is a normal family'. This contrasts with the frequently favoured adult rationalisation that children are resilient, adaptable, unaware or readily readjust to parental divorce. Neither Kate nor Kristian pretends this to themselves, or to each other. Kate's book is a model of damage limitation, of the importance of communication, cooperation and compromise, when 'consciously' uncoupling in the real world.

There are many examples of the courageous way in which Kate acknowledges, listens to, sits with and absorbs her children's pain. She feels their visceral distress. In a touching description her daughter says 'Mummy I have a pain in my heart' and Kate answers 'oh darling. I know that you do. We all do.' Also recognised is the need for community support, 'that parents can't be all things to their children, that sometimes they will need another pair of hands to guide them, a different shoulder to cry on, and that having a grandmother, aunt, teacher or others to turn to when they feel the need' can make all the difference.

Uncoupling always involves money 'rearing its ugly head' with that dreadful dilemma between income lost minding children and income gained at the expense of time with them. As Kate says, 'I am doing all I can and he is giving all he can', and when Kate and Kristian arrive at a financial arrangement with which neither of them was totally happy they knew it must be fair enough! What a clever insight.

But apart from the pragmatics of separation there is the 'shame' of separation; the secret inner psychological world, of loneliness, loss and 'guilt in permanent residence' as well as the alarming loss of identity that occurs. Kate describes it as 'horrendous, like someone has taken a photo of me and ripped it to pieces in front of my face' so that as she lies scattered at her feet she sees the need to put herself 'together again, the same but different'. For Kate and Kristian there are moments of helplessness, hopelessness, depression, disassociation. With the dismantling of identity, there is a task to recoup, recover, accept and re-invent the self in a new way.

Kate describes the classic post-separation emotions, the search for stories like her story, for someone who felt as she was feeling, for someone who could show her hope and most importantly someone to reassure her that everything would be okay. Not finding that reassurance, she decided to be *that* person for others and to write her story to reassure other people. Because as she floundered she also discovered that being vulnerable invites other people who are unhappy to drop their masks, their pretence of perfection and to confide if they were trapped in unhappy marriages that they needed to end. This book is written for them too.

Books about marriage breakdown and divorce litter the self-help shelves of shops and online resources. There are personal narratives and professional analyses; tips on how to know if it's over; advice on healing the broken heart. There are instructions on how to uncouple and rebuild life; how to survive and thrive in a post-divorce world and how to get through this adjustment that merits the second highest place on the famous Holmes–Rahe inventory of stressful life events.

But Kate Gunn's book is different because it is crucially multiperspectival. It tells her story. It includes Kristian's most important commentary which provides insight into the less frequently heard male reflections from the sidelines, so that we listen to him, hear him and admire him too. And then Kate has recruited a wonderful multidisciplinary team of professionals, each expert in their understanding of the different dimensions of divorce to guide the reader from Kate's personal account to the professional perspective and back again. Within Kate's book lies another, of practical information and advice from some of the finest experts in psychology, child psychotherapy, finance, legal matters, mediation, positive psychology and mental health. Books within a book, this is a book that contains all that one needs to navigate the difficult territory of broken marriage and personal repair.

What books have you ever read in which a couple whose marriage has ended both speak without anger or rancour to share their experience in amicable honesty with mutual care? What books give you what this book gives you: the gift of the personal to guide the general reader seeking help for self or others in a sad situation? What books add direct professional advice? Where has such information ever been collated in one publication?

Yet at the end of the book there are some observations that also must be made. Perhaps 'uncoupling' is too bland a word, too clean a cut, too neat a wound to describe the million messy emotions and intricate negotiations that separation and divorce entail? And if Kate and Kristian and their children suffered considerably, despite the incredible practical, emotional and active support of family and friends, how doubly traumatic and seemingly undoable must it be for those people who separate who do not have the many 'gifts' and multiple supports that Kate and Kristian received. Anyone who buys this book, who knows anyone going through the breakdown process, will now be on double alert for the reality of the danger and distress that divorce entails.

Kate and Kristian knew that whatever messages their marriage and its end gave their children, that the overriding message children need is that of united parental love. And so this foreword ends with extracts from Kate and Kristian's letters to their children. Kate writes 'we will both continue to smother you with buckets and spades full of love for evermore, kissing the cuts on your heart until they heal.' Kristian tells his children 'I hope you feel swathed in the love I have for you constantly. I love all three of you equally and without condition. I will be here for you until my final breath.'

It is love that continues to bind this family even while they live graciously apart. No ruptures of living conditions, reorganisation, reconstitution or recoupling with others can ever disrupt this. It is the simple, singular most significant psychological message that parents can give children during separation and divorce: that their love for them does not end.

Dr Marie Murray,
Consultant Clinical Psychologist and Systemic Family Therapist

Introduction

There was no big moment. No juicy story or unforgivable deception. There was no difference of opinion that couldn't be resolved, or future dreams that we just couldn't get past. It was just a long, slow, sad falling out of love with each other. A familiar tale. But one that we didn't want to tell each other. Or even admit to ourselves.

We had moved abroad to see if sunshine could thaw the ice, but when we discovered that our problems had hitched a ride too we finally admitted defeat. It was a painful relief. We hugged and cried together, and wailed into the wilderness alone.

And then we came home, although we didn't have one anymore. First me and the children, and then their dad. Our families rallied around us, their own loss and feelings sidelined for ours.

There were bad weeks and good weeks. There was licking of wounds and drowning of sorrows. There were mistakes and successes. And slowly, slowly, we came through it. Not sworn enemies fighting it out in court, but co-parents and friends, gently muddling through the big decisions as well as the little ones.

Our story of the breakdown of a marriage is not unique. Naturally there are some aspects that only we two know and did and lived – but in essence it is a timeless tale. Just not the fairytale kind unfortunately. The Beginning saw us fall in love; the Middle was filled with chapters full of travel, children, hopes and dreams; but at the End the happy had disappeared, and we were left with a potential ever after that neither of us wanted.

But this isn't about the breaking up. This is about the moving on. Two adults, three kids, twelve years, five sets of needs and emotions, one-and-a-half salaries, three homes, countless bills – and a black dog.

1

Telling the Children

MY STORY

Conversations with My Daughter

We sit on the cold brown tiles of the very top stair of our Spanish villa, looking down into the darkness. It is two days after Christmas and there is something that needs to be said. I am afraid of what my daughter, Kaya, is learning about relationships. Frightened that one day she'll choose this for herself.

Yesterday I had spent all of the morning and most of the afternoon lying in bed in my in-laws' house, struck with a hellish hangover. The relief of actually making it to Christmas Day as an intact, though desperately frayed, family had seen me drink far too much cheap Spanish cava, and now I was paying the price.

Each movement of my body sent me stumbling to the toilet to heave bitter nothing from the pit of my stomach. I would then collapse back into bed, cold and sweating, until the next wave of nausea rose up.

By lunchtime Kristian had had enough. 'Get up, we need to go now', he said, his big shadow standing in the doorway.

There was no point in arguing, and yet the goal he had set me seemed like an impossible task. I levelled my breathing and rolled out of the bed, listening to the rising stress through the ceiling above me as he angrily gathered both our belongings and our children. I hobbled in my pyjamas to the car, smiling weakly at his worried parents as I left. Sorry. Sorry. Sorry.

The trip was only twenty minutes but felt interminable. So many bumps and holes and sharp inclines and swooping dips.

I held a plastic bag in front of my face and vomited the yellow bile from the very pit of me. Hunched forward in the passenger seat, praying for an end – an end to the sickness, an end to the journey, an end to all this tension and unhappiness.

'Are you ok Mummy?' a small, scared voice asked from the back of the car.

So here we were. Me explaining to my daughter that no, I wasn't ok.

But of course she knew that already. None of this was ok. None of us were ok. This was not just about one hangover; this was about our whole lives. We were living in a toxic waste ground which was slowly killing us all. Killing the light. But now a switch had been turned on, and the bulb shone with mega kilowatt force – this couldn't go on or the damage would be irreparable. We had to get out. All of us.

The Talk

My broken heart is pounding in my chest and a heavy stone sits in the pit of my stomach. Dread and guilt claw at my throat. It's still December. Just three days after Christmas, and the sun is shining.

We've been living in Spain for five months now. Five months of hard emotion that there is no more running away from. Five months of crushed hopes and heavy pain.

We gather the children around the huge kitchen table and tell them we need to talk to them about something. They are nine, seven and five, and their wide innocent eyes look at us with trust and curiosity. My own fill with tears that I fight back with matter-of-factness. I stare at the breadcrumbs on the rustic wood table. Crumbs left over from lunchtime sandwiches. The last meal we would eat together before their world is shattered into pieces. Breadcrumbs. I need to throw down breadcrumbs and follow them out of this dark forest.

'We have something to talk to you about … something important.'

I take a deep breath and look to Kristian for support, but his head is bowed. He's not really there. He's in protection mode. Eyes cast to the floor, no breadcrumbs there.

I explain that we are going home, back to Ireland. Just not together. It feels almost deceitful saying it now, but I hoped that it would cushion the blow. The emotions of their parents' break-up tempered by the joy of being homeward bound. We tell them how much we love them, and how that will never change. We explain that we will always be their mum and dad, and that they will still see both of us all the time.

I'm not sure that I can take the pain if they start raging and crying; perhaps that's why I skim over the details. In one way I am lucky – I have a way to sell it to them. Living abroad hasn't worked out for any of us. Not only has the marriage taken a fatal blow, so have the children's happiness and confidence. While they love the big house and swimming pool that the move has afforded us, they hate school and miss their old friends, family and our pretty hometown of Greystones on the Irish east coast. They are understandably thrilled at the prospect of returning to Ireland, so we focus on that – clinging to it desperately and squeezing it for all it is worth. Our conversation is built around the return, not the break-up. We are cowards with our children's best interests at heart.

We try to respond to their questions as honestly as we can, but in truth neither of us has any of the answers. Where will we live? When are we leaving? When will Dad come back? Will we be going back to our old school? To our old classes?

Are you getting a divorce?

It is asked in a tiny, terrified voice, full of disbelief and fear. I am caught off guard, and don't know what to say. A single second ticks past slowly. I silently pray that Kristian won't lose his cool, his anger and hurt answering the question that none of us want to think about. I am forever grateful that he manages to stay silent.

'No. We're just spending some time apart from each other.' I promise vaguely. 'We're still one family'.

Their varied understanding of what is happening is spread across their beautiful faces: the five-year-old happy to be going home and wondering if he can go out and play now; the seven-year-old seemingly accepting, but bigger thoughts fleeting across his eyes like dark clouds through deep skies; the nine-year-old scared and relieved and full of grief.

After The Talk we disperse into various parts of the villa, digesting what has just happened in completely different ways.

It is done. Whatever happens now we can't go back on it. We have just irrevocably shifted the entire lives of our three young children, and I know that it can't be for nothing.

Supersaturated

That night I lie awake in my queen-sized bed, all three children curled up into me like question marks asking unanswered and unending questions. What is happening? Why don't you love each other? Do you still love me? Where will Daddy live? Why does it hurt so much?

I stare into the darkness, wide awake and praying for sleep. My arms surround them but will never be wide enough to hold all of their pain. I think of Kristian, alone in a different bed in another room of the house. No children's quiet breathing and peaceful faces to comfort him. He is fighting his own demons in silence and solitude. My heart sinks to unknown depths and I push him away, shielding myself from more suffering with their small warm bodies.

Over the following days there are angry outbursts from some, bitter tears from others. Five sets of huge emotions bursting from our bodies and escaping into the Spanish hills.

Soon I begin clearing out their bedrooms in preparation of the move back home. Dust and toys are swept out from cold tiles under cosy beds. I cry as I pick up a small teddy bear at my feet. It is one that we had brought with us from Ireland, one of the prized possessions we had squeezed into the boot of our car – something to make them feel connected with home when we moved over. The move they hadn't wanted to make. The move that was a gamble that hadn't paid off.

The words 'What have we done to them?' go round and round in my head as I hold the teddy, both of us staring with glassy eyes at the pile of dirt that represents how I feel about myself at this moment.

A sound disturbs me. Kristian stands quietly at the door, watching. Looking to comfort and be comforted. Sadness meets in our gaze. We hug each other and weep together.

Days merge into one another, hazy now. I am simply focused on getting from one crushing morning to the well-earned relief of sleep each night. I have no idea whether I am there for our children as they need me to be. Each day is like wading through dreamlike water, an unreal reality.

'I have to go', I burst out one afternoon. 'I have to get out'.

I push through the front door not knowing where I am going, just with an irresistible urge to leave. All I know is that if I stay still any longer I will simply combust – too much emotion for one body to bear. I get in the car and drive wildly down the hillside towards the glittering sea on the horizon. Tears stream down my face as I scream into the windscreen. No! No! No! No! No! Oh God. No. Please, No. I am railing at the pain. Pushing it away. Ordering it to leave. I don't know how long I am gone for or where I go. I come back hours later. Blessedly exhausted and empty.

Four years later, I will find a scrap of paper from those first days. A friend had told me it was useful to write down all the emotions that I felt, to try to make sense of everything. The feelings I had written down were: confusion, loneliness, isolation, fear, sadness, despondent, hopeless, guilty, despair, I can't stop crying. And beside them was another list. The practicalities of what needed to be done now: call school, cancel tenancy, packing, shipping, car, uniforms. The vast chasm between the two seemingly unbridgeable.

The children are dealing with their new reality as best they can. I listen to their fears, but I don't encourage them to open up about them. Not yet. My own pain is so great that I don't think I can take on any more. I build a protective shield around myself so that I don't absorb more feelings than I have in me already. I am there for the children but only in the capacity that I can manage. I am there physically. I am there to hug and talk and listen and support. But I'm not fully present emotionally. I cannot take on their pain. I cannot own it and understand it and imagine how they feel. I am supersaturated in emotion already. Nothing else will fit inside me. I do as much as I can and that is all I can do.

Kristian is of course dealing with his own anguish. In those early weeks we are like two ghosts moving past and through each other. Both in pain, coping however we can. Staying alive. It's enough to know that we are both suffering. We both love our children more than anything else in life. And we both do as much as we are able with what we have in us.

Throwing Down Anchors

In those first few days, after The Talk, I speak only to my sisters. Our families know what is happening, but no one else. I can't bear even the thought of speaking to my mother. It's not that she won't be supportive. I just can't. My older sister, Siobhán, sends a constant stream of messages, knowing exactly what to say at precisely the right time. At the same time she listens, consoles and supports Kristian. Not judging, not blaming, just there for both of us.

My younger sister, Maria, kicks into practical action, booking a flight over to help me with the children when the time comes to return.

Somehow a date is fixed to go home. The arranging and paying of flights completed by someone, though I can't say who. Was it me? The grief is such that decision and action is almost impossible. For once in my life I surrender and let others carry me, while I try to do the same for the children.

My family has also begun the motions of finding us a home to return to – a difficult task in the current climate; rental houses are almost non-existent in Greystones. But luck seems to be on my side. The first estate agent they check with has a new listing on the market. When they ask for the details they reel with disbelief. The house in question backs on to my brother's home. They even share the same back wall. It appears that Fate is shouting loud and proud at us across the waters: 'It will be ok.'

My sisters and mother visit the house and take pictures, delightedly sending me the photos. We have a home.

But the pictures leave me dead inside. This was not our home. I have not chosen this house. My whole being is immediately flooded with guilt. How could I be so ungrateful? I know that I am unbelievably lucky to have my family helping me, and I know that this is a perfectly good house to move into. They have even paid the deposit and first month's rent for me.

I know I am lucky.

I just don't feel lucky.

But whatever I feel inside I must push down for now. I need to put my game face on and convince the children that everything is ok. Better than ok. It is going to be great. I show them the photos and tell them they can pick their own rooms. I tell them that their cousins will be at the end of the garden, and that we will be just up the road from their Granny and Maria. Although we don't yet know for sure what Kristian will be doing, or whether he will even be coming back to Ireland to live, we at least know where *we* will be. It is something to anchor us when we all feel adrift in the stormy seas of the unknown. So, we focus on that and begin to see what other anchors we can put down. What else will pull us toward a safe and secure harbour?

The school is next on the list. The children needed to know if they will be returning to their old school, and if so will they still be in their old classes with their old friends. In their world this is everything, so I force myself to write to the principal and explain the situation. When we had left Ireland I had told her that we were moving with Kristian's work. We weren't sure for how long, we weren't even sure if it was the right thing to do. 'Keep the family together' were her words that ring in my ears now, as I explain that in fact it hadn't worked out and we needed to come back. Not together after all.

Thankfully the school is amazing – allaying fears and welcoming the children back to their previous places. Another big anchor to keep us in place

I focus on all the positives with the children. Look at our new house! Are you looking forward to having your cousins as neighbours?! You're going back to your old school! Your friends can't wait to see you! Maria is coming to visit us!

Perhaps I try too hard.

The guilt is still crippling me.

Telling Others

I still haven't spoken to my mother. My sisters are passing on messages but I'm not ready. Even though I know she won't judge, and in fact may think it is the right thing for us all, I can't bring myself to hear her voice.

I begin to tell friends by private message and text. Close friends first. Some school mums next. My oldest friends and I have a Facebook group and I tentatively tell them what is happening. Supportive messages flood back to me and make my eyes fill with tears.

'We'll look after you', they say, and I want to believe it. One of them posts a link to Gloria Gaynor's 'I Will Survive'. I shut the lid of my laptop immediately. Too soon. I am still deep in my hole of suffering. Gentle, understanding messages are all I can handle from the outside world. I am not ready for jokes or girl power chattering. I shift back into my cave.

I reach out to people I barely know to help pull me through instead. I need someone who has been here before. Felt this before. Can tell me that it gets better. I write to Anya, an online friend I have met only once, very briefly, several years previously. She becomes my lifeline. 'You did as much as you could for as long as you could', she writes when the guilt becomes too much. I hold on to that line for dear life, using it as my mantra for months and even years to come.

'Be sure Kate. You need to be able to live with this decision for the rest of your life. Your children will challenge you on it.'

They are hard truths, but I dig deep and make peace with knowing that not just I, but 'We' are sure. It has taken a lot of time to get to this point, and now we must push through. Through the river of torment and on to the bank at the other side, where hopefully one day the sun will shine again.

'It's a process', Anya says.

'How long will it hurt this bad for?' I ask. An impossible question.

'Sometimes it gets worse before it gets better. I'm so sorry but it's best that you know.'

My stomach knots up in pain as I read the words, but I feel something deep inside me shift. An added strength makes itself known. There if I needed it. Way down deep. Deeper than I could have known was in me. There is some solace knowing that I have coped with everything so far, and if I can cope with all that perhaps I can cope with more after all. I nurse her words as I lie in bed at night, nose pressed close against blond, childhood locks.

Alice writes a blog. I have never met Alice, but she becomes a hugely important presence in my life. She is much younger than me and she writes openly about her divorce. I devour the details of her story. Sitting down for dinner with her two small children – the lone adult at the table. Conversation nul. The small moments of normal family life that she misses. I read on and on, searching every post, looking for answers, looking for guidance, but most of all looking for someone who had come through the other side, someone who could tell me 'It will be ok.'

It will be ok.

I haven't really had time to make proper friends in Spain. Even the thought of it has been exhausting. Starting from scratch all over again when I already have a ready-made community back in Ireland has seemed almost futile. Perhaps I knew all along that I wouldn't be here for long.

But I go for coffee with one of the mothers I met when our daughters had struck up a friendship. She is an expat too. English. I feel I owe her an explanation. Why we are now leaving and why our daughters will no longer be best friends.

'I knew something was wrong. There was just something about you. Something in your eyes ...', she says to me when I explain.

It turns out that complete strangers could see the unhappiness, even before I could look in the mirror and see it for myself.

LOOKING BACK

Guilt with a capital G.

No parent plans for this conversation to happen. Like nobody goes into a marriage thinking that one day they would be working out who takes the dog and how many of the 963 CDs are actually yours.

But if you are separating then it's going to happen sooner or later. We knew that the children needed to be told in an age-appropriate way, preferably with both of us there together, showing a united front. We knew there would be tears and fears and disbelief and blame. That there would be emotions thrown at us and others hidden – pushed down into the depths of bellies that would become sick if we didn't handle them carefully.

One of the biggest things that children need in life is security, and when that security is threatened the fear is immense. We tried to give the children as much information as we could in terms of how the changes would affect them. Where will they live? Where will Dad live? Where will they go to school? When will they see Dad? But we didn't know the answers to many of the questions during that initial conversation.

It can be incredibly hard to care for another's emotions at a time when your own are raw and hurting. Sometimes

I could only offer a fraction of what I knew the children needed me to. These were the times I tried to lean on others. I had to just trust that the crippling pain wouldn't last forever. I gave what I could and called on those around me to provide the rest. There were times when Kristian had more leftover in him to give than I did, and times when I shouldered the burden. Both of us were suffering and what we had left over on any given day wasn't always equal. We both gave as much as we could when we could.

But kids are amazing. Their resilience never ceases to surprise. Among the heartbreak and uncertainty of those early days our children still laughed, fought, talked and hugged. And although we boarded a plane a few weeks later without their dad, they knew that we were still a unit. Still family. It would be weeks until they saw him again, but we spoke about our feelings every day and kept in constant contact – checking in with him whenever they, or he, felt the need. Communication lines always open.

And that was one of the keys to success. Listen, talk, communicate. A never-ending loop of checking in. Not just 'how are you feeling?' but 'how are you feeling *today*?'

Although I can't say we did a perfect job on this. While I thought we had been having constant check-ins of everyone's emotional needs it's hard to know how much is understood at each point. Information that one child grasps can be completely overlooked by another. So it was that two years after returning home an unexpected conversation occurred. My youngest and I were in the bathroom together. He was having a bath and I was taking the opportunity of having him captive to have a little one-to-one time. I told him, as I had so many other times, how much I loved him, and how much Daddy loved him, and that even though we weren't together anymore that would never change.

His head shot around.

'You and Daddy aren't together anymore?!' he asked incredulously.

We sat looking at each other in stunned silence. He not understanding how this unexpected turn of events had occurred. And me unable to grasp how he had missed it.

'Well of course we're not', I spluttered. 'Daddy has a separate house and doesn't live with us anymore. What did you think?'

'I don't know', he replied, head down, a brand-new reality setting in.

I wondered then whether this meant we had done this whole separation business really well (there clearly hadn't been lots of fighting and bad mouthing about each other), or really, really badly (how had we missed that he hadn't grasped the concept of us being separated?). I'm still not sure. But it was a huge lesson in how age affects understanding and how as our children grow understanding develops, so the same conversations need to happen again and again on different levels. Probably forevermore.

Another lesson I learned is how important it is to listen to their needs, even when they're not saying anything out loud. When they were upset, but couldn't or wouldn't identify why, I would start asking some gently probing questions. 'Do you miss your dad being here at night times?' 'Did someone say something to you in school?' 'Have you got a pain in your heart?' We made a point on making bedtime earlier and I would lie down with them. It's often at the end of the day, when the hustle and bustle of the day is done that the stillness and darkness allows their troubles to surface. I made quiet time a necessity and gave them opportunities to open up.

If they needed their dad to say goodnight to them then we would see if we could arrange for him to call. If they were upset that everyone in school had 'normal' families, then we would make a hot chocolate date to talk it through. When they were just feeling really sad, I should have simply listened, acknowledged and loved them. I think I tried too hard to spin their troubles round. Not every cloud has to have a silver lining; sometimes a cloud is just a cloud and you just have to say 'Hey Cloud, I see you' before it can pass on by.

In those early days there were moments when hurt and anger were thrown like daggers. There were days that I screamed into a pillow and bit my knuckles till they bled. But I did everything in my power to keep my frustrations and pain to myself, not to transfer any of it onto them. I hope I was successful, but I can't be sure.

Throughout the early days I was dealing with four sets of huge emotions – my own, and those of my three children. But I knew that Kristian was also dealing with his own pain, guilt and fear, so while I had to care for my own well-being, and of course the children's, it helped to try to understand his perspective too. Nobody wants to go through separation and divorce, but unfortunately it happens. Working together means a whole lot less pain and fewer long-term issues for everyone. Watching the hurt and confusion in my children's eyes when I was partly to blame was one of the hardest things of all. Seeing them try to work out what was happening crushed me. But it got better as time passed. I got stronger. They adjusted. That raw pain passed, and before I knew it I had a new normal.

I'm not saying that it was easy. It absolutely was not, and we made plenty of mistakes along the way. But our end goal was to cause our children as little upset and emotional strain as possible – that is our continued common goal, so we work towards it together.

KRISTIAN'S WORLD

It's funny, I didn't actually realise our marriage was officially over. It took a while for it to become clear. My depression had caused a rather prolonged period of emotional turmoil with associated outbursts, and it was following one of these that Katie proclaimed 'I can't do this anymore. I'm going home.' There was no 'I'm leaving you' nor 'I want a divorce', Katie just wanted to leave Spain and so did the kids. My mind clouded the whole separation issue with the decision to leave the country. All of us were unhappy. The children's school experience was really upsetting and the cause of a whole rollercoaster of emotions for us all. I can't recall specifically when it became clear that this was actually a break-up, it was gradual I guess. Deep down, I realised, I knew I wanted a separation too.

Our rented house had a two-month notice period and as Katie was pretty much off home with the kids on the next possible flight, I had to remain in Spain until the notice period was up. I couldn't afford to lose the deposit. I would need it for wherever I was going to live next. Do I stay in Spain? My folks are down the road, but I don't know anyone else. Do I move back to the UK? It's where my friends are, my support structure. I'd never planned on living in Ireland forever and I guess that's why I had pushed so hard for our foreign 'adventure' in the first place. My friends are all spread out across the southeast of England now though or living abroad, with families of their own. It's not like I'd see them every day. Any notion of a rekindled student lifestyle was quickly dispelled. More to the point, how on earth would I cope with seeing my children maybe only once or twice a month? How would they cope without having me around? My depressed self told me everyone else would be better off without my negative influence in their lives.

A month or so before the big split, a (useless) psycho-therapist had referred me to a local psychiatrist who had the power to prescribe medication as mine was clearly not working. He prescribed something new alright. He warned me that this medication could make me worse before it makes me better and told me to ride it through. As Katie will attest, it was the blackest period of my life. I was often in the throes of utter despair, walking around on my own with no specific destination in mind and feeling suicidal. I was completely unable to cope with being inside my own head. I guess I felt hard done by that she chose to leave me at such a time, but she had the children's best interests at hearts, she always does.

My behaviour and emotions were too erratic for me to be depended on as a positive influence in their lives.

EXPERT ADVICE

...ON TELLING THE CHILDREN

Dr Sara O'Byrne is a senior clinical psychologist with over fifteen years' experience working with children and their families.

Telling your children about the separation can be one of the most stressful aspects of the process. You might find yourself worrying about the impact on the children and the act of telling might somehow make the process more real. With good preparation and communication and by considering what your children need in this process, you will find ways of adapting to this 'new normal'.

How you talk about separation will depend on the age of the child. Younger children will sometimes need more concrete information such as where everyone is going to be living whilst older children might need information that lets them know that their relationship with each parent will be ongoing. Regardless of the age of the child, here are some important points to bear in mind:

Planning

- Try to have the conversation in familiar surroundings, so that the child is comfortable.
- Where possible, have both parents present for the conversation so that your children will see that you are still working as a team and to avoid blaming one parent. Try to do some preparation together in advance so that you are both maintaining the same script.

- Do not expect children to take in all the information in one conversation; you will likely need to return to it several times to make sure that they have the right information.

Delivering the Message

- Keep the message simple and focus on the basic facts.
- Give your children a script that lets them know what has happened. For instance, you might say something like, 'Mummy and Daddy have made some mistakes and have been fighting a lot so we have decided that it is better that we live in separate houses. We think this will help us to get along better.' Let your child know something about where they will be living. For example, 'You will live in this house with Mummy during the week when you are in school and you'll spend weekends in Daddy's house.' What is important is to briefly acknowledge past mistakes and focus on future changes and similarities.
- It is amazing how many children (particularly younger ones) hold themselves responsible for the break-up. So give them the clear message that they are not at fault and there was nothing they did to cause this outcome.
- It can also be helpful for your children to hear that other children in these situations experience a range of emotions (and list some examples) and that you will be there for them to hear about some of their experiences.
- Protect your children from information and feelings that might be overwhelming for them, for instance information about affairs. When children are involved in these discussions, we are potentially affecting their relationships with one or other parent.

Return to the Conversation Again

- Set aside one-to-one time with your child in the weeks and months ahead. This time does not necessarily have to be used to talk about feelings, but can be a good opportunity for the child to do so if the need is there. Use open-ended questions.
- Don't feel like you have to offer solutions or problem-solve with your child. Simply listening and 'being with' them in these difficult emotions is enough.
- Some children might need help with emotional vocabulary so you might need to describe what you see (for instance, 'You seem worried about what your friends might think').
- Your child might experience a range of emotions, ranging from guilt, sadness and loneliness to anger and frustration. Your child's understanding of these emotions might also vary. Some children will present with regression in their behaviours (such as toileting accidents or sleep disturbances), and be more inclined to express needs indirectly. Your child might also try to be a mini-adult and act as a support to you.
- Avoid critical talk about your ex-partner and don't use your child as a go-between. Avoid exposing your child to conflict between each of you.
- Consider your own self-care. Your child might be raising difficult issues with you. This is not the time to be trying to manage alone. Seek support from family, friends and a professional if needed. Be patient with yourself and your child. Loss and hurt take time to heal and this might be a gradual process for you all.

Importance of Stability

Adjusting to multiple changes at once can be very stressful for children. Adaptation to parental separation is enough for now. Try to avoid other changes (such as starting a new activity) and maintain routines as much as possible. Routine also means consistency in boundaries and limits – your temptation might be to spoil your child but hold back; what they need is a balance of warmth and boundaries.

Finally, make communication regarding separation and divorce as normative as possible. Children benefit both from having a narrative that explains a particular event and from opportunities to return to the topic with further questions over time.

Some Books to Help Children

- *I Don't Want to Talk about It* by Jeanie Franz Ransom
- *Living with Mum and Living with Dad* by Melanie Walsh
- *Two Homes* by Claire Masurel
- *When Mom and Dad Separate: Children Can Learn to Cope with Grief from Divorce* by Marge Heegaard

2

The Family Home

MY STORY

'Maria!' The children's faces light up with a delight that I haven't seen in weeks. Their favourite aunty coming through the door. Our knight in shining armour. Our guardian angel. Our rock. They fall on her and cling around her neck as if she is a life buoy. She is. She is here to save us all from drowning in our tears and despair.

The Icing on the Cake

It is a bittersweet reunion. She has come to help us bag up all the belongings that we had packed with such hope and trepidation only months before. Our car had been our carriage when we came to Spain, and we had packed it floor to ceiling with our 'must haves'. Now we must pack up not just all of that, but everything that we have accumulated in the past five months of trying to build a life in Spain. There is no car returning. Just a broken woman, her hurting children and their smiling rock taking a final flight home. Hard decisions will have to be made on everything from T-shirts permeated with memories, to toys, towels, books and beloved garden chairs. Bring or leave. When we begin the indecision is crippling.

I start in the kitchen, working through the belongings, trying to see what is ours, what will fit in our cases, what will save me money rebuying on our return. I stand frozen, sunshine pouring in on me. A box of fifteen coloured food dyes sits in my hand – a gift from my brother before leaving. Pirate birthday cakes, Hello Kitty buns and swirling rainbow icing have been made with these dyes. Happy memories have been created by them. If I throw them away will I be throwing away those memories? Belittling them somehow? Will I be able to create new ones? Images of wholesome birthday parties with smiling children and a normal family swim in front of my eyes. I hold that box like a talisman. It is my crystal ball looking into the past. Trying to see into the future. I don't know how long I stand there. Unseeing, unhearing, undoing, until my sister touches my arm and I come blinking back into the world – a box of half-used food dyes in my hand. I push them across the counter, unable to make so great a decision right now.

Over the next few days I sort through all of our belongings for the second time in a few short months. Piles begin to emerge – what will come now, what Kristian might (or might not) bring later, what will be left behind for good. Huge sports bags are purchased from discount stores, zips catching and breaking as I shove just one last thing on top of the over-spilling contents. When I am done I look at the massive pile of luggage and wonder how my sister and I will manage to get six bags and three children through two airports and multiple car journeys. I can't even get to the garden gate without weeping.

But we will. We have to. The time has come.

The Long Goodbye

Kristian has been talking about returning to England to live, and visiting the children over the weekends. He feels he needs to put down his own roots in a place he belongs, not in my place, not in my town. I try not to think about it. I say nothing to the children, not yet. I can't. I'm not sure what they would do with the devastation this would cause.

This is a decision only he can make. I pray that he will make the right choice, children over country.

And of course he does.

He makes plans to return to Ireland after us. He will follow in six weeks' time, once our tenancy and his work commitments are settled. The relief is immense. The children need him, and even though we are no longer together so do I. I need him to pick them up and make them feel secure. I need him to help deal with their sadness and fear. I need him to help support me supporting them.

Maria, ever the rock, has also found him a place to rent, just up the road from us. It is only a one bed, all that could be afforded, but it is handsome and welcoming. He will be living just fifteen minutes up the road from us and although I know we will both need distance, it still feels comforting. Most of all we know it will be best for the children this way.

So we say our goodbyes, nursing our grief and hope and guilt. We have spent the past weeks preparing ourselves and it feels almost anticlimactic. 'See you in a few weeks', I make a point of saying loudly, so that the children will hear. Six weeks sounds like a lifetime to them.

I think about Kristian on the way to the airport. I have my tribe all around me. Blond heads and tanned limbs, grubby hands holding mine. I have my sister sitting strong beside me, carrying the weight when I can't. Joking and stroking, raising much-needed smiles.

But Kristian. All Kristian has is an empty house and the overwhelming silence that comes only when chaos and noise have been taken away. No screeches of delight as the boys jump in the freezing pool. No tantrums over homework they don't understand. No running barefoot through the house chasing each other with nerf guns. No balls being kicked against walls or scooters whizzing over tiles. No warm sleepy bodies to nestle into. No comforting hugs to give and receive. Just silence, which only his unwelcome thoughts and regrets will fill. My heart aches for him. For the briefest of moments

I put myself in his place and an overwhelming panic shoots through me. My children being whisked off home while I remain, alone and lonely. I shut down my mind and concentrate on the green and brown Spanish countryside whizzing past the window.

Home

When we touch down in Ireland we drive straight to my mother's house. It is an unspoken decision. I don't even know where we will be sleeping tonight. Though I know it can't be alone. I am not ready for alone yet.

I walk into the kitchen and there stands my mother, as she always is, beside the Aga with a tea towel in hand. The familiarity of it is comforting, but at the same time disconcerting – how can everything be just as it was before when nothing actually is? Everything has changed, and yet …. Our gazes meet and she embraces me, silent and soft and warm. Everything that needs to be said is said in that moment. There had been no call required before now after all. Perhaps I had known that all along.

Dinner is made and placed in front of us. We will stay for the night, or the week, or as long as we need. Relief sweeps through me, then guilt, always the guilt. All these people helping me cope. But what about Kristian? I try to hold on to the fact that his parents are close by watching over him, so I quietly hand him to them in my head and trust that they will all get through the next six weeks in their own way. I can only carry myself and the children right now, and even then I will need all the help I can get.

The doorbell rings and I freeze. I am not ready for the outside world yet. But then Emma, one of my oldest friends, breezes in, a big smile on her face and a huge hug proffered to me. There is no pity, just support, and the fact that she is there if I need her. I hadn't even realised that I had. The little glimpse of the outside that she brings inside and the knowledge that I can in fact face other people is her gift to me.

Other friends get in touch over the coming days – a heart-felt card, a text, a call. Little branches of support held out to me. 'Just in case you get tired treading water, grab hold of me', each one says.

The next day I must leave the house. The thoughts of walking down the main street and meeting anyone I know makes me feel physically sick. But I have to get to the bank. No way out. I put on a big coat with an even bigger hood and, head bowed, march down the road. I can't say for sure if anyone sees me or recognises me, and if they do they probably have bigger things going on in their own lives to care. I make it to the bank unscathed. On the way back I look around me at the shops and the cafes and the people. The hometown I had grown up in feels different somehow. Like something has shifted. Like a veil has been lifted. Like I am seeing it as an outsider for the very first time. Perhaps now that I don't have a 'normal' family I *am* an outsider. Perhaps I don't belong here anymore. But I have nowhere else to go and nowhere else I want to go. So I will stay. Broken family and all.

My first challenge has been completed. I have successfully run the gauntlet of the terrifying main street. Give the girl a medal. I have paced 500 metres there and 500 metres back and I have survived. It is a tiny but somehow momentous occasion for me. The tank that has been running on empty for so long now has a tiny bit of fuel in the bottom of it. I promise myself that I will keep taking those baby steps, keep filling that tank, until I am overflowing with strength and have enough to properly share with both Kristian and the children. I will be the strong one. I will make this ok.

House

Later the same day my mother and Maria bring me and the children up to see the new house they had all so kindly gone in search of just days after Christmas.

I walk through the half-filled rooms, the sickening feeling returning to my stomach, the petrol tank swiftly depleting. I try to smile and show my gratitude. Maria has made up each of the beds. She has bought bedding and blankets and plates and bowls and knives and forks and kettles and toasters. She has measured spaces for new tables and chairs. She has done everything she possibly could to make it homely. But it is not our home. It is a cold empty house with cables coming out of the walls and ugly rugs on the floor. I hate myself for being so petty.

The children run through the house, the boys whooping with delight as they spy my brother Liam's house out the back window. 'Can we climb over the wall and call for them?' they ask excitedly. 'Yes, I think so?' I answer falteringly, looking for someone else to agree. I don't feel in a position to be able to give that sort of permission. This isn't my house. That isn't my wall.

They race down the stairs and hoosh each other to the top of the back garden wall. Pushing bums and pulling arms. At the top they look back at me in the upstairs window and wave with delight. I can't help but give a tired smile back. My poor brother doesn't know what's coming.

'Are you sure it's ok?' my mother asks again. She has been awake in the night worrying that the house isn't good enough for us.

'It's perfect Mum', I say, turning to her. And I will it to be so.

It is strange and unsettling moving into a place I have not seen before or chosen to live in. I lie in bed at night and cry softly. The house is cold and filled with someone else's furniture. I go through the list of things that I hate about it. The walls are bare and unused cables hang from ceilings. The sofa is ugly and uncomfortable. The kitchen table is too small. The bathroom is 80s pink. It's cold and grim; grey walls surround us. The whole place feels alien and wrong. We don't belong here. But what other option do I have? I know things could be a lot worse and I know that I am lucky. Why do I not feel lucky? I list off the positives to myself again and again. I am close to family and friends. The children's school is just up the road. Rental houses in the area are virtually impossible to come by, and yet I have a great one in a perfect location.

I will my heart to catch up with my head and see the silver linings. But it refuses me.

And then there is the money. How on earth am I going to pay for this house that I hate?

I have managed to keep my part-time, working-from-home job throughout our international moves back and forth from Ireland. I love it; it is perfect for me, and now I am terrified that I won't be able to keep doing it. I don't earn enough money to pay the rent and bills, but if I have to look for a full-time job that will mean childcare costs, unhappy children and even more stress.

Splitting up means now two rents will have to be paid. Not to mention the significant part of the mortgage on the negative equity home we had bought, like so many others in the boom, in another part of the country. It was supposed to be a starter home, but it stopped us in our tracks. Refusing to let us move on. We can't sell it as the debt would be crippling.

It seems impossible. I wake frequently in the dead of night wrapped in terror and darkness, numbers swirling around my head and none of them adding up. Absolute fear grips me whenever I think about it. A knot in my stomach and a pain in my heart take up permanent residency.

Kristian and I haven't even sat down to talk about money yet. We have both been in survival mode, just moving from one daily task to the next. Getting to this point that we are at now. It already seems like we have travelled a thousand miles from that conversation at the kitchen table. The vast distance between us physically mirrors the emotional chasm that has opened up. Heads down, getting through our suffering alone. I have to just trust that we will work out the finances between us when the time comes. I hope in my soul that we can be fair and honest about it. I hope that pain or resentment doesn't control our hand. I hope that we can put the children's needs and emotions before our own. I hope that I can stick to my own beliefs. I hope that Kristian will feel the same. I say many prayers and put my trust in the universe.

Some days it is easy; other nights I lie frozen in terror of what might be.

Over the next few weeks I obsess over making the house into the cosy nest I know we so badly need. I spend money I don't have on rugs and throws and cushions and bedding. I frantically bang nails into walls to hold lopsided pictures and mirrors. I unbox books and unload TVs.

Eight-Armed Lullabies

Every evening the children and I all pile into one of the double beds and talk about how we feel. 'Fine' is the standard response when they don't know what emotion to put on themselves. 'Sad' comes to visit often. 'Angry' has a mention. But by far the most common reply is 'I miss Daddy.' Those words are a stab to my heart every time. A pain I can't take away from them. A pain that I, in part, have caused. I mutter meaningless replies and try to soothe their wounds, but they need their dad back in their lives to really heal them.

As we lie there in the bed, I spread my arms out wide, trying to fit them all under my wings. I sing them lullabies until they drift off to sleep. Sometimes they belt them out with me. I enjoy these moments. I feel that I am doing something right at last.

After they drift off to blessed sleep, I kiss their peaceful faces and promise them that everything will be ok. Then I creep back downstairs to the chair in front of the fire. I pour myself a glass of red wine and settle in to watch the boxset of *Downton Abbey* that someone clever has loaned to me. This nightly ritual is my balm. My time to stop feeling for the day, stop protecting, stop worrying, stop hurting and just escape.

And somewhere along the line in the busy days of unpacking goods and calming fears, of stroking heads and banging nails, of lighting fires and buying blankets, our house becomes a home. Our safe place. Our new nest.

And I love it.

A Dad-Shaped Hole

The past six weeks have been filled with anguish. The children are hurting and they miss their dad. So much. I have done what I can, but I can't be all things to them. No one can fill the Dad-shaped hole in their lives except their father.

And now he is coming back, not to our home but to our town at least.

I am relieved and nervous in equal measures. Will the calm I've created around us be upset again? Will all the work I've done to heal hearts be undone? Will the fighting begin? Will I finally get a much-needed break? Some time for just me? Forty-two days of constant caring to high emotion have taken their toll. I need to breathe. I need to get out. I need to find Katie again.

There will be difficult conversations coming and I have to regain my strength for them.

And suddenly he is here. Setting up home fifteen minutes away from us. Broken but encouraged, the deep love of his children evident as he nestles their joyful faces into his neck.

'We missed you Daddy!'

I know that whatever happens those children need to have him near, to see him every week or even every day. Whatever we can work out. Whatever is best for them.

Kristian's new house is clean and proud and organised – the opposite of my chaotic, messy home. We now have our own spaces to live in as we choose, no exasperated sighs about lost documents and unwashed clothes. No resentment about uneven divisions of tasks. Ironically, I've never been tidier. I am now in charge of every job in my home, and knowing that lifts the unspoken arguments from my shoulders. I do the bins. I change the lightbulbs. I cut the grass. I'm in charge of the admin, the cleaning, the blocked toilets, the coal. It's just the way it is, so I get on with it. Surprisingly, it is so much easier this way.

Later that first day we talk to the children together again, explaining what the arrangements will be. My house will be their base: the family home. We will work out special times when they will stay with their dad, and they can see him whenever they miss him, if it is at all possible.

I see cautious joy returning to their faces.

LOOKING BACK

We were fortunate with our change of living arrangements. It wasn't a case of anyone moving out – we were moving *back* – back to the children's hometown if not their home. My family had already activated into disaster recovery mode and found me and the children a house to rent. Not a luxury most people have.

Looking back, I will be eternally grateful that they swooped in and took control. They paid the deposit and first month's rent for me and I knew I had a safety net if things didn't go according to plan – not that I actually had one of those.

We had left Aughrim in 2010 when Kaya was six years old, rented in Greystones until she was nine, and then upped sticks and headed to Spain. To be back in Greystones was a huge relief. We were home again.

I know how lucky I was, but even so all I felt at the time was fear. We had two homes in Greystones, one of the most expensive towns in Ireland, and a negative equity house in Aughrim to pay for, and I had no idea how we were going to do it. Three sets of rent into one-and-a-half salaries do not go. In desperation we had pushed the practicalities to the back of our minds, but very quickly the reality set in. How would it all be paid for?

In my fear and despair I called a family friend who was a family law expert. In no way did I want to start any legal proceedings, but I had no clue what rights I had or what I might have to live on each month. He was practical and matter-of-fact.

'The situation is untenable', he said. 'You will be looking after the children 80 per cent of the time, so Kristian will have to move into your negative equity home in order to give additional money to you to look after the children.'

It was said as if it was the most natural thing in the world. So obvious. And while in terms of money it probably was, it in no way took into account the emotional needs of all of us. What would be better for us all in the long term? If Kristian moved 45 miles away to a village where he knew no one he would be miserable and likely to either spiral into depression or hitch a flight back to England. If Kristian moved 45 miles away he wouldn't be able to take the boys to football training during the week. If Kristian moved 45 miles away the children wouldn't be able to have impromptu sleepovers when they needed them. If Kristian moved 45 miles away I would lose my support, their other parent, the only other person on the planet whose duty it was to care for them. Weighing it all up it was as obvious to me as the alternative was to the lawyer. There would be nobody moving to the negative equity house 45 miles away. Even for the sake of 700 much-needed Euro each month. We would have to find another way.

For most couples going through a separation, one of the earliest and most difficult factors to agree on are the living arrangements.

When one parent has to move out of the family home it can be massively traumatic. Going from a chaotic family home to a small apartment or bedsit is a major change. Similarly, if a move back in with parents is on the cards it can be extremely tough to regress from being head of a household to a visitor in your childhood home.

Some feel they need to sell up and move away to get the space and closure they need. Others have no other option available. This can mean moving schools and leaving friends. It can be a massive upheaval at a time when children are already insecure and hurting. We tried to use their needs and our gut as our yardstick – sometimes we succeeded and sometimes we inevitably failed.

All children will be upset by the changes. It's inevitable. Ours missed seeing their dad every day. They missed the private moments and the goodnight kisses. My job was to talk them through it. Soothe their fears. Come up with a coping plan together.

One thing they won't miss is the fighting or silent resentment, because no matter how well we think we hide it from them, they always know. I hang on to that when the guilt takes hold. It is far better for the mental health and future of our children to have two calm homes rather than one angry, bitter one.

The early days following the announcement to the children were filled with fear. My own, Kristian's and our children's. Many of these fears stayed silent. Rolling around in minds and eating into happiness. I did my best at calming the scary unknowns facing my children, and I thought they were doing fine, as well as could be expected. Better even. It was three years later that they told me with tears in their eyes that those lullabies I lovingly sang to them each night, the same lullabies that they asked for, bring back so many painful memories now that they can't listen to them anymore.

KRISTIAN'S WORLD

The two months passed alone in Spain, mainly in drunken silence. My decision was made: I was going back to Ireland. I was missing my children so much already that the idea that I could live in another country from them was frankly ridiculous.

My wonderful sister-in-law Maria found me a place to live, only a fifteen-minute walk from Katie and the kids' new abode. My daughter sent me a set of countdown cards, one for every single day until I departed. My heart was in so much pain.

I booked a ferry home and began to look forward to the road trip across Spain with the car and what was left of our family belongings, including everything I owned in the world. I began to think about our other home – the one we had bought in the height of the boom. What to do with that home now?

Due to the prohibitive pricing of the Irish housing boom in the new millennium, the possibility of buying a house in Katie's hometown of Greystones or surrounding areas had been an impossibility. We had driven through the pretty village of Aughrim in the deep south of Wicklow one (rare) sunny day and decided we could see ourselves living there. Before I could blink, Katie had organised a house viewing and we began the painful administrative journey of actually buying a house.

We lived there between 2003 and 2010 and our three children were born with the Aughrim house as our family home. Peak boom time, our house valuation had increased significantly, and we released equity to build an extension. The house wasn't as big as we needed with two children at the time. We built a modern wooden-based extension with underfloor heating and all the bells and whistles you are convinced you need to be really 'happy'. The subsequent valuation of the extension versus the amount actually spent on building it is not something I can dwell on objectively without becoming nauseous.

Once Kaya started school and we had to start thinking ahead to their educational futures, I just couldn't envisage a future there. I'm from the south of England and it was just far too alien. We had been feeling far too isolated from the modern world and (Katie's) friends and family, so the urge to move back to Greystones was strong. We rented a house, got some tenants, got the kids' school sorted and were back in the twenty-first century.

Both the decision to release equity on the house value and the decision to move back to Greystones are now clearly evident as having major impacts on our separated financial futures. Hindsight is a wonderful thing.

Whilst we were trying to come up with an agreeable financial plan in those first months of being separated, and plenty of times over the years since, the notion of moving back to Aughrim has been strong in an economical sense. The amount of rent we received from the tenants there was equal to half the mortgage. Therefore, on a monthly basis, I was paying my own rent, paying a set maintenance amount to Katie, paying half of the mortgage on the house in Aughrim as well as sharing the usual ongoing associated costs of having three children. This is some future I thought. We have to sell the house. But the house was so far into negative equity following the equity we had released, along with the severe economic crash and subsequent house value decrease. What was the point of selling the only notable asset we had, to be lumbered with nothing but a significant debt to be repaid into a black hole if we sold it?

At the time of writing, after paying the mortgage every month for fifteen years, the market has recovered to an extent, the tenants have moved out and we have the house up for sale. Valued just above what we bought it for.

Banks, housing, mortgages, solicitors, 'the market' – what a load of rubbish. We were spectacularly unlucky – like so many of our generation. Buying in the hope of 'getting on the ladder', but remaining stuck on the first rung, with a big banker's boot holding us down there forevermore.

EXPERT ADVICE

...ON DEALING WITH THE FAMILY HOME

Deirdre Burke is a trained family law mediator, qualified barrister and practising solicitor. She is a member of the board of the Legal Aid Board, and of the Family and Child Law Committee of the Law Society. She was also the founder of the Guardian Children's Project, a charity which provided essential support services to children and young people coping with the effects of separation and marital breakdown in their families.

In my experience, second to worry about the children, what happens to the family home after separation or divorce is the key concern of most of my clients. Will the home need to be sold? If so, what will happen to the proceeds? If the home is not sold, who will get to live there and under what circumstances?

Without a doubt, to resolve this issue by agreement rather than court gives a couple greater flexibility and allows more creative options to be explored. However, in general, there are a number of key scenarios which most couples will have available to them.

It is important to note that the legal definition of 'family home' is the home where the couple reside during the marriage. Therefore, other properties, such as investment properties or holiday homes, will not be considered the family home. While these properties are family assets, and must be dealt with as part of the overall separation, they do not attract the same level of protection as the marital family home.

Most couples own their family home jointly. However, because of the special status which the family home has, even if the property is in the name of one spouse this will not diminish the claim of the other party when separating. In deciding the matter, a court must consider the future accommodation needs of all dependents, including both spouses and any children.

In general there are three options available when considering what to do with the family home:

1. The home can be sold and any equity arising on sale can be divided between the couple. 'Equity' in this instance means the net proceeds of sale, following payment of any mortgage, legal and auctioneer costs, and any other associated costs. How this equity is divided will depend on the requirements and circumstances of each person, and most importantly on the requirements of any children to be

accommodated. This is often the cleanest option for a couple separating.

2. The second option is that one person 'buys out' the interest of the other by paying over a lump sum. The lump sum to be paid will depend on the available equity in the property, i.e. the value less any mortgage. (Many people mistakenly believe that they are entitled to a percentage of the market value.) If there is a mortgage on the home, then the person taking over the home will be expected to have the other person removed from the mortgage. This is the ideal situation but will entail sourcing sufficient funds to a) take over the mortgage and b) pay the lump sum. This can be challenging for many individuals. If this is not possible then the person keeping the home must at a minimum give a legal indemnity (promise) that they will be solely responsible for the repayment of the mortgage. There are varying disadvantages to this situation, but it must be weighted up against the overall situation and circumstances.

3. A couple can agree to a 'deferred sale' of the family home. This means that the fact of sale is agreed, as well as the future division of the equity, but the sale itself is postponed. This is particularly useful if there are very young children, as it can secure their accommodation needs, for example for the duration of their education years. The sale can also be postponed for a short period of time, for example to allow one spouse to secure an independent mortgage. If a deferred sale is agreed, there must also be specific agreement about who lives in the house and how the outgoings of the property are discharged in the meantime.

There is also a fourth option, albeit one that only suits very unique situations. This is that the family home is physically partitioned, to create two independent homes, with independent access and separate legal titles. In general the house needs to be quite large to facilitate this, and certainly the couple need to have an exceptional level of communication, but it has been done.

To help shape this decision the following information is needed:

- A current up-to-date market valuation of the property
- Redemption figures for any mortgage upon the property
- The approximate cost to each party of buying another home – noting that if there are children the priority will be to ensure they have a primary home, however both parents need accommodation to facilitate overnight stays with both
- The borrowing capacity of each person

The above comprises a simple overview of the general options available in respect of the family home following separation. However, every family is different and every situation is different. Further, the family home is only one of many issues to be decided. Therefore it is vital that legal advice and guidance is obtained at an early stage.

Legal advice is also essential at an early stage if a person is considering leaving the family home before matters are fully agreed. Very often this is a reasonable thing to do, which will 'create space' to foster negotiation and agreement. However it is important to be clear that this is done without waiving or relinquishing any interest which the person has in the home.

3

Money Matters

MY STORY

'How about you take them Friday nights and I'll have them on Saturdays?' I say, keen to get a set routine going.

'Why can't we alternate the Friday and Saturdays instead?' he responds.

We are dancing, like fighters in a ring, skirting around the ropes. Neither of us wanting to land a punch yet, but fully aware we need to protect ourselves in case the other does.

I weigh it up in my mind and it seems like a perfectly fair arrangement for all. The children will still know exactly where they will be each week and we will both get a variety of weekend days with them. Neither of us missing out on Saturday football matches or Sunday lunches.

'Yeah, ok.'

And just like that our weekend arrangement is agreed. Nothing is written in stone, but it is a beginning. The children know when they will be seeing their dad each week, which gives some much-needed structure to their lives.

It is the start of 'The Plan'.

But now it is time to start talking about money. And I am scared. There's simply not enough to go around.

As I will be caring for the children the majority of the time and only have a part-time job we agree that Kristian will bolster my monthly income. A figure is suggested, pulled from a hat and placed into our heads. Is it enough for me to live on? Will it leave enough for Kristian to live on? Will all the bills be able to be paid?

The shortfall on the mortgage from our negative equity house swallows up a massive chunk of available funds. We will effectively be paying three separate rents with one-and-a-half salaries. It feels like smashing a square peg into a round hole, like a belligerent toddler with a wooden hammer. Perhaps the lawyer is right and the situation untenable after all?

We agree to give it a try, see how it works out. I don't feel it's enough and Kristian feels like it is too much. I come to the conclusion that this is probably a good indication that it's close to fair. It works for a while. We are 85 per cent of the way there, but money keeps raising its ugly head. Getting in the way of moving on.

Girl on a Train

It's a midweek morning when we board the train to Dublin. We've decided to try mediation. We're not really sure exactly what mediation is, but we want things to be fair and neither of us want to get involved in any legal stuff yet. Legal stuff is scary and expensive. The grey sea and dark sky meet on the horizon as I stare out of the carriage window. How did I get to this point in my life? This was not how things were supposed to be for me. I am good and clever and balanced and positive – my life was supposed to reflect all that. Where is my house in the country with five sets of coloured wellies lined up outside? Where is my Aga in which I bake warm buttery scones? What happened to the big dinner parties I was supposed to throw, with good red wine and laughter flowing? What about those happy family holidays abroad? Picture-postcard smiles and tans on each of us. Where is the dream I was promised by myself?

Not here on this dusty train carriage that's for sure.

I am now a single mother. My children are from a broken home, and we are broke. The words stick in my throat. Single mother. I haven't yet been able to bring myself to say it out loud. It is not who I am, and I am not what I associate a single mother to be. For all my nice, middle-class liberalism, the term is still loaded with negative notions for me. I am the worst kind of fake liberal. Supportive and understanding, as long as it doesn't come too close.

I look around the train carriage, half-listening to Kristian talk about new albums and the state of the country. I nod absentmindedly while I imagine tapping the lady next to me on the shoulder.

'Do you know we are separated?' I would say to her. 'We don't look it do we? We're actually on our way to mediation to talk about splitting up. We have three children together. I'm now a single mother. You'd never know though, would you?'

'That's nice dear', she'll say, as she pats my arm and moves to another seat.

But it's not. It's horrendous. It's like someone has taken a photo of me and ripped it to pieces in front of my face. And now I am scattered at my feet and need to put myself together again. The same but different.

Kristian talks on and I look out of the window again. A very faint reflection of myself stares back.

Mediation

We walk up the steps to the dirty white Georgian door on a busy street in Dublin. I feel hugely self-conscious, as if all the busy people walking by are watching – judging me and my broken marriage. We have been told to bring details of all our available funds so that we can review the incomings and outgoings clearly. The mediator who has been assigned to us tells us that unfortunately these usually don't add up. Normally they are way off in fact. But when our figures fill the whiteboard we can see that we just about manage to scrape a pass. She questions the figures we've come up with. Is that really all you spend on clothes? What about entertainment? Is that shopping bill realistic?

It has to be I think to myself. There's no other option.

I dissect the figures written up on the board in front of us and quietly seethe with resentment. The €90 outgoing for Sky TV every month which is on Kristian's list is hard to get past. We manage on the basic €24-a-month package, and soon even that will be gone. But I swallow it down. I know it will sound petty if I mention it, and who knows where the argument might take us. I let it lie, but can't really let it go. It is one of those small, seemingly insignificant, facts that I can't get past.

It is only now, four years later, when I recount the story to someone I barely know that I finally see the other side. She is older and wiser and much, much further down the divorce track than I am.

'But that was all he had', she says, smiling kindly. 'You had the children to cuddle up to at night, all he had was some sports on a screen.'

And at last I understand. After all these years I can let it go. And I am oh-so-thankful to myself that I stayed silent that day.

Other Voices

Other voices aren't so forgiving.

'*How much?*' a friend asks aghast. 'I can't believe that's all he gives you.'

'Yes, but he pays the shortfall on the mortgage too. It's significant …' I trail off, looking into my coffee cup for answers.

Her lips purse together and she folds her arms across her chest. She raises an eyebrow but manages to keep any further feelings on the matter to herself. However, now she's transferred her thoughts into my head and they are trying to bed down and set up camp on the shaky terrain.

Another woman tells me to file legal proceedings immediately. 'Do it now and do it quick. Before he moves some Polish woman and her kids in and the money stops arriving.'

I smile and shake my head. That would never happen. And yet a rising fear creeps up my throat and lingers there.

I am angry with everyone – people I know for raising doubts, Kristian for not giving more, me for wanting more, the government and the bankers and the estate agents for our godforsaken money pit of a house that we can't get rid of, and the universe for not giving me the life I always thought I'd have.

Later that week I bump into another friend of ours outside my house. He asks how we're both doing. I explain that it's all going well, but we are both broke. He waves his hand in the air and discards the notion. 'Sure it's only money', he says, as if it doesn't matter in the slightest. 'A good relationship between the two of you is what counts.' It seems so simple in the bright clear light of day. But at night Fear and Trust play tug-of-war in my head for hours, and I wake up exhausted.

Changes

After a couple of months tensions begin to show. Kristian is struggling with the outgoings and I don't have time to work any extra hours to earn more. So we go back to the drawing board and came up with a new plan.

Every Tuesday he will pick up the children from school, keep them overnight and drop them to school the next morning. This gives me the flexibility to work extra hours and top up my incomings a little, and the children get to see their dad more regularly. We agree to reduce Kristian's monthly payments and test out the new arrangement.

If this life experience has taught me any major truth it is this – do not rely solely on any one person when it comes to the family finances. I am so thankful that I kept that toe in working waters. I now know just how important it is to be in charge of my own finances, so the new arrangement suits me. I don't want to be forever dependent on a cash flow I can't control. I don't want to be beholden to my soon-to-be ex-husband for the food I buy and the house I live in. Yes, the children's welfare is and will always be our shared responsibility, but the more independence I have, and the less reliance I have on another person, the more I will get my much-needed strength back. It will diminish the power of The Fear.

Thankfully the new arrangement seems to work. I take on some more work with my long-term contract and also gain some midweek headspace. Kristian becomes more involved with school procedures and hellish homework.

The Future

If I could have seen into the future I would have been sick from the shock.

Losing your job is never a nice experience. Rejection, depression and fear are all normal reactions to being 'let go', but losing your job when you are a single mother brings that fear to a whole new level. It's not just your career you're talking about – it's your income, your rent, your roof over your family's head, their food on the table. That's fear with a capital F right there.

When I began working part-time for a UK online parenting site it was my way of gently testing a return to work after taking time out to raise my family. It was far removed from my previous role as a customer relations manager for a big American finance business. But it gave me a sense of purpose beyond school runs and toddler tantrums. It gave me a reason to use my brain again and a community of other mothers to meet. And as an extra bonus it also gave me a bit of money to add to the pot of family finances.

However when Kristian and I separated it became much more than a nice-to-have sideline – it became my lifeline, my main income each month, my safety net. As the primary carer of three children I desperately needed that income to keep afloat. Belts had been tightened, agreements reached. I had put my head down and I hung on for dear life.

And then the unimaginable happens. The phone call comes. They are very sorry, it's nothing personal, the role is just moving in-house. Ironic, I think, as I wonder if I would soon be *out* of my house.

And so just like that my world turns upside down.

There are tears, and wringing of hands, and ringing of friends. And there is, of course, wine. There is lots of wine.

While that helped a little, it didn't change anything. I am still out of work, unemployed, broke, broken and scared.

I quickly kick into panicked action. Grabbing freelance work wherever I can and using my emergency fund to get by. But the situation can't last. I question the current arrangement with Kristian and silently wonder where his obligation to us begins and ends. Does the change in circumstances mean that he needs to carry us completely for a time? Or is it all my responsibility now? It upsets the status quo between us and I can see the delicate net we have created unravelling. I am scared.

Legal Eagles

For the first time in the whole break-up I seek proper legal advice. I need to talk through the current situation with someone, lay it all out on the table so that I knew my rights and what would be expected of each of us if it came down to it. But still I feel guilty and ashamed entering the office.

'It's very admirable, what you are doing', he says to me when I explain the current state of play. 'But you have to protect yourself.'

But I want to protect more than that. I want to protect our relationship, whatever that is now. Protect our children. Protect what we've built. By protecting all that am I not protecting myself too?

'There are shared debts', he goes on, explaining it to me as if I were a simple child who doesn't quite get it. 'The joint mortgage needs to be paid and you have no income; therefore your ex-husband has to pay for it. The children are your joint responsibility and you have no income; therefore your ex-husband has to pay for them and the roof over their heads.'

I know in theory what he says is true, and yet my gut is telling me that it's more complicated than that. I know that we will never be cast out onto the street, I'm fortunate enough to know that I have the safety net of family if it ever comes to that – not something that everyone has. But at the same time I know that the money that comes into my bank account each month is not enough to pay the rent, let alone the food bills, petrol costs, doctors' fees, and general outgoings of keeping a family home going. I am actively looking for work, but what happens if it takes a year to find something?

He tells me that in a court of law it would be a walkover. But I don't want to walk over anyone. I want it to be sorted out in a reasonable and responsible manner between two adults who once loved each other. And I still think it can be. I just don't know how yet. I leave the office deep in thought.

The meeting does give me something though. It gives me confidence. It gives me security. If it comes to it, it gives me an ace to play to encourage negotiations. I say nothing to Kristian but I pop the business card in my back pocket, to be produced in dire straits. I will only use it if I'm forced to.

Luckily I never have to. Within a few months I secure employment and I'm back in the driving seat – heading in the right direction once more.

LOOKING BACK

For us, dividing up the limited pot was our greatest challenge and most frequent stumbling block. There is so much fear and uncertainty swarming in the beginning that it can quickly become like a game of Hungry Hippo. A bag of cash dropped on the living room floor and each person snatching for as much as possible before it's too late.

But it doesn't have to be that way.

I'm not saying our way was perfect. There have been plenty of bumps along the road, and money is still always tight. But we have what we have and we work with that. It might not be the best deal either of us could have fought for – but it also meant there was no fight to be had.

There are of course additional expenses that still crop up every few months – football boots, school books, Christmas gifts – but we tend to work those out in the same manner. Kristian takes responsibility for the lion's share of club fees and sports goods; I cover birthday parties and the majority of the extra day-to-day costs. If one of us is really struggling the other usually steps in to lend a hand. It's a movable feast (or more likely famine).

A huge part of managing to get to a place where we could quietly sit and observe, rather than hyperventilating into a paper bag, was the fact that we were both earning. The money coming in was heavily weighted on one side, but the difference in having a small income of my own – both in terms of an increased fund and my own mental health – was immense. It gave me something to cling to and improve on. It gave me hope and took away some of the helplessness.

I know that many women give up work entirely after having children – I did that myself before somehow managing to build a new career. I went from a good job in financial services to baking buns and making cardboard volcanos. And I loved it. I was very grateful that Kristian's income allowed me to do it. But I often wonder how things would have panned out if I hadn't gone back to work. First a newspaper article, then a blog, then freelance writing for other businesses and on and on until I had a whole new career experience to focus on. A future income stream of my own. If I hadn't returned to work at all, and had no money of my own to fall back on, our story of separation could have been very different.

All of our life situations and opportunities are different, but when my relationship was breaking down having my own income became vital. And I'm not the only one. I know a woman who takes in foreign students to help pay the rent, and others who started crèches in the playroom. I know women who stormed back into the boardroom, doing more in three days than others could do in three weeks. There are ways to get means; it can just take a while to find your footing.

Childcare

A huge part of any separation – and the major focus for most – is who has the children and when. Broken down simply, we had to decide where the children would live and when they would spend time with each parent. However these things aren't always simple; tied into these decisions was who would earn money when – which is where it got tricky.

Creating a parenting plan with the help of mediation helped. There are some great online resources too. A parenting plan can be as detailed or loose as you want it to be. It can include day-to-day arrangements, financial agreements, education, religion and decisions about the future. Flexibility is key when dealing with the lives and needs of multiple people so, in my experience, it can be better to keep the parenting plan simple.

The children often need one-on-one nights with their dad, and he and I both need nights out and days away. We accommodate each other as much as possible. A weekend away, a work trip, a shifting of dates – they are each taken on a case-by-case basis without note-taking or point-scoring. Yes, there may have been eye-rolling at times. 'What? You're going away again?!' but a flexible arrangement benefits everyone, not least of all the children.

Nothing Going On But the Rent

Money is often the deciding factor in how the new living arrangements unfold. There is usually a limited pot and it needs to be fairly distributed. Often fear guides decisions at this time, with both of you scrambling to get as much as you can to protect yourself. It's a natural human response to a stressful situation. I tried to continually remind myself of the limited pot available – how can it be divided fairly, or added to in the future? Lawyers will fight for your right to as much as possible – but fair is usually better in the long term. A good relationship between myself and Kristian for the next twenty years is worth more than a couple of hundred Euro a month or an extra bedroom in the home.

A mediation service could be the answer if you are having trouble coming to an agreement yourselves. It was for us. The mediator helped us list out all our assets, debts, savings, income and outgoings, and helped us agree a fair division. The €3,000 I had squirreled away for a rainy day was to be used for joint house repairs; the extra funds Kristian received in his monthly salary was to help subsidise additional rent or mortgage costs. Having someone neutral in the room helps both parties come up with a fair deal for everyone. If there simply isn't enough to pay for two houses, other arrangements can be discussed. 'Nesting' – the practice of both parents moving in and out of one home – is successful for some. Living 'together apart' is the only option for others. Sometimes you have to boomerang back to your parents at 40 years of age.

Each family situation is different, but for most what is at the heart of everything is the desire to do what is best for the children with what you have available to you. Although that is easier said than done at times.

Others' Views

It is only natural for your family and sometimes friends to take sides. Everybody wants the best for you. They want to heal your hurt. I know some people who thought I wanted them to give out about how unfair it all was. I tried not to get sucked in and listened to my gut instead. If someone told me he should be giving me double what he was, yet I was happy with the arrangement, then I left it well alone. I know one man whose best friends told him that his wife didn't deserve to get the house after everything she did, but he was happy for the children to keep some stability by staying in the family home, so he stuck to his guns. He knew how his relationship worked and what arrangement he was happy to live with.

That's not to say we don't all need to protect ourselves and our futures, but that can be done our way, not anyone else's.

KRISTIAN'S WORLD

Katie and I were still friends; there was no major acrimony between us. I was living alone in her hometown in her home country purely to be near to the children, so access rights were never going to be an issue. Money always is an issue though, no matter how people get on. I'd been the chief earner so of course I would be expecting to pay a monthly lump sum to Katie and had no issue in doing so. I also had my own rent and the other half of the mortgage to pay that went uncovered by the small rent we received. Then there were all the associated costs of my own, in being a single man in his own place.

I drew up a budget and Katie drew up a budget and to be honest, we weren't a million miles off. We negotiated and negotiated and got to a place whereby we were both happy enough. Well actually, neither of us were particularly chuffed so I think this must have been a good indication that we'd found some (fair) middle ground. The negotiation was hard though and I would ruminate continually. I hadn't asked to move back to Greystones. There was no negotiation there. Here's our new house, this is how much it costs. This is basically how things seemed to go. As the dad and chief earner in this circumstance, I felt like I basically got told what my situation was and had to just get on with it. Here's where we are living, here's where you're living, here's when you'll be looking after the kids and here's how much money I need from you to get by. That's what it felt like sometimes anyway. It's all quite a lot to take in when you are battling with depression and have no immediate support structure to hand. Katie had all the friends and family in the world to talk things over with over coffee or rant and let off steam. Mine was a continual internal dialogue and it was extremely draining.

Whilst formally the kids were with me twice a week, the reality was much more. Everyone wanted their one-on-one night with Dad and we got a rota going. It was usual to have one or two one-on-one nights a week, plus the two nights with them all. I mention this only in that the budget for daily child costs was drawn up as 5/7 nights with Katie and 2/7 with me, but the reality was much different. It still is, which I love – it means the kids still value time with me, which I can already see changing now our eldest is in the throes of becoming a fully fledged teenager. But it did mean I was incurring a lot more costs than were budgeted for as I wanted to make them feel special for one-on-ones, so we would always go out for something to eat and go to the cinema or get a takeaway delivered. It all adds up. Though the value of money can become less when focusing on providing loving, bonding special experiences with your child who is dealing with the whole mental and emotional impact of the separation themselves.

But overall, I am just thoroughly grateful we did not have to go the legal route. The cards are stacked in the mum's favour and I would have just been legally instructed to pay a certain amount per month as her legal team saw fit. I cover a lot of ad hoc expenses for the kids and so does Katie. My uncle passed away not long after the move back to Ireland and I was kindly left some money. With it I bought each of us a much-needed second-hand car and paid for the annual insurance (up until that point we were sharing one twelve-year-old seven-seater – whoever had the kids had the car). I only point to this to illustrate that if there's money, I share it. I am never going to make my kids or Katie go without for the sake of selfishness. I think time has allowed us both to recognise this and appreciate we still share so many of the same values regarding the key drivers in our lives.

Neither of us ever had any intention of having more children with other partners in the future though. This must make things particularly difficult to agree and I am just glad we haven't had to go there. Yet …

...ON DEALING WITH MONEY MATTERS

Mary Miles practiced as a solicitor in both commercial practice and with the Legal Aid Board before training as a mediator. She has ten years of experience working with separating couples and families and is a strong advocate of mediation as an alternative to court.

Mediation – A Better Way to Separate?

Every conflict will raise its own set of particular issues that are unique to the people involved, so mediation doesn't always follow the same path. Typically, a mediator will work with a separating couple to facilitate a discussion and an agreement on all aspects of their separation. It is possible, however, to engage a mediator to assist with just one or a few specific issues that are causing conflict. For example, a couple may find they are in complete agreement about co-parenting decisions but need a facilitator to help them to agree on how to approach finances. Or perhaps a couple do not have any shared assets and the only thing in dispute is scheduling time with their children. Every mediation is different, but the most common type in my own experience is all-issues mediated separation, the central themes of which are discussed below.

Co-Parenting – How to Parent When Separated

In an all-issues mediated separation there will be multiple sessions with the parties. Where co-parenting issues are a priority (and they commonly are), then the co-parenting sessions will come first. These sessions will deal with all parenting-related matters. An example would be how to schedule time with the children (sometimes referred to in the legal world as 'access'). The objective of such a discussion is to generate and trial a child-focused weekly schedule, where both parents have good quality time with the children.

In conjunction with this schedule, there might also be a discussion of how to effectively parent together when separated. The couple will look at how they can safely share parenting values and suggestions with one another. Once a means of information-sharing is agreed and put into practice, the couple will become more confident in making parenting decisions as a cohesive unit. One of the most useful side effects of using mediation is the requirement that parties collaborate. By using practical problem-solving activities the couple will be more focused, not on the hurt and pain of the relationship breakdown, but on the objective of finding a resolution to the specific problem identified. The process will unearth the supportive tools already present in the relationship and use these to empower the couple to work towards the shared objective of being the best parents they can be. Common co-parenting decisions to be discussed in mediation might include schooling and education, health and diet, extracurricular activities, how to spend holiday time, childcare preferences, and the role of new partners in parenting. The list of parenting issues to be discussed and included in a mediated agreement is very broad and will vary with each family.

Financials – Money and 'Maintenance'

As part of the mediation process a couple will be asked to carry out an extensive family budgeting exercise. This will involve the completion of a monthly budget sheet, detailing all income coming into the 'family pot' and all expenditure coming out of it on a monthly basis. This provides the couple with a snapshot of their financial reality at a given point in time. It will assist them in deciding how family funds are allocated and how to plan for the future. The monthly cost of both the parents' and their children's needs will be identified. It will then become clear if the family pot can continue to maintain all parties or whether changes need to be made in light of the separation. Maintaining two separate family units will always be more expensive than living together as one family. This can often be a challenge for separating couples to accept and prepare for. The legal term 'maintenance' is often raised by the parties in these sessions. How much maintenance should be paid by one parent to the other to ensure that the children's needs are fully met? Is spousal maintenance also required? It may be helpful at this juncture to look at what the term 'maintenance' means. In legal terms, maintenance is financial support paid by a person for the benefit of their spouse (or civil partner) and/or their dependent children. When looking specifically at child maintenance, both parents have a legal obligation to maintain their dependent children in accordance with their means. With the assistance of a mediator and armed with the results of the family budgeting exercise, it should become clear to the couple how much money will be required to ensure that they and their dependent children can continue to have a reasonable standard of living post-separation. That sum will be the amount transferred voluntarily in the mediated separation agreement. The sum will need to be reviewed at regular intervals. A review will also be required where there are any fundamental changes in either the financial circumstances of the parents or the needs of the dependents. It is important therefore that the separated co-parents have the ability to recognise when the need for a review arises and how to find a suitable new solution.

Family Property

Dealing with the family home and other jointly held property is another important and obviously very emotive topic for discussion in a separation. Decisions concerning family living arrangements and how these might need to change on separation will be the starting point for any agreement on the family home. There will be time to reality-check all options available to the couple with regard to their family property and a decision will be made jointly with the welfare of the children as the primary objective.

Other Issues

All-issues mediated separation agreements will also need to cover a number of other matters. Other joint assets such as savings/investments, insurance policies, shares and pensions will need to be discussed, usually with the benefit of expert advice from a pensions specialist and/or an accountant. Debts and potential tax liabilities will also need to be discussed and explored. Finally, the parties will be encouraged to get legal advice with regard to inheritance issues, succession rights and the making of wills on separation.

4

Mental Health

MY STORY

Mind

The therapist looks at me like I should know what I'm supposed to do. I don't know what I'm supposed to do. That's why I'm here. My mind and emotions are like two big balls of wool that have become so tangled up I don't know where one starts and the other ends. I don't know what I want. Or who I am.

'Let's take a different approach', she says, realising that I don't know my problems well enough for her to help solve them. 'Close your eyes and still your mind.'

I do as I'm told, pleased not to have to look at her helplessly anymore.

'Now, picture yourself in your mind's eye', she says. 'Can you see her? Look at her eyes, her stance, the way she moves. Now, tell her to take a seat in the corner for a moment. Tell her it's ok, that you will come back for her soon, but that you just want to take a moment out for a bit.' The therapist's voice lifts up and down like a quiet tide coming in and out of my brain.

I do as she says, surprised at how easy it is to put myself in a corner. I am a very compliant guest.

'Now come back inside your mind and tell me what you see.'

I immediately see a young woman in a cornfield. Her curls gently brush against her face as she twirls and dances in the sunlight. She is carefree and happy, swaying with the breeze. The girl is me. Or was me, once upon a time. She is who I should be, my true self, the person I have lost. I watch her closely and time passes. The therapist asks me questions and I reply easily, as if in a trance. While my thoughts and emotions are hard to get a handle on, this is simple. I know what this girl feels and thinks and dreams. I know her fears and her desires. I see her hopes for the future and her regrets of the past.

After what feels like minutes the therapist tells me to go back to myself in the corner of the room to say thank you. Thank you for being so patient. Thank you for waiting. Thank you for trusting. A lump forms in my throat and my eyes swim. I am grateful and yet I don't want to come back to her. I want to stay in the field and go dancing in the corn.

I leave the room confused and energised. I've been given a glimpse of whom I was and whom I want to be again. But how do I find her and bring her back? Or is it too late to try? Nobody has told me that part yet.

The next week I return to close my eyes again. This time a mountain appears. It is grey and green and rises up from the sparkling sea below. It's as clear to me as if I was looking at a photograph. There is a person climbing the mountain. A girl. She is halfway up and leaning on a stick. She has come a long, long way and she is tired. She looks down the mountain at the path she has travelled. It has been hard, but there have been plenty of beautiful moments too. She's proud of how far she has come. Then she looks up – up to the top of the mountain with clouds gently passing in the blue sky. It seems so far away. She's not sure if she can make it. Does she need to make it? Is there any shame in stopping where she is? She has come as far as she can on this journey and now it is time to rest. I open my eyes. The girl of course is me, and the mountain is my marriage. I cry, feeling sorry for myself and all that has been lost.

Each week I return and paint new images from my mind. A kidney, a crutch, a caged animal. I know instantly what each of these pictures mean and they come easily to me. I am both fascinated and exhausted by the weekly sessions. But at the end of it all I know my mind better than I have in years. I understand how I feel and now the choice of what to do next is up to me. Decisions will now be made in the full knowledge of how I feel. The messy ball of wool has been untangled. It is liberating and terrifying at the same time.

Panic Attack

Finally summer has arrived and I am lying on the local beach with the children. They laugh and dig while I watch from behind my sunglasses. The warm sun melts into my back and the blue sky is clear and endless. And then it hits. It is as if my body has finally relaxed enough to allow the trauma of the past months to surface. The intensity of the moment sweeps over me and I begin to feel dizzy, then my heart and mind start racing until I manage to talk myself down. It's not the first time this has happened. In recent weeks I've started getting these panic attacks. They occur in random places – talking to friends, walking down the road, at this beach that is my home. Fortunately, the moments are mostly mild, fleeting and controllable. No one observing me would have any idea what is happening inside my head, but that's the problem with mental health. It's hidden until you tell someone.

Body

The immense pain that immediately followed the break-up has lifted. I feel stronger. And yet other feelings have come to visit. Loneliness and Loss linger. And Guilt has taken up permanent residency – never far from sight.

A good friend tells me she is doing yoga classes on a Tuesday night in the old convent. Tuesday nights – my childfree night. I instantly know that this is what I need and I sign up that day. I have never done yoga before. That week I arrive with a borrowed mat and ancient workout gear. I hope that I'm not the oldest, scruffiest, least bendy yogi in town. The room is bathed in an orange glow, the wooden floors and centuries-old walls cocooning us in. The other women are a mix of old and young, slim and rounded, stressed and peaceful. There are no ponytailed yoga bunnies here. Just talk of crappy days and aching backs. It's perfect.

I had always thought yoga was a cop-out – pretending to exercise with a bit of stretching. No red faces and sweaty brows required. Halfway through the class muscles I didn't know I had are aching. My shoulders burn as I'm twisted into what is supposed to be a resting pose. My arms are on fire. How is that old woman making it look so easy? I'm supposed to be fit dammit. I grit my teeth and hold position. It feels wonderful escaping into a physical pain instead of an emotional one. All of my energies are focused on some-thing other than my mind. It is like an oasis when I have been dying of thirst. It is everything I need. Each Tuesday from thereon in I religiously recharge myself, topping up the tank with enough fuel to keep me going for the week. It becomes an obsession, a lifeline, my new go-to therapy that I can't be without.

I also start running. Physical exercise is like a secret weapon now. Warding off feelings before they impact, batting them away with lively endorphins. Within six months of returning home to Ireland I do something stupid. I sign up for a triathlon. I learn that there is nothing like fear to focus the mind.

My weekly routine now involves running three mornings a week, cycling when I can and swimming in the freezing Irish Sea. One hour a week is spent with a group of wetsuited figures on a cold grey beach. I put my face in the water and instantly lose my breath. The icy sea stops my heart and my skin aches. I try again. Five seconds this time. Then again. Before long I am swimming, fast, panicked strokes that leave me quickly breathless. Over the weeks I learn to slow down and in turn speed up. I progress from 100 metres to 1000 metres, through hard waves that slap my face and smooth glass that lets me glide. I get caught in strong fishing lines and am assaulted by terrifying seaweed. One of the nights I over-commit and have to get out at the other end of the beach, panting and exhausted, my lonely pile of clothes lying shamefully on the sand in the distance. I walk back dejectedly, feeling like a failure. Later that month I sign up to do a one-kilometre sea swim challenge. I complete the two-kilometre one instead and feel like a queen, a crown of seaweed sticking to my face.

Soul

My love affair with the sea started long ago, and my mind and mood depend on it. I grew up just a five-minute walk from the shore, and although I don't remember those toddler trips to the beach with my mother I do know that the sea air seeped into my tiny being and became part of my soul. So much so that if I'm ever away from it for too long I have an ache in my bones and a longing in my heart to return to its vast embrace.

I have early memories of sunny days and soft sands at Brittas Bay. The thrill of my parents giving the nod that yes, we were going. The race around the house for togs and towels, while my mother made the picnic to see us through the day. White-bread sandwiches, hard-boiled eggs, crisps, Marietta biscuits and the all-important flask of sweet coffee.

Although we lived beside the sea, going to Brittas brought extra excitement. The hot sand that squeaked under bare feet, the huge dunes that we would spend long hours running up and tumbling down, the seashore that was warm and shallow and inviting – it was a million miles from our own stoney grey beach with its dangerous dips and crashing waves, even if it was just a thirty-minute drive from our door.

We would spend the entire day there, roaming through long reeds and in and out of the twinkling water. Until, skin prickled with sea and sun, our parents would collect us up and lead us back to the car, all tanned limbs and sea-sprayed hair.

Aged eleven I did a local swimming challenge – one mile in the sea in exchange for a medal and bragging rights forever more. I remember the waves engulfing me and salty water filling my gasping mouth. I remember wondering whether I'd make it to the finish that seemed as far away as adulthood. I remember finally reaching the end, and how on the way back home my dad told every person we met what I had done. Proud as punch.

My childhood summers were spent in a constant flow up and down to the beach, just like the tide. Whole days were spent jumping and diving off rocks, diving boards and bridges into the welcoming sea. The deep intake before launching off the edge, the hard smack of entry, the shock of freezing water as it engulfed body and head, the bubbles streaming past open eyes, before finally coming up for air.

Then swimming back in to do it all over again. And again. And again.

My early adulthood was spent travelling. In Mexico I languished in the turquoise water, looking up at the sky as I drifted on the gentle waves. A red bandana, tied around my tanned wrist, cut through the infinite blues.

I lost my heart to the incredible sparking seas of Australia – sometimes tinged with the possible danger of sharks, saltwater crocs and killer jellyfish.

The picture-postcard water of Thailand didn't seem real; I would spend long hours on a hammock staring into it. Glowing blues and greens carrying brightly coloured wooden boats. Like the entire country was bathed in a chrome filter. HD views for all. When the storm hit we dashed into the sea, escaping the stinging rain beating our faces by diving under the huge waves. Water on water. I'm not sure I ever felt so alive.

New Zealand's seas were wild and grey and reminded me of home. I went swimming with dolphins off the coast of Kaikoura, and the depths of the dark water around me sent a rush of fear through my veins. The dolphins raced up and past me, swerving and ducking at the last minute so we didn't collide. It felt like being rooted to the middle of a motorway while cars flew at me in every direction.

When Kristian and I moved back to Ireland to settle down we bought a house where we could afford one. It was not near the sea. There was a river and a lake in the village, but no ocean at the end of the road. We spent the first six years of our daughter's life there, but it never felt quite right. When we finally moved back to seaside living it was like a deep exhale.

Now I take my own children down to my beloved sea. We walk barefoot through the same town, down to the stony grey shore. Sometimes I'll swim; sometimes I'll just breathe it in, so as to remind my bones that it's still in touching distance.

The sea is a part of me. A part of my mind, body and soul. I had forgotten how much I need it. I make a pact to take to the freezing water at least once a month for a full year. Every swim is a cold, invigorating, life-affirming, de-stressing dash of happiness. Each time it's as if the person you trust most in the world is telling you that everything will be ok, and sure what are you worrying about that for anyway? The best and cheapest therapy in the world.

Simple Pleasures

I feel a little bit of that carefree girl returning and begin to daydream about what else makes her dance. I am all the time looking for answers, looking for her.

It is a year later that I spend an evening with Kristian at a gig. We are still good friends and we still enjoy much of the same music. The tickets were a birthday gift. I sit in the packed room full of strangers listening to an old guy playing on a guitar. As I lean forward with an involuntary smile on my face, all the stresses of the week fall away, my heart soars and I realise *this matters*.

For me music is one of those things that make my soul come alive. Whether it's live music, car-blaring music, drunk-dancing music – it is one of those big life things that are just important to me. And yet somewhere among that collection of 963 CDs my love had been lost, usurped by Kristian's greater passion and keener knowledge. I had relinquished my right to it, but I am now ready to take it back.

Other simple pleasures that lift my spirit are noted down as they come to mind. Listed so that I don't forget their power or importance:

- Running – the joy of the crest of that hill and how you suddenly come alive as your heartbeat thickens
- Mountains – the pinnacle of the great outdoors. Where you get to throw your arms out wide and hug the world
- Flowers in a vase on the kitchen table
- Clean white bedding
- Fresh coffee and homemade pancakes

I decide to fill my life as full as possible with these things. Small pleasures that have a huge impact.

And my children. They are my low, slow lullaby of love. Especially when they are sleeping ….

The Big D

While my own mental health is about trying to keep on an even keel, keep the ship sailing smoothly through turbulent waters, Kristian's is about survival. It's about desperately grabbing hands to pull him out of the quicksand that drags him under, enveloping him, suffocating him, sucking joy from his bones and leaving nothing but darkness. There has been a third person in this relationship from the very start, but I didn't learn his name until many years later. Depression. He is cruel and greedy and moves without empathy.

Depression has robbed us of many things over the years. When it first reared its ugly head we were in New Zealand, travelling through one of the most beautiful countries in the world. We were full of freedom, youth and love. It should have been perfect. But the affair was about to begin. We called it the Blues for want of better understanding. Kristian didn't know why he felt like he did, lethargic and sad, drinking

Scotch alone in the middle of the night. Maybe it was me. Maybe it was the weather. Maybe it was New Zealand. We packed up our backpacks, sold our van and moved back to Australia where we had lived and travelled previously. We knew we could be happy again there. But the big D had followed us, and was to stay with Kristian throughout his life from that point. It wasn't until years later, when the children were small, that he was officially diagnosed and the long, winding and exhausting path of managing it began.

Depression robbed us not only of that year-long trip around New Zealand; he became the cause of uncharted unhappiness and pain over the years. He lashed out at the world in despair, hurling hurtful insults. He endured Christmas gatherings and marched us home early from Halloween parties, little witches and devils trailing sadly behind. Sometimes, when he was really settled in for a long stay, Kristian would lie in bed, unable to do more than just breathe. Depression sat heavily on his chest, making even that difficult. There were times when Kristian would spend 12 hours sleeping and then still be in bed at 1 p.m. the next day, simply surviving. Meanwhile, I would have been up every hour of the night, feeding babies and tending to nightmares. My day would begin again at 5 a.m. and by lunchtime the exhaustion was all-encompassing. I would be delirious with lack of sleep and would curse my husband, lying like a great lump for hours and hours in a comfortable bed when all I asked for was a 30-minute nap while he tended to his own children. I knew he wasn't doing it on purpose, but the injustice still stung. It was toxic and painful and very, very hard. For both of us.

Soon I didn't know where Depression ended and Kristian began. The lines blurred by the tears in my eyes.

When our lives began falling apart in Spain, Depression had rubbed his hands in glee and settled in to watch the show. Kristian spiralled into terrifying depths we hadn't experienced before. A real fear of what might happen took hold. There were days I returned to the villa and opened the doors with my breath held, not knowing what I would find. Kristian was out of his mind with both the sickness and a major change of medication. He wasn't himself. He was liable to do anything.

I was out of my depth and Kristian was sinking fast. I talked with his parents in hushed tones so that little ears wouldn't hear. There were thoughts processed and suggestions made. There was crossing of fingers and wringing of hands. But none of us were qualified for any of this. Eventually I could only pick up the children and carry them to a better place, leaving Kristian's parents to pick up their own son and carry him through.

At least now some positives to the split are evident. Kristian had always needed more peace and space than a small house and three children allowed. The chaos of family life did not come easy to someone who loves books and music and his own time alone. Now that we are living apart he has that space. When the children visit him he is ready for them, recharged and excited to spend time with them. He is more open to the wonder they bring to life. He is, in my view at least, a better father this way.

LOOKING BACK

That old adage of putting on your own oxygen mask first when the plane is going down comes back to me again and again. Your instinct as a parent in a crisis is to tend to your child before yourself, and while this may be true much of the time at some stage you have to look after your own needs. You can't look after your child if you have stopped breathing yourself. I found putting myself first for a while became a necessity. I called it living selfishly, but in fact it was what we all needed at that time. If I had gone under we all would have drowned.

The Little Things

Life's simple pleasures are not to be underestimated. What I've learned since my separation is that we need to regularly stop and ask ourselves: What matters? What makes me happy?

Life can be one hard slog if we let it, but by seeking out these moments we can sprinkle our days with magic.

'You are allowed to enjoy life you know', my sister often reminds me when I am living a little too earnestly.

And she's right. There is no need for us to be always at the bottom of the heap. Each little pleasure boosts our mood and our strength; it shines a little light of happiness into our broken hearts. And happy heart = happy me = happy kids = happy life.

Mental Health

Of course not everything is that simple. When my panic attacks hit it felt like my mind and body were letting me down. I had come so far, why were they surfacing now?

The more I talk to women of a certain age the more it seems that anxiety and panic attacks are an unspoken pandemic of our generation. Background, situation, personality seem to have nothing to do with it – admit to anyone that you've suffered from mild to extreme anxiety and the floodgates open: everyone, it seems, has a story to tell. Add a separation or divorce into the mix and it seems almost inevitable.

I had my first peep into the world of anxiety about ten years ago when I found myself in a packed conference room with a large number of my then colleagues. Despite having had numerous similar meetings in the very same room, with the very same people, I had a sudden urge to get to the door and get the hell out of there before I collapsed. The more I thought about collapsing in front of everyone the harder and faster my heart began to beat until I sure I was going to pass out. And there I was – stuck in a vicious circle of fear feeding fear.

After that, every time I had a meeting scheduled in that room I would be anxious the same thing would happen again.

I have no idea what brought on that first attack. And to be honest I still don't know if it was an anxiety attack or a panic attack or even what the difference is really, but once the evil little creature had found its footing it lived there at the back of my mind, biding its time until it felt another appearance was warranted.

The next time was in a church in the middle of Mass. Again a packed room. Again the door too far away. And so I began to recognise the possible flashpoints and would try to avoid them as much as possible (apologies God and past bosses).

It seems odd admitting to it in public. It's still a bit of a shameful secret amongst sufferers I think. It's almost like an admittance of not coping with life. Although I believe strongly that I am. If I'm honest I don't consider myself the type of person who would suffer from such things. Whatever that 'type' is.

But there is it. Not my fault, but my problem. And I'm not the only one.

On a recent discussion on the subject one friend admitted to me that 'Lately I've had the constant feeling of butterflies, like I'm anxious about everything. And then I've started feeling near panic attacks about some things that shouldn't make me feel panicky.'

Another said, 'Earlier in the year I found myself straying into feeling anxious again; I felt like I had this huge pressure on my chest all the time and was crying at the drop of a hat.'

One poor woman told me of the guilt and fear she suffered over them: 'I suffer from panic attacks; they got so bad earlier this year that my daughter started to imitate me when they happened in front of her. I got a good doctor so they have abated for now. I never ever felt ashamed of it. It is the most frightening experience to go through in that moment and time seems to stop, so much so that I feel that my mind and my body are going to stop.'

Sara, who writes openly about her diagnoses on her blog, *Not Another Book Blogger*, also went through major issues with her condition: 'It was a surprise finding out that that was what was wrong with me. I thought I was dying; my attacks caused me to go unconscious each time. I felt like I couldn't tell anyone outside of my immediate family, and only now after seven years am I starting to open up about it.'

These women are not all going through divorce and separation, but they are living with their own demons.

Why Do They Happen?

Although each case is individual, many sufferers believe that it's down to the frantic pace in which we live our lives. We run from one task to the next, trying to squeeze in just one last thing – 'I'll just do this and then I'll sit down …', 'I'll just finish this before I take a break …', 'I'll just go here before I have a rest …'. And of course the sit-down/break/rest never comes because the tasks are endless – especially as a single parent.

My friend Annie says that:

> I've decided I live life too frantically. I try to fit too much in, I try to get one more thing done on the to-do list and I try to catch up with one more email and everything overflows into the next until I stay up too late and get up too early and end up feeling like I never do anything well enough. … The crappy pseudo-strength we call 'multi-tasking' has a lot to answer for. The idea that women are good at multi-tasking is such a dangerous myth. A few people multi-task well but never for long periods. No one can do several things at once really well for any length of time. This idea that multi-tasking is a strength is an anxiety-generating, production-reducing roadblock in the path of normal, healthy living.

Annie rocks.

Of course major life changes, a particular traumatic event – such as separation or divorce – and grief are other key triggers.

What Helps?

Because my condition is mild, many simple things help: slowing down, disconnecting, breathing, meditation, mindfulness, yoga, cutting back on coffee, drinking herbal teas, Rescue Remedy.

Others with more debilitating symptoms are advised to book in with a doctor. There is plenty of help out there and plenty of people experiencing the same thing.

Equally, if depression may be coming to call then it's time to see an expert. I've realised that sometimes we need to put ourselves at the top of the to-do list. There is nothing more important for our children than us, so we need to prioritise ourselves sometimes.

Mental health issues are nothing to be ashamed of. The mind, just like the body, needs to be cared for and looked after.

Physical Health

During that first year I become healthier than I had been in a long time. Possibly ever. I grabbed some of those childfree hours and spent time running, doing yoga, swimming – and it felt wonderful.

Off the back of that my food choices became healthier. It's a virtuous cycle of good and it is so important. Being fit and healthy changes everything. My very being became stronger, allowing me to take on the extra weight and deal with the additional stress. Mental and physical health are so linked for me that I can't deal with one without the other. I can't say it better than Nike – just do it.

KRISTIAN'S WORLD

Depression affects so many of us these days it seems, or at least people are more comfortable discussing it now. It can be a debilitating beast, and whilst submerged in its darkest depths I would not wish it on my worst enemy. I've been on medication longer than I can remember and it's just part of my morning routine now to pop pills at breakfast. After all of these years, I have no real grasp of what this medication is doing for me.

All I know is that when I have tried to taper down my usage or stop the pills I would get 'brain zaps' – strange electrical-like flashes across the brain. These aren't nice and so I would return to the tablets, cap in hand.

As previously explained, I had my blackest episode ever in Spain. I was trying out new medication as I did not feel as if the medication I had been taking was really doing anything, and I was on the top dose. I've also been hospitalised whilst in a depressive spell, while on medication also. So if I can go to the furthest points of despair whilst medicated, it obviously leads to the question 'so what's the point?'

I've read plenty on the illness and have tried many lifestyle changes to try to alleviate the symptoms. Like so many ailments or dietary advice in the modern age, there is often a lot of conflicting advice, and many new fads proclaiming to be the new fix in the Sunday supplements. It really is just trial and error for the individual. I have used mindfulness/meditation techniques, regular exercise, diets, abstaining from alcohol, forcing myself to join clubs or start new hobbies – and none of these things in isolation is the fix (for me), but a combination of activities is what is required to keep my head above water.

Currently, due to high cholesterol and not wanting to be prescribed more pills to be taken eternally, I am experimenting with veganism. The knock-on impact of this after six weeks is that my energy levels are higher, I've lost weight, I'm eating better, but most of all my mood has really stabilised and I have a lot less 'brain fug'. I know it's too early yet for any formal conclusions, but I have genuinely noticed the difference to my all-round well-being. I found that the more I read and learn (and the current spate of Netflix documentaries is particularly hard-hitting), the more obvious it is that removing dairy and animal products from my diet makes sense. So I am to stay on this train for a while yet.

...ON MENTAL HEALTH AND STAYING POSITIVE

Shane Martin is a psychologist dedicated to teaching the very best self-help psychology to empower people to enhance the quality of their lives. His Moodwatchers psychology course has been delivered at community venues throughout Ireland. His book, Your Precious Life: How to Live It Well, *teaches us how to bolster our mental health in order to be as happy and resilient as we can be.*

Life is imperfect and crisis is guaranteed. There will always be setbacks and misfortunes. Resilience is the ability to adapt to the challenges of life. It's about bouncing back rather than falling apart. If you are strong in resilience you have this 'bouncibility' and can harness your inner strengths and coping mechanisms. Resilience is crucial. It's a life skill. We all need it and have to work on it.

If you are low in resilience, you will focus too much on your problems and deficits and be overwhelmed during challenges. You will be drawn towards unhealthy conclusions and become more vulnerable instead of stronger.

Becoming more resilient will not mean that problems disappear. It does not mean that you have to become 'as hard as nails'. Resilience is more about learning how to cope – tapping into your own resources and fostering more strengths in order to stay 'standing' after crisis. It's about managing stress and keeping health and crisis in the same room as each other. You can learn to be more resilient. Resilience is not about 'digging deep' and burying your feelings. It's not about 'weathering the storm'. It's not about 'keeping it all in'. Resilience is about experiencing natural emotions, like anger, grief and pain, but being able to go along with daily tasks and getting on with your life. It's about being your own best coach in crisis rather than your own worst enemy.

Some Tips for Resilience

Connect with People

We are stronger by connecting with other people. We need this connectedness. Invest in positive relationships with family and friends. Accept their support. Reach out to them. They are a powerful resource during crisis. Get involved in your community. Surround yourself with people during tough times.

Harness Your Sense of Spirituality

Try to see beyond the crisis. Do not let yourself be defined by the challenges you encounter. Have something meaningful to focus on. If you pray, pray more. Tap into your spiritual self and put your problems in context. No matter what you are going through there is someone going through much worse. It's hard to see it that way but try. Is there anything that you are grateful for? Focus on that too.

Have a Laugh

Seeing the funny side of things is not disrespectful or self-denial. Science has shown that laughter has mental and physical health benefits. If you cannot find humour during challenge, turn to other sources to create the sparkle. Dig out a funny book or movie. Buy tickets for a comedy show. Ring your good-humoured friend and tell him or her that you need a good laugh.

Tap into Your Own Resources

You're not a total weakling. In the past you have tapped into strengths to carry you through other challenges.

Build on these strategies. Look back on a previous challenge and focus on the things you did right during that period. Revisit the things you did wrong and commit to learning from these mistakes this time. Don't repeat the same mistakes.

Harness Hope

It's never too late to get stronger. It's never too late to surprise yourself by how well you cope. But don't just 'wish' for more strength. Find something from each day that suggests that the situation is improving or that you are coping better. Try something tomorrow that will make you even stronger again. Start believing in yourself and expect yourself to cope better rather than waiting for yourself to fall apart.

Mind Yourself

Start daily exercise. Start doing the things you love best and are best at. Starting some new activities, for example yoga or a weekly game of football, as a distraction is very powerful Get adequate rest and eat well. These are basic things, but many people ignore them in crisis.

Keep a Diary

Sometimes we need to 'chat' to ourselves. We need to let the lid off the bottle rather than keep shaking it. Writing down how the day went, how we feel, and so on helps us unleash some thoughts/feelings that may be repressed. It can help us see situations in a new light and discover a new path.

Embrace Change and Get Ready for It

Life will always mean change. It's a journey of twists and turns. Expecting change makes it easier to adapt when it happens. We have to learn to become more flexible and not become engulfed with anxiety when change beckons. Seek advice about pending change and how to make the best sense of it.

Set a New Goal

Set goals to accomplish for each day. These will help you get through each day and at night you can review these small successes and take strength from them.

Practise Relaxation Techniques

Stressful situations are hard on us. We go through a lot of physiological changes when we are stressed. It's important that our bodies do not become too used to pumping adrenaline and other stress hormones. We need to calm ourselves down and let our bodies know that we want 'calmness' as well as 'preparedness' during challenge. Deep breaths, visualisation, prayer, relaxation and yoga are good for us. Maybe join a relaxation class to help you through the crisis.

Becoming resilient takes time and practice. If you do not feel that you are making progress - or you just do not know where to start - consider talking to a counsellor or psychologist. Sometimes the best of us need this kind of help.

5

Finding My New Identity

MY STORY

The School Run

The first time I have to do the school run following our return from Spain is terrifying. I have done this task three times a day for the past four years, which equates to … well, a lot of school runs. It is nothing out of the ordinary. Same school, same people, but different me. I wonder who already knows that we have returned from our failed Spanish experiment, and who knows we were now separated.

The older two children are nervous but excited – finally returning to where they belong. The youngest is starting school for the first time, again. His initial foray into a class-room experience, through a language he didn't understand, is now a painful memory.

They have all been through so much in the short time we have been gone. Long school days away from their mum and dad. Long school days not understanding what people around them were saying. Long school days crying in toilet cubicles and begging to go home. Long school days holding each others' hands through bars in the yard to comfort one another. I feel physically sick whenever I think about it. Their eyes fill with tears when they do.

And this is one of the many reasons we are home. Here. To bring them back to a sense of belonging.

I put on a smile and grab the car keys. 'OK, who's ready?'

They jump in the car, the older two throwing old school friends' names between them as they do, wondering what classroom they will be in, who they will be sitting beside. They are returning to the school year in January having missed the first term. Another challenge.

They are unaware of my own challenge: meeting the school mums with a broken marriage now under my belt.

As we walk into the school my heart is pounding. I hold Baxter's hand tighter than I should, squeezing reassurance both into and out of him.

'Marley!' a child I don't recognise shouts aghast. 'Marley's back! Marley's back!' she calls, running through the corridors like an eager town crier. An excited murmur goes through the school as Marley smiles shyly from my side. Secret's out.

A mother I know comes up to me. 'You're back', she smiles without question.

'Yeah, we're back. The kids are delighted.' And that's all I need to say for now.

I adjust my story depending on how well I know the other parents. No one is anything but lovely. Welcoming and understanding. The few I share all with give me strength to tell others.

'You're so brave.'

'It's the best thing for the children in the long run.'

'Do you need any help?'

Stories begin to pour forth. A sister trapped in an unhappy marriage. A friend who is staying for the sake of the children, but destroying herself and them as she does. An unhappy childhood ruined by fighting parents.

'You're doing the right thing', says one woman with real belief shining from her eyes. 'My parents stayed together for far too long and ended up despising each other. It was toxic. I would have been much happier if they had gone their separate ways years before.'

It is everything I need to hear and I fight back tears of gratitude and relief.

Another invites me to go for coffee. 'How did you do it?' she asks quietly, the unhappiness weighing heavily on her shoulders.

And this is something I hadn't expected. The number of people around me who are stuck in unhappy marriages – looking for answers, wanting to find the way out. They contact me by phone and email and Facebook. Looking for guidance and reassurance. 'You did it and you're ok', they all seem to say. 'What's the secret?'

But I'm not an expert. There is no secret. I'm just muddling through as best I can, fortunate that no one is being bitter and unreasonable. I try to give them a little advice, but most are just nuggets of truth that were passed on to me. The divorcee's phrasebook. Words of meaning that are gifted between members of the club no one wants to be part of: 'Exhaust every avenue first', 'You need to be really sure', 'Talk to each other', 'It takes two to make it work', 'Get quiet, dig deep, know why you are making this decision', 'You did as much as you could for as long as you could', 'You never know how strong you are, until being strong is your only choice.' I sound like a walking fridge magnet.

I'm not sure I am passing on anything useful, but I am getting something in return. Each of these conversations gives me strength. I am proud of what we have achieved. I am no longer ashamed of my single mother status; I carry it as a badge of pride. I survived.

I am finally ready for Gloria Gaynor.

The Guy in the Bar

I follow his eyes and peer behind me, wondering when they installed a TV in the bar, and am surprised to see there isn't one. Just the usual bar with the usual barmen serving the usual drinks. It's dark and the music is loud. I turn back, wondering again what he is so obviously staring at. If it's not a screen over my shoulder then it must be …. Oh! It hits me like a bottle to the head, smashing my beer-tilted brain to pieces. Me. He's staring at me.

I laugh out loud at my shock. I've been out of the game so long – unseeing, unlooking – that I hadn't even realised what was happening.

Later he stops staring and decides to talk to me. Emboldened by alcohol, I feel flirtatious and confident. He tells me he's from Bray, the neighbouring town.

'Bray!' I scoff, as if the town is worthy of a thousand putdowns. There has always been a competition between our two neighbouring towns – so close in proximity, so different in perception. My town is quaint and pretty, his is sprawling with rough edges.

We go on to a late bar where he is affronted to have to pay in. 'Don't mind him', I say to the girl taking the money, 'he's from Bray.'

'*I'm* from Bray', she deadpans back to me.

'I *love* Bray', I gush, hurrying up the steps.

Later we walk home together, strolling up the middle of the road holding hands. I feel like I've left twenty years of me behind on a bar stool. We spend the next part of the night fooling around, waiting for the inevitable to happen. When it does I can't handle the moment. It seems so very odd to be in an intimate situation with someone I don't even know. This different body, these different hands.

And yes, there he is again, my new best friend, leaning on my shoulder, whispering in my ear. 'And what do you think you are doing?' Guilt says to me. 'Who do you think you are? You're forty years old and you have three children to care for, and look at you – acting like a drunken teenager.'

Guilt is not a good friend to me this night. Sometimes I need him – he pulls me back on the straight and narrow and makes me try harder – but tonight he is full of cruelty, dragging me down from dizzy heights I haven't seen for years. Putting me back in my place, back in my box, closing the lid on my becoming anything more than just a single mum treading water. He takes great pleasure in cutting off freedom. He is too strong for me to argue with tonight.

I explain my situation to my new suitor and make my excuses. He leaves and I fall into a heavy sleep. But the next day I awake and everything has changed. A new window has been opened and through it a fresh light has been cast on to my life. A long-sleeping part of me has woken up, slowly stretched and is now looking sleepily around to see what she will do next. She's in no hurry; she's just happy to be strolling by, watching through windows. Looking at all the opportunities opening up.

The thought of her brings a smile to my parched lips.

Going Out Out

After a decade of rarely going out I am now a regular in the local pubs at the weekend. One night every weekend the children are safely tucked up in their dad's house so I can either sit at home licking my wounds and worrying, or I can go out with my sister and friends to drown my sorrows. What begins as a necessity becomes something that I haven't been party to for a long time – I am having actual Fun.

For so many years the unspoken and invisible umbilical cord of motherhood tied me to the home, and I had forgotten all about grown-up fun. But now that cord has been stretched, allowing me to remember the taste of freedom.

At first this gentle pull has to be emboldened by alcohol, but little by little every new extending of the cord, every night out, every childfree hangover, every moment re-bonding with friends and family has finally brought me to a place where I can walk out that front door with a click of my heels and not feel that heart-wrenching pull of the cord backwards.

I spend Saturday nights sitting outside pubs on balmy evenings hearing strangers' life stories. I head off on midnight adventures with new-found friends. I dance wildly and badly in pubs and clubs and have shouted conversations across tables filled with good food, old friends and buckets of red wine. For one weekend in the summer I twirl around Barcelona doused in glitter and happiness.

But each time I leave I come home afterwards, pick up my 'Mum' hat, and gladly slot back into my most important role. Renewed and reinvigorated. It's not that I love my children any less than before, it's just that I love life more now.

Working Girl

It's been a bumpy ride.

I began with a part-time working-from-home job that I thought was the pinnacle of what I could hope for. The perfect balance of home and work life, even if I knew it would never really take me anywhere. And then that job was gone and I became not just a single mother, but an unemployed single mother, filling out forms and begging for welfare. It turns out being self-employed doesn't guarantee you very much security in society. I'm not ashamed of looking for support from a government I have helped fund for many working years, but sitting in the welfare office waiting for my ticket number to be called doesn't exactly fill me with pride.

I'm looking for work and freelancing as much as possible. I do up my CV and LinkedIn profiles and realise that I know more than I thought I did. The experience I've built up in the past six years bears little resemblance to my qualifications, so I sign up to an online course to fill in that gap. I am hopeful but still hugely anxious of what my working future will be.

And then an email pops into my inbox. Would I be free to come in and discuss an opportunity?

This job is so perfect for me I could have written it down in a 'Dream Job' profile. The offices are, incredibly, within walking distance of my house. I would get to use my writing, creative and digital skills, and could fit it in within school hours. I grab it with both hands and send a massive cheer to the Universe. I'm back on track and the future looks beautiful.

You're So Vein

Which is more than I can say for myself.

I inspect my face again in the magnified mirror. The thread veins around my nose are all I can see when I look at myself these days. How did I not notice them before? Yes, I definitely need to do something about them. I make the booking and tell nobody.

When the time comes to get them lasered I tell the woman my life story. Midway through I realise that I am a cliché. I had convinced myself that what I am doing doesn't qualify as getting 'work' done – it's not like I'm getting botox or anything. But it's the same thing. Newly single woman seeks help in looking younger. I realise in that instant that this is an inside issue; the work I need doing is in confidence and self, not in skin and blood. When I inspect myself afterwards in the magic mirror I see little or no difference and I'm glad. Besides, I couldn't afford it anyway.

I do, however, find money for clothes. My wardrobe had been whittled away with the house moves to a skeleton of ancient jeans and ill-fitting T-shirts, so I feel it is a justified necessity to get some new pieces. Plus I need to up my game now that I am single. Boots, tops, dresses and more are purchased. I spend time doing my make-up and get my hair dyed. I allow myself a small sense of pride when I look at myself in the mirror before going out. It feels good.

'You!' A woman I know vaguely grabs me outside a bar one night. 'You look amazing. Your face …'. She swoops in close so that I can feel her beery breath on my skin as she peers into my eyes, '… it's like a huge weight has been lifted off your shoulders – whoosh!' She steps back to action it out, waving her hands from shoulders into the night sky above. She looks again, contemplating something. 'You look like you again', she decides, before squeezing my hand and walking off into the night. I have rarely spoken to this woman before, but she has seen something in me that others have mentioned too. I have carried a heavy weight around with me for so long that it had become a part of me. I didn't even know I was carrying it until it was lifted from me. And now I feel lighter than I have in years. The girl in the cornfield turns and smiles at me.

Danger Danger

I used to be fearless.

When I was ten years old I did running dives off slabs of cracked concrete over seven cold, hard, grey steps that led into the deep sea. In my mind I saw only my small self flying over the steps and into the cold water, my head hitting blue glass, never the last step, or a slip before take-off that would see me bruised and battered before crashing to my end. Teenagers used to watch, gearing up the confidence to follow suit. I wondered what all the fuss was about.

At twelve I took my brother's skateboard and brought it to the highest hill I could find then took off without a second thought. The air flying past me got faster and faster. I felt exhilarated and alive. Until the corner came into sight and I realised that I had no idea how to turn this ship. So I jumped off. Like alighting from a moving car. My feet couldn't keep up and I took the corner on my belly. Black tarmac scraping my skin raw. Hips and elbows in tatters. When the world stopped spinning I picked up the board and hobbled home. Hiding the wounds from my mother, in case she tried stopping me doing something else equally as stupid next time.

At just eighteen I headed off to Minneapolis to work in an office. At 21 I was pulling pints in a bar in Malta. At 22 I headed off to Mexico to help families from a border shanty town.

When I was 24 I strapped a backpack to my shoulders and jetted off to Australia for a year on my own. I learned how to fly a plane while there and did aerobatics with a co-pilot sitting beside me. Loop-the-loops and rolling dives to earth. The next plane I got in I jumped out of. Free-falling thousands of feet before the parachute kicked in and brought my gliding body back to earth.

Fearless.

But when Kristian came into my life I let that person go. Not his fault; I guess I didn't fight hard enough for my own self to shine through. Instead of forging my own path

I followed his. He would drive when we went anywhere, he would choose the music, he would talk and I would listen. When we travelled I would follow his steps through airports, not even knowing what flight number I was on. It was such a gradual process that I didn't realise it was happening. I left my independence on a luggage carousel and forgot to collect it.

After the break-up my first solo trip abroad filled me with terror. I couldn't sleep thinking about how I would get to the airport. Bus or car? Drive or be driven? Did I know the way, and where would I park? What if I couldn't find the car when I came back, or if it wouldn't start? All the what-ifs filled my brain until I was frozen with indecision. Someone put me on the bus. I hope they told me to get a grip because I don't think I was in a position to tell myself. I began worrying about which terminal to get off at almost immediately, rechecking my ticket every ten minutes, and my passport in between.

I found the airport. Clever me. And the flight times and gate number. A little glow returned with a tiny speck of self-belief. I wandered around the shops and had a coffee.

I'm not sure what happened in that spare hour, but I somehow managed to walk myself to the wrong terminal just at boarding time. I realised barely in time, and had to run back through the airport, sweating and cursing my ineptitude. I got the flight. Ruminated at how low I'd sunk in my Independent Woman status, and vowed to do something about it.

The Love of Music

Kristian and I first met in a hostel in Byron Bay, Australia. He had been stopped there a while and had a group of ready-made friends. I was travelling alone and was at the start of my journey. We immediately bonded over music and shot glasses of Irish whiskey.

I had brought a bag of CDs with me, lovingly chosen from my collection to see me around the vast country. He was a music addict and knew more about bands and genres than anyone I had ever met. He introduced me to music I had never heard of, swapping his knowledge for my CDs, devouring with delight the new tunes after being so limited to his own small and over-used travel collection for so long.

We would lie in his single dorm bed sharing one pair of headphones, as he gave me the backstory of this group and why the samples on that track worked so well together. We fell in love to the Charlatans, Morcheeba, Way Out West, Jurassic 5 and Ben Harper. In later years he would make me mix-tapes, graciously including tracks that he knew I would love – even though they didn't live up to his very particular standards.

When we left Australia a year later we moved in together, combining our collection, passing on our doubles of the Stone Roses and the Rolling Stones. In London and Ireland he worked in record shops, furthering his collection and his love of all things music. And somewhere amid all the moves and months my love of music got sidelined. It became inferior to his. The CDs became his collection. He chose what we listened to in the car, at home, on holidays. And I fell out of love. I no longer got excited about discovering new bands and didn't bother trying to commandeer the stereo with old ones. And so I let music quietly slip away from me. It was 'his thing', not mine anymore.

When it came to dividing up our collection he dug deep – handing over much-loved ones such as the White Stripes and Jamie T, but there were plenty of glad-to-get-rid-ofs too. Coldplay and the Pigeon Detectives still grace my shelves, despite my best efforts to return them to him.

But now that I have my own collection again I begin re-listening. I remember how I feel when I listen to Neil Young's *Harvest* on a sunny Sunday morning. I sing along to Bright Eyes in the car and discover brand-new bands on Spotify. Music is mine again.

The first summer after the break-up my sister Siobhán invites me over to London to stay with her for a weekend. There is a festival and one of my favourite bands is playing. I still get anxious leaving the children for more than a night, especially if it is a whole plane ride away, but I talk myself around, clear it with Kristian and book the flight.

The sun is shining as we sit on the grass with our plastic cups of beer. Drop-dead cool young things swirl around us and we happily people-watch until a group of pretty boys sit down beside us. They introduce themselves and we chat amicably from behind our dark glasses.

'Married?' says one.

'Separated', I reply.

'Why are you wearing a ring then?'

It's a fair question and I instantly feel like a fool. They now either think that I am a married liar or a pathetic divorcee who can't accept her fate. How can I explain the complex emotions of removing a wedding ring to a group of buzzed-up kids? How can I tell the story of my grandmother's antique ring that was passed down to me, used as my engagement ring and is now steadfastly stuck to my hand forevermore. Never to be removed because it is mine. I twist it around my finger and look off into the crowd.

A couple of hours later the melancholy is long forgotten as I climb onto the broad shoulders of the guy beside me. The band look out into the crowd and begin to sing just to me. It's my song: 'What Katie Did'. I belt back the lyrics with fifty thousand strangers. I look down at my sister and she grins back at me. 'Look at you. Look. At. You.' she is saying to me with her smile. 'Look how far you have come.' A moment of understanding passes between us and I feel my whole body fill up with joy. As I climb back down to ground I am fifty feet tall. I am ok. I have survived. I sway to the music and an image flashes into my mind. I have become the girl in the picture again. Dancing in a field in the sunshine – young, free and happy.

LOOKING BACK

It can be a slow shift from broken to whole. From shame to pride. From weak to strong. I'm not able to pinpoint when exactly I realised that I was ok, but there are many flashes of moments that moved me forward. One minute I was drowning in a well of sorrow and the next I was laughing hysterically with a bunch of my old school friends wondering why we had ever lost touch in the first place.

In two short years I went from working-from-home married woman, to unemployed single mother, to career girl. I swapped writing at the kitchen table in my pyjamas for client meetings, high heels and conferences. I thought I had no more to offer the world, but was shown that the world had so much more to offer me.

The Ordinary

The first weeks and months are the hardest. And it's often the smallest moments that have the biggest impact on the self. Evenings alone on the sofa, no one to have an adult conversation with. Who am I? Running out of milk and realising that I am going to have to get out of my pyjamas and put three kids in the car to go and get some. How did I get here? Filling in forms where my new identity becomes real. Mrs to Ms. Marital status: Separated.

In the early days I remember trying to hush the children if they asked in public whether they were going to 'Dad's house' that day. 'Stop judging me', I would think, feeling the eyes of strangers boring into the back of my head. I would usher the children to somewhere more private to talk, or answer with whispers into their ears. Four years on I'm mostly over that, but in truth a little of the shame still stings. I want to explain to the room full of people that, 'actually everything is fine thank you very much. It's a very amicable separation if you must know. And, yes, they will be staying at their dad's house tonight. It's FINE.' I never do of course, but it says a lot about our perception of separation and divorce that even after all this time I still feel that way. The term 'broken home' has a lot to answer for.

The Wedding

I can only presume that Kristian struggles with it too. This change of self. This letting go of your old identity and the search for a new you. It is two years after the break-up when we are both at a family wedding with our children, not together but not completely apart. A friend begins to introduce us to a couple I haven't met before.

'You know Kristian?' he says and they nod and smile at each other.

'And this is Katie, Kristian's …', there is a long pause as the word 'wife' drifts over our heads in wispy smoke and lingers in heavy silence. It is on the tip of his lips and in all our minds. Unspoken, hanging over us all.

'Wife! She's still my wife!' Kristian jibes, trying to make light of the lead weight.

My head shoots up from shoe-gazing and I stare at him confused. No. No I am not. I may still carry his name, we may not be officially divorced yet, but I am certainly not his wife.

We all shuffle uncomfortably, and I carry the conversation and a furrowed brow with me long after we quickly disperse.

The Journey

I can almost break it down into phases, my journey from lost to found. Family got me through the first phase, carrying me when I needed it. My children pulled me into the next – because when you are responsible for making dinners and doing school runs there's not much else you can do but get on with it. Friends brought me out and helped me enjoy the third phase, showing me that there was fun to be had and even boys who might be interested in a single mother of three young children. Who knew? I raced through the final phase – dodging loneliness on my morning runs and evening swims, remembering old hobbies and life loves that made me feel alive.

These phases blended into one another, and I can't say when each one began and ended. Some were short and over before I had a chance to take stock and realise. Some were longer than I thought they should be; others are still ongoing work. 'Time is a great healer' they said. I wanted to punch someone each time I heard it in the early days, so I can only apologise now – but time is a great healer. I needed to feel the pain and take the support to move on through each stage of becoming me again. And whether it is five months or five years later – it will be ok. Better than ok. Almost all of the separated and divorced people whom I have shared stories with are happier now than they were in their marriages. Life may be harder in terms of survival and money and chores, but nothing is harder than living under the weight of a dead marriage. Feeling hope dissolve into despair. These are the things that will destroy a person – not a broken marriage. Although it seemed like the greatest pain I had ever felt, the breaking of that bond let the light back in. It showed me strength and depths I never knew I had. It uncovered friendships I had forgotten and helped forge new relationships I didn't even know I needed. It made me a better person – more empathetic, more forgiving, more loving, more alive, deeper, stronger, freer and, yes, happier. But it's a process. You can't just rush to the finish line. Re-building a person takes time.

KRISTIAN'S WORLD

Firstly, not a single member of Katie's family or wide circle of (our) friends made me feel at all uncomfortable or awkward when I returned to Greystones. I will be forever grateful for their openness and generosity in treating me 'normally'. People were genuinely concerned for me and it meant a great deal.

The awkwardness was brought on myself in large paranoid dollops. I was back living alone in Katie's hometown, working from home and dealing with the fallout of a broken marriage, all with my constant companion, the black dog, to keep me company. Anywhere I went I was plagued by an inner commentary of who was thinking what if they saw me. I averted my eyes and wore headphones whenever I needed to go to the shops, protecting myself from unnecessary inter-action. Greystones has grown significantly over the years with new housing, but the main street is still the same size and there is always someone to say hello to (a blessing for most people).

Fortunately, the kids have hectic enough lives to prevent me from becoming a total recluse: school runs, football training, horse-riding, hockey, birthday parties, etc. - all requiring pick-ups, drop-offs and spectating when it comes to matches. Gradually, I came back out of my shell, but not having my own long-standing friends to hand for a pint or a coffee when I really needed to unload was sometimes hard. But in hindsight I struggle to find the energy to discuss my own personal feelings too much anyway, though, sadly for others, not my opinions when I am in good form! I did find myself drinking in pubs alone more than would be regarded as healthy however, especially when it comes to one's own sense of self within the world.

Where in the past we were obviously invited to social occasions as a couple, now the invites have dried up on my side. The couples scene doesn't fit for a single man when there are dinner parties or meals out and the 'going out' scene doesn't exist either as the guys I knew who would have been game have all found wives, started families and become part of the couples scene.

On the bright side (kids taking over aside), I do watch as much sport as I like without any complaints. I read a huge amount and watch lots of films. Not the same as being out for pints and a laugh though is it? Fortunately, once or twice a year, the stars align and a few of my best mates from home and I manage to agree on a weekend and a location and actually get it together to actually meet on said date and location and cut loose. It's the only time I actually feel like my old self again and for a short spell I am blissfully happy. It's taught me to never, ever take the relationships of those oldest, closest friends for granted. The shared histories, experiences, laughs and being able to speak to each other with a simple look of the eyes is one of the most valuable things in the world.

EXPERT ADVICE

...ON FINDING YOUR NEW IDENTITY

Emma Kenny is a resident TV psychologist (This Morning), presenter, writer and expert commentator in the UK media and press.

Get to Know Yourself Again

When we get married, have kids, move through careers and go through a million different life experiences it changes us. This means that when you end your relationship you are only whispers of who you used to be and that is exciting, because you will have developed and learnt and grown, and that means you need a period of rediscovery. Time alone matters, whether it simply involves reading some fantastic books, or allowing the stillness of silence into your world when the kids are finally in bed. Creating space allows a new day to break and a new self to emerge from the chrysalis.

Ditch the Fear

So you are divorced, a little older and maybe you are carrying that designer baggage called kids, but that shouldn't make you feel as if life has passed you by. The only thing that stops people being vital and attractive is their attitude. You can consider this situation a failure, or simply a step towards the life that you truly desire.

Be the Best You

Okay, getting fit, eating well and reinventing yourself may seem a little shallow, but I promise you that has nothing to do with the way others see you and everything to do with the relationship you have with yourself. You are a one-off, a complete masterpiece, and you need to take the best care of yourself to reflect the worth and value you have for your body and your being. Decide how you want to look whilst living your new amazing life and make the changes required to achieve it.

Feel the Love

Surround yourself with those closest to you because being loved and feeling bonded makes us feel safe and happy. It has been proven throughout psychology that loving relationships help to release the happy chemicals in the brain, and being in the company of good humans increases the happiness index.

Be Mindful

Learning that the only thing we have or can control is the here and now is liberating. Whether you sign up to some yoga classes, start gardening or begin taking long walks with nature, creating space to look after your mental and physical well-being, whilst reminding yourself of the miracle of being, can make a huge difference to your mental state.

Take Some Risks

Whether that involves pursuing a secret passion, or signing up for a charity freefall, anything that involves pushing us outside our comfort zones will result in us feeling liberated and courageous, and more importantly it will remind us that the only limitations we have are the ones we place upon ourselves.

Say Yes

Seriously, say yes to as many new opportunities and experiences as you can possibly say yes to. This world is an utterly awe-inspiring and beautiful place, but we often believe it is full of obstacles and negativity. Creating an open mindset by agreeing to socialise with colleagues or accompanying your mum to that wine-tasting night she keeps asking you to creates a sense of adventure – and that changes your world.

Create a Bucket List

And make sure that it is time-limited. Think about all the things you have ever wanted to do and then write them in a list. Put the ones you know you can achieve at the top and the ones that require planning, or are more financially challenging, at the bottom. This way you can start ticking the initial ones off ASAP, whilst planning and saving for those that require a little more thought or time.

Be Open

Don't believe there is a right and wrong time to date again; there are no rules to life, only the ones you decide for yourself. If Mr or Ms Right stumbles into your life and asks you for your number then go with how you feel as opposed to what convention suggests. Life and luck sometimes collide so grasp yours with both hands.

Practice Being Self-Full

You have spent however long meeting the needs of others and that often means putting your own on the back burner, but not any longer! Say no to people and things that drag you down and instead say yes to what you want for your life. By looking after your own needs you will always have plenty of energy and love to share with others. That means by saying yes to you, you're actually protecting the needs of those who rely on you.

Practice Gratitude

Every day, no matter how tough, write down three things you were grateful for and one thing you struggled with but that you learnt from. Keep all these in a box somewhere safe and when you are feeling a little bruised and worn by life open the box and remind yourself of just how lucky you are.

6

Moving On

MY STORY

The Gig

It's the end of the summer, on the second year of being a single woman again, when it happens.

Year One had been a rollercoaster of emotions, going from lost to found, finding me, finding fun, enjoying life and becoming a new person. It was at times wild, sometimes selfish, and often confusing, but all exactly what I needed at that time. Year Two has so far been a little quieter, a little more considered. I have stepped back from my new-found freedom and surveyed the landscape. A silent sadness has drifted down and rests over me. Not the heart-breaking despair that consumed my very being in the early days, just a reflective pause that I need to take. A noting of what has been lost and an acceptance of what I can no longer have. My weekend flights of freedom are still fun, but they no longer sparkle with the wonder of a rare and precious jewel. The shine has been slightly dulled and in my more considered moments I wonder whether they will become sad and pathetic if I continue week-by-week, month-by-month in this cycle.

'Just buy the bloody ticket', Rebecca orders down the phone.

I am walking home from an evening in my brother's house, and the summer air has the scent of adventure in it.

Rebecca and her partner, Lee, had mentioned months previously that there was a guy. Aodhán. Separated too. Into sport and music. You never know ….

It had seemed fine in theory. Fine when we were laughing about the possibilities over dinner and red wine in their cosy kitchen. Now? When there was an actual chance of meeting him? Not fine. Not fine at all.

I try to throw back excuses, but her mind is set. Finally, I acquiesce. I will do it. I will go to the gig with them all. He definitely won't know anything about the setup though, right? And there will definitely be lots of others there too, yes? Ok. I'll go.

When the moment comes, weeks later, my heart is thumping so loudly in my chest that I feel my whole body moving to its beat. Stay calm. He walks in and is introduced to everyone. Sitting down beside me and Lee – easy, calm, casual. My chest slows and settles, and the conversation continues.

Later, after too many drinks, we sit on bar stools in an over-crowded room. Our friends have melted into the busy hum of the pub, and we are the only two people left in the world. We swap stories of favourite gigs and bond over favourite bands. Time evaporates into empty pint glasses. I put a foot on his stool. He puts a hand on my leg and moves closer.

There is something so easy about being with this guy. Like family. Like we grew up together. It is comfortable and familiar, and I glow just knowing that there are people out there like him. It's not that I immediately know he's 'The One', it's just that I know now that there is the possibility of 'A One'.

By 10 a.m. the next morning my sisters and Rebecca want to know the full story. I do my best to bat away their questions as they ping through my phone, hurting my hungover head.

'Well?'

'What happened?'

'Do you like him?'

'Does he like you?'

'Did he stay?'

'Are you seeing him again?'

I don't know the answers to most of their questions and I'm not willing to answer the ones I do.

'We need to find out what he thinks of her', decides Siobhán from London.

'I'll ask Lee when he comes in', says Rebecca.

'Oh, I've already spoken to Lee!' Maria gleefully adds, in the most perfect example of small-town life there has ever been. They had bumped into each other on the main street. It's still only 10 a.m.

She regales us with what she's found out so far, and they jab and jive like boxers, weaving stories from thin air.

The buzz of the phone eventually slows and stops until, tucked up in bed that night, I get the only message I had really wanted to get all day. 'I had a really nice time last night …' it begins.

Second Date

We have both been travelling alternate weekends, so it is weeks later when we manage to meet up again. It's a different kind of nervous. The dread nerves have been replaced by excited ones. I'm looking forward to seeing him again. Don't let me down Universe.

I'm getting the train and hoping with everything in me that he doesn't get onto the same carriage. I safely make it past his stop and then a text comes in. My heart jumps but he is simply telling me where he's sitting in the pub. Three big fears are immediately laid to rest:

1. He's not going to stand me up.
2. I'm not going to be there first.
3. Truth be told I was also a little afraid I wouldn't remember what he looked like, so at least now I know I won't be wandering past him while looking for him.

A smile creeps onto my face. It's confirmation that, yes, he *is* a good guy.

When I walk in there he is, looking even more nervous than me. But the familiarity quickly wraps itself around us like a blanket, and the conversation flows with the beers. By the end of the night it is clear to both of us that there is definitely something in this.

Looking at Stars

In the very early weeks of the break-up, before the pain had eased, before any thoughts of moving on, before the notion of ever being with another guy had even poked its head into my brain, Kristian had very clearly brought up the subject.

'Just promise me that if you meet someone you'll tell me. I don't want to be the last person to know.'

I had agreed instantly. It was so far from my thinking that my reaction was along the lines of 'well *that'll* never happen.' But now it had.

Even though Aodhán and I had only been out together a handful of times we both knew it was more than just a dalliance, more than just a couple of weeks of dinners and date nights before it phased into a quiet memory. So, not long after that second date, when Kristian dropped the kids off one evening, I followed him out of the front door.

'I need to talk to you', I said, despising the fact that a smile crept onto my lips as I said it.

'You've met someone', he replied instantly. I still don't know how he knew. I guess that's what fifteen years of living with someone will do.

'Well maybe. We've only been out a few times, but you said you wanted to know so ....' I trailed off; it wasn't easy to say and must have been harder to hear.

'Well you know pretty quickly if it is something or it isn't something', he shot back.

I couldn't argue.

We looked at each other in the darkness and I searched the sky for more words.

Kristian nodded, got into his car and drove away.

Telling the Children – Take Two

We decide to take it slowly. There's no hurry. There's no need to involve the children yet. We need to ease ourselves into this new world, enjoy the newness and the excitement, share our stories and tell our tales. We go to gigs and meet each other's friends; we go out for dinner and prop up our favourite bars.

'I'm not going anywhere', he says to me, and gradually I begin to believe him.

By Christmas we have met each other's families. I don't want to tell the children before it's necessary – their world has been rocked enough without another bombshell. But I also don't want them finding out from someone else. The longer it goes on and the more serious it gets, the more I know it must happen soon.

'I think I'm falling in love with you', Aodhán whispers one night as we stand, foreheads together, not quite believing what is happening between us.

I feel the same way. It's extraordinary and perfect and wonderful and frightening. It's everything I didn't let myself believe could happen.

Telling the children becomes loaded with importance. I am afraid. Afraid of their reaction. Afraid this newfound joy will be taken away from me. I tell myself that I will always put their needs above my own, but what if I really must? I decide to wait a little longer.

Finally, weeks later, I sit down with them at another kitchen table to have another difficult conversation.

'So. I met someone …', I begin, and once again cowardly skirt around the truth. The children are confused, knowing that I am talking about someone special but not fully under-standing what it means. I don't dwell on the questions or answers too long. Planting the seed is all I want to do for now. The rest can come later. 'What's his name then, this someone?' they ask.

'A-on?' says Kaya.

'A-on?' says Marley.

'A-on', says Baxter, rolling it around, testing it out. 'That's weird.'

The irony is not lost on me. As someone whose own mother refused to tell her friends what her new grandchild was called I know a thing or two about weird names. Their reality of name-giving has been flipped since birth. When introduced to 'Paddy', the most common of all Irish names, the boys fall about laughing, helplessly clinging to each other with the hilarity of it. 'Paddy!' they call delightedly to each other. 'Paddy!'

So we focus on his weird name instead of the fact that their mother has an actual boyfriend.

As the days go on, Kristian is nothing but supportive. Guiding them through. He takes one of them out for pizza and leads the conversation.

'You know Mum has a new friend?' he says.

'Oh! What's her name?'

'It's not a her, it's a him. It's a boyfriend.'

The penny drops. The boy bursts into tears.

Kristian repeats the mum-met-someone story to the children again and explains that he is ok with it all. Gently does it.

When we all feel that the time is right we arrange for them to meet with him. We decide that the boys will go first. I show them a photo of him, smiling beside his sister.

'He's a really nice guy. You'll like him', I say. 'And he's really good at football – I'm sure he'll have a kickabout with you.'

It's all the cards I have. Marley is sold immediately; anyone who can play football is welcome in his world. Baxter is a little more cautious. Now it's just burgers and milkshakes that can sell it to him. As the day approaches they are both nervous and excited, but nothing to what Aodhán is experiencing. It's like going into an interview with a couple of four-foot-tall CEOs. And you really want this job.

They meet, we eat, and other than some random chip-throwing everyone behaves themselves. Two weeks later we repeat the procedure for Kaya and another major milestone is finally passed.

All the Fun of the Fair

We try to do fun things with them if the weekend allows us. In between collections, football matches and chores there often isn't much time. But it's summer now and the fair has come to town, so we decide to make a day of it. We go out for burgers and stroll around the stalls in the sunshine. The boys want to try their hand at the darts game. There's plastic tat and cheap teddies to be won. Marley goes first and wins a prize. The pressure is on now for Baxter. He throws a dart and misses wildly. He wants that toy but knows he's not going to be able to get it himself.

'Will I throw for you?' Marley offers, keen to get another go.

'Here, do you want me to get it for you?' Aodhán asks, stepping in. Baxter silently hands over his darts.

The first throw isn't good. Neither is the second. Within seconds the darts are all gone, and he hasn't even won the lowest prize on offer. Aodhán looks mortified; Baxter devastated. The woman at the stall leans over the counter towards us; even this English gypsy who has spent her life conning people for coins feels sorry for him.

'Ah love, your dad's not great at darts now is he?'

'He's not my dad', Baxter fires back.

My eyes meet hers and an understanding fleets through their icy blueness.

'Ok then! How about we give you one of these anyway? And your mum's friend can practice for next time.' She winks at us and hands over the crappy toy he had wanted to win. I silently thank her with praying hands behind their backs as we leave the scene of the crime.

Marley looks up at Aodhán as we walk away.

'You're really bad at darts', he says.

Husbands and Boyfriends

The sun is shining and Aodhán is sweating profusely. We walk down the hill and past the harbour towards the pub where we've all agreed to meet up. Kristian will be there already, the two boys with him. Kaya doesn't want to be present when it happens; she thinks it's weird and unnecessary. Maybe it is. It is certainly strange and unsettling. It's a situation that none of us ever thought we'd be in. Not something we could ever prepare for.

'Are you nervous?' I ask and am surprised when he says no. It makes me feel a little better though. Perhaps I'm making this bigger than it needs to be. I'm nervous. Though I wonder just how awkward it will be. Toe-curling-silences awkward or just stilted-conversation awkward. I want to hold Aodhán's hand, but it doesn't seem appropriate. We cross the road and I scan the tables outside, looking for Kristian. There he is, arms waving like an Italian as he recounts a story to his captive audience – a few of our mutual friends are sitting with him. We arrive at the table. There are pints and sunshine and the mood is good.

Kristian stands up, towering above us both.

'Alright mate? It's about time we met!' He grabs Aodhán's hand warmly and pats him on the back. I want to hug him. It's going to be ok.

Drinks are bought, and conversations begin. Straight to the crux of everything – football. The great leveller.

'So, does she still watch football matches with you and pretend to be interested?' Kristian asks with a wink.

'Ah yeah, but it's still early days', Aodhán jibes back.

I squirm in my seat. It's uncomfortably close to relationship talk. Swapping notes. I am the butt of the joke, but I am so proud of them both. It is all said without being said. Kristian has given us his blessing. The boys swoop in and out, extorting money for crisps and drinks between playing football on the grass. They watch and process from under blonde fringes and wet curls. 'Well Dad's ok with this' I can see their brains messaging, before picking up the ball and getting on with more important matters.

Later Aodhán tells me that the sweat wasn't just because of the hot day. He was sick with apprehension; he just didn't want to make the situation any worse for me so stayed silent.

Twelve

Kaya is twelve and doesn't need another man in her mother's life. Or hers for that matter. She was curious at first, wanting to meet him to make up her mind about this stranger who was suddenly taking her mum away from her. At the first burger and milkshake meeting she was delightful. Smiling and charming and showing just how lovely she really is. But now the novelty has worn off. Now Aodhán has started appearing on Friday nights for dinner and movie time. She doesn't like that at all.

'Is he going to be there?' she asks before we go out one weekend.

'Yes. Is that a problem?'

A rise of the eyes heavenward, a bag slung dramatically over the shoulder. 'Why does *he* always have to be there?'

It's far from the truth. We have been so slow and careful about how he has been introduced to their lives. Never staying over. No holidays together. Just odd days or nights that we try to make as fun as possible. Waiting for them to get used to the idea, comfortable with having him around. It seems that moment hasn't come yet. While the boys are accepting and often even pleased by his presence, Kaya is struggling.

She gets into the car and I take a deep breath. I don't want her to be unhappy. God knows she has been through enough upheaval in her short life, but I also need her to know that she can't dictate my happiness without good reason.

'You don't have to like him', I say to her as she stares steadfastly ahead. 'But you cannot be rude to him.'

No response.

'Do you understand?' I push a little further, needing her to know her feelings are valid and important but that there is a line she can't cross.

'Fine', she says. And we all know what that means.

Bribes

Aodhán brings chocolate when he visits at the weekend. Buying children's affection is lesson one in every 'mum's boyfriend' rule book. It has serviced him well.

'Is Aodhán coming?' the boys ask with shining eyes as I'm preparing dinner. They always know because for once it's not pasta. They might as well be asking when will the treats be arriving.

Before long though, Aodhán begins to realise his new role in their lives and decides he wants to be more than a walking vending machine. The first night he rolls up with nothing but a smile he is cast aside with disgust – doesn't he know the drill here? But before long they get used to the idea of just Aodhán, no bribes in pockets. He keeps them on their toes, occasionally brandishing huge bags of minstrels or giant chocolate bars.

'*That's* the Aodhán I'm talking about!' shouts Baxter as he jumps on the couch for a high five.

PDAs

We stand outside the restaurant saying goodbye to each other. Pizzas eaten. Kids bundled safely into the car. Another outing survived. We check in with each other – that went well, yes? We feel we are making progress. Very slowly inching the situation forwards toward some sort of normality. Aodhán leans in for a quick goodbye kiss. We've been careful not to show any Public Displays of Affection with the kids around. We don't want them to feel awkward. And God knows your mother kissing someone who isn't your dad is awkward. Actually, your mother kissing *even* your dad is awkward.

As his lips brush mine there is shouting from the car; my heart sinks until I turn and see three laughing faces, banging the windows and cat-calling at us from the parking spot.

'Oooo, kissy, kissy', one teases as I climb in, trying to hide the smile on my face.

'We saw you! We saw you kissing!' they call delightedly. Those kids of mine. They never cease to surprise me.

Sleepovers

It's over a year after meeting that Aodhán finally stays overnight when the children are there. I've left it up to them to decide when it's ok for this to happen, checking in every couple of months.

Sometimes two are ok with it, sometimes only one. Never three. So we hold on. When Kaya is going to Granny's house for a night I try again. The boys look at each other.

'Yeah, I'm ok with that', Marley nods and Baxter shrugs his shoulders as if to say 'Whatever. No big deal.'

That night they are excited. Something new is happening. Sleepover time. It all goes perfectly – just as I had hoped it would. But in the middle of the night I wake, a little face at the door, nervous about coming into his mummy's bedroom for the first time. Unsure what to do now that there's a stranger in his place in the bed.

'Come in sweetheart', I say. But he just stands there in the darkness, unable to come to me. I get up and bring him back into his own room, climbing into bed beside him and cuddling his little warm body close to me. We drift off to sleep together as we have done thousands of times before.

LOOKING BACK

Slowly Slowly Catchy Monkey

It happened so gradually I don't remember when the kids became ok with Aodhán staying over, but before long they were climbing into bed with us in the middle of the night or bringing us tea in bed in the morning. In fact, the entire process of 'integrating Aodhán' has been a slow evolution over a lengthy period, and I think that was the key to making it work.

It's exciting meeting someone new and falling in love, but that doesn't mean everyone else is going to be thrilled about it. We tried to hold back and wait, reasoning that if it's meant to be then there's no real hurry anyway.

We waited over six months before arranging the first meeting. We waited another two before holding hands in front of them. We waited a year before he stayed over for the first time. We waited two before he took them out on their own for the first time. We have waited almost three years before planning a holiday together. One day we may all move in together, but only when the time is right. Financially, of course, that was years ago, but emotional security is more important than swapping two rents for one. It must be for the right reasons.

Even after almost three years together, the kids still blow hot and cold with Aodhán – sometimes cheering when he walks in and sometimes whispering angrily to me, 'What – again?' But there is no fear in them. No worry that he has come to take their father's place. They like spending time with him and they are all forging their own relationships with him, on their own terms, in their own time.

All I'll say about Aodhán is this – it takes a special kind of guy to graciously navigate around a single mother, her three children, an ex-husband and a heavy swell of choppy waters, with nothing more than an internal compass for guidance.

First Meetings

I waited until the children were ready to meet Aodhán before arranging a lunch date at their favourite restaurant. We did it separately – boys first, then Kaya – so that it wasn't too overwhelming for Aodhán and the children had a chance to review him on their own terms. Looking back, I think that was a mistake. The lunch dates went well, but it put a lot of pressure and nerves on the moment. Some people advise having a few group meetings first – an afternoon barbeque with friends for example. That way they get to meet your partner without the pressure of 'meeting your partner'. Others recommend introducing the new partner as just a friend first. I think this depends on the age of the children. Maybe if they are very young this would work, but older children see and hear everything. That touch of the hand, the teasing from your best friend – I feel it could confuse them and cause them to distrust you when the truth comes out.

Better, I think, to be honest, but not to put too much pressure on them (or the new partner). If I had my time again I would have gone for a walk, or to a play park, or the beach. We could have done a fun activity together so they weren't sitting opposite one other in a busy restaurant interviewing each other with awkward questions and answers while I held it all together with a fixed smile, praying that they didn't hate each other. (They didn't.)

Confidants

When Kaya was struggling with the news in the early days she didn't know whom to talk to. Although I had quietly told her many, many times that she could tell me her thoughts and worries about the relationship, she didn't want to have to explain why she felt angry or sad or confused. She didn't want me to feel bad or guilty about having a boyfriend. She couldn't talk to her dad about it either, as it was all too strange and awkward. So, she sought out her sixteen-year-old cousin, Lauren, who took her out for hot chocolate and a chat. I had no idea this was taking place, but Lauren sat in our local coffee shop with her, listening, talking, explaining. Teasing out Kaya's feelings and showing her some of the positives. Later, as Kaya wiped away the tears and put a smile back on her face the man sitting next to them got up, leaned over and said to Lauren, 'She is very lucky to have you. Well done.'

And he was right.

It taught me that, much as we want it, we can't be all things to our children. Sometimes they will need another pair of hands to guide them, a different shoulder to cry on.

Having a grandmother, aunt, teacher or slightly older cousin they can turn to when they feel they need to can make all the difference. That conversation in the coffee shop was a turning point for Kaya. If everyone else thought this situation was ok then maybe, just maybe, it actually was.

Kaya soon went from not wanting mum's boyfriend to exist to sitting down to dinner with us, merrily chatting about her day. Marley never seemed to mind him being around – the 'good at football' sold it to him almost straight away. And Baxter, the youngest, needed plenty of reassurance that Aodhán isn't and never will try to be his dad.

I learned that this was never about Aodhán; it was about their mum being taken away from them. It was about their dad being sidelined. It was about fears for the future. Aodhán has stoically weathered it all, his skin growing thicker by the day. One in a million.

Split Loyalties

When I began thinking of introducing the children and Aodhán, I ran it past Kristian first. If he had refused or caused a fuss I'm pretty sure I would have gone ahead with it anyway, but we might have delayed it a while longer. I know Kristian wasn't thrilled with the news – another valley of fear and regret to wade through – but he never said.

Being open and honest from the start helped me. Every new step away from what was is hard, but being as considerate and upfront as possible – even if it's scary – certainly helped. It makes life slide forward a little more smoothly, rather than rocks being thrown in the way at every turn.

Kristian has been paramount in making my new relationship as non-traumatic as possible for the children, and indeed all of us. He has sat down with them several times and explained that he is ok with it all, that Aodhán is a nice guy and that he makes Mummy happy.

He also shows them, each time we all met at a drop-off or pick-up, that he likes this guy – Mum's boyfriend. Often, they will chat together, as the children secretly observe, taking it all in. Finding their new normal. I'm sure Kristian struggled with his own feelings at times, but he never showed it. The only two things he ever asked of me were 1) honesty and 2) not to take the kids on holiday with us that first year.

Split loyalties can be really hard on children. I know that at times each of them feels sad for their dad, who is living alone most of the time. I also know that this in fact suits him. I know that they sometimes feel guilty that they are spending time with Mum and Aodhán, as if we are a family, when Dad is not there. 'He's not part of our family', they have said to me many times. And each time I have had to agree, that no, he is not *exactly* part of our family. To be honest it's the one conversation I never have a proper response for. Denying that Aodhán is part of my family doesn't sit right with me. He's not and yet he is. It always leaves me feeling guilty, like Peter denying the relationship exists.

Recently, Kristian came around for dinner with us to discuss this year's summer holidays. It would be the first time that Aodhán and I would be going away with the kids and the plan was for Kristian to do the first week with them at a campsite in Italy, and then for us to come over and do the second week.

One of them repeated the phrase again. 'He's not part of our family. Why does he have to come?'

These days it tends only to come up now when a major shift is occurring – sleepovers, special occasions, whole weekends together, holiday plans. He probably wanted to show his father where his allegiances lay: 'I'm still on your side Dad.' I must admit I was surprised by the response. Kristian put down his knife and fork and said very slowly and clearly.

'He is your mother's partner. Why wouldn't he come?'

Boundaries

I'm a huge advocate of putting children's needs first. As parents that's what we do. Or try to at least. But not to the point of martyrdom. I told the children very clearly that they didn't have to like Aodhán, but they had to show respect. I told them that they would always be my number one, but that this relationship was important to me and made me happy. I told them that it is ok to be sad or angry or jealous about it, but they couldn't act out on those feelings. They had to talk it out with me or Dad or someone else, because I wasn't going to end this relationship just because they didn't like me being with someone who wasn't their dad.

That might sound selfish. But becoming a martyr for my children wouldn't have done any of us any favours. I would have become unhappy and they would have learned that my feelings aren't important. But I am a person in my own right. Not just Mum. In the long run I hope that they will respect me for putting my needs on the table alongside their own.

Only I and my internal compass can know what is best for my family in this regard. I check in with it regularly, and take those quiet moments to acknowledge the path we are all on. It's no use blindly sleepwalking into new relationships. We picked our way slowly, considerately and carefully – guiding our family to a new life chapter.

KRISTIAN'S WORLD

Katie was the one to find a new partner first and I never had the slightest issue with this. Provided he was a decent guy and didn't think he was about to become the surrogate father of my children, I was happy enough. He is and he doesn't. He's been nothing but a calm, positive influence and I want Katie to be happy. I'd like to be happy in a new relationship too, but this is harder. It's a small pond to fish from locally where everyone knows everyone or someone who knows someone. Plus, most people have some shared history with Katie or her sisters or common friends and it would feel odd to begin dating someone Katie had a connection with. Though, that's probably just a hang-up in my mind.

So, meeting people organically has been hard. I have forced myself to join meet-up groups and started various activities in order to try to branch out to meet new people, but when I'm juggling the kids' schedules with work too it's hard to find both the time and the energy to venture forth alone into pastures unknown with my 'A-game' on. I've dated on and off using online dating (which filled me with absolute horror to have to admit I needed to engage with at all), but that too just becomes another commitment to juggle and fit into the week. It's also quite a draining experience, trying to sell yourself to strangers online. One woman I was dating simply said, 'If this is going to work, I have to see you more than once a week.' Maybe I enjoy my freedom too much when the kids aren't around. Or maybe I just haven't met the right person.

I know my mum frets about me being alone. Especially with me having dealt with depression, but despite the occasional trip into the future envisioning myself living alone as an old man or thinking of not being able to start afresh somewhere new until I am well into my fifties, I am generally quite resilient.

I'm comfortable on my own and being here for the kids comes first and that's all there is to it.

I guess I feel my place is a nearby sanctuary that any of the children can come to as often as they need or like and the thought of having to introduce a new partner who may be here and disturbing the equilibrium they are used to is something which makes me anxious. Kaya is thirteen now and already carving out her independence, so naturally I see her less, but the moment she texts me to see if she can stay over she knows that 99 per cent of the time I will say yes. That makes me feel I am doing my job as a father and I do not want to remove that safety blanket without good reason. It's my safety blanket too.

EXPERT ADVICE

...ON MOVING ON

Stella O'Malley is a psychotherapist and best-selling author of Cotton Wool Kids *and* Bully-Proof Kids.

Telling Your Ex

There is no hard and fast rule about any break-up. For some couples it would only be natural to tell their ex-partner when they meet someone new while with others it can be a significant new problem – everything really depends on the kind of relationship that has developed since the split. Ultimately, it is probably more important for your children that your ex is well aware before you meet anyone new that you have a new life that involves meeting new people and that this may impact on your children's future in many different ways.

Some couples choose to maintain a cool and almost professional relationship with their ex and, in keeping with the spirit of this new relationship, believe that there is no need at all to divulge any personal details of their new life. And yet, if your child is to visit your ex's home on a regular basis, then perhaps it is in your interests to make sure that you are kept abreast of any details that might impact on your children's lives. If this is the case then a certain quid pro quo is essential and so it is advisable to take the lead in sharing any personal but important events in your life.

If there is calm acceptance between both of you that the romantic relationship is dead in the water and all that can be salvaged is a healthy co-parenting partnership then it should be easier to divulge the news. If you are in a healthy place and you're confident your ex is over you and getting on with their new life, then you might be free to tell your ex about your new partner the same way you might tell them about any new developments to the time that your child will spend with you: this is something that's happened in your life and this new element might impact on your child's life.

Alternatively, if you're worried that your ex has been having trouble getting over the relationship you might choose to subtly introduce the news that you are now living a new life that entails meeting prospective partners. Some exes will simply close down the conversation; they won't want to hear anything about your new romance – and that is entirely within their rights. There is no need to insist on shoving the news down your ex's throat. 'I'm dating X and it seems to be going well' might be enough. The main detail that you have a new partner is enough – sometimes there is no need to elaborate further, especially if your ex is showing a distinct lack of interest in the conversation.

Social media can often 'out' new relationships before any serious decision has been made about the relationship and so a certain level of discretion should be used so that pictures of the new happy couple don't inadvertently give your ex a horrible shock.

Telling Your Children

Children will very quickly taunt their siblings with any new or secret information that they might have and so it is often more appropriate to tell all the children at the same time. This is not the time to be gushing or over-enthusiastic about the fabulous personality of your new partner. Instead, it is much more appropriate to gently tell them that you are dating someone new, that it's going well and that nothing much will change in the immediate future. Then, it is imperative that nothing does change in the immediate future so that the children don't feel usurped, dethroned or insecure about their position in the family.

Eventually, preferably at the child's request, you can add some more information about your new relationship and add some bare details – the area where they live, whether they have kids of their own, what they work at, etc.

Over time your child will hopefully learn to trust that this new partner has had no significant impact on their lives and then you can slowly introduce the new partner – initially on an irregular basis. If the partner is introduced on an irregular basis then your child won't feel powerless in the face of the adults' routines – it will also give them the opportunity to tell you if they don't like any aspects of the new partner or the change in routine.

A child's mindless or even astute criticism of a new partner can feel very hurtful and it is important to ensure you don't immediately jump in to defend your new partner. Instead, giving your child the time and space to work through any instinctive and even primal emotions can set them up for a much healthier and positive relationship with your new partner in the future.

Managing Your Child's Reactions and Emotions

Children can respond in a whole variety of ways to the news that you have met someone new. Some children might be absolutely devastated that this new brute or witch has come to wreck all future hopes that Mammy and Daddy will get back together. Of course, this rage might not present itself explicitly – instead it might come across as stubborn, mulish or awkward behaviour or else it could emerge as passive aggression. In situations such as these, endless patience, gentle understanding and consistency are crucial for the child to retain their sense of importance in the family unit.

Some children may choose to unleash all their rage upon the new partner – even when this is entirely inappropriate. If this happens then it is imperative that you provide some counselling or therapy for your child as they work through their difficult feelings. It isn't appropriate for children to use the new partner as a whipping boy – this merely sets your child up for future complicated feelings of guilt and regret.

Other children might be thrilled that there is a new hope for a Hollywood ending to their broken family and so can have an over-the-top exuberance to the new romance. Again, keep in mind the Latin motto *festina lente*: make haste slowly. Any child who has experienced the break-up of their parents' marriage, and thereby the break-up of their typically conventional family unit, can appear to be ruthlessly keen to get rid of the old unit and hurry in the new with unseemly haste. But this positivity might be a refusal to accept their more complicated feelings and instead focus on a more simplistic view of life.

It is more helpful for children to be introduced to the concept that life is often difficult, usually complex and seldom simple. This can be done in a variety of ways but usually consists of a variety of conversations that point out the complexities of life. You should seek to steer your children away from versions that pinpoint villains and saints and rather focus on how we are all fallible but usually kindness, understanding and love is enough to see us through.

The Ex-Partner's Role

The author and motivational speaker Brené Brown tells us that 'Rarely can a response make something better – what makes something better is connection.' There is no need for the parent to make the child feel 'better'; indeed it can often be significantly more helpful for the parent to authentically acknowledge just how unbearably complicated and difficult this is to your child. Empathic understanding is vitally important. Pretending that it's 'all good' might make the parent feel good in the moment but it might make the child feel that their feelings of uneasiness or disturbance are 'wrong'. It is much more helpful for children to be given the time and space to feel sad and regretful whenever they are asked to face the fact that the family unit as they once knew it has been irreversibly changed.

Introducing a New Partner

It is essential for the well-being of the child that their parents' romances are kept within the adult sphere until the hot heat of a new relationship had cooled down to a more domestic relationship. Children really don't need to be witness to the sexually charged atmosphere of a new relationship – that period should be kept for the time spent away from your child.

A new partner should only be introduced if there is a realistic chance that there is a future for this relationship. Nevertheless, there is no need for your child to be immediately told that this is a serious relationship – having already experienced the break-up of their parents' union, it is unhelpful for children to be subject to further romantic separations.

It is more helpful for the new partner to be introduced on a casual, irregular basis for the first few months so that your children have some time to process the concept of your new relationship before they are asked to begin to accept it.

The New Partner's Role

Again, at the risk of being tediously repetitive, slowly does it. Although many adults might feel in a huge hurry to make up lost ground and to quickly find a new partner so that they can, once again, enjoy the dreams of a happy family with the promise of a companion in their future lives and old age, it isn't fair to inflict this upon children.

New partners need to be understanding of the complexity of their position - for the first few months, and even the first few years, the new partner's role might be to support the biological parent's position: 'Your mother doesn't allow you have so many sweets and so I'm going to take them away. / You'll have to talk to your mother about this.' Eventually, especially if some serious commitment is taking place in the new relationship, the new partner will gradually begin to take charge of certain aspects of running the household. It is at this point that you need to sit your child down and explain that your new partner now has some say in the adult decisions of the household. Connection, gentle understanding and empathic understanding are very important if your child is to feel that their voice is heard in this new situation.

7

Dealing with Conflict

MY STORY

Lessons from My Father

My father was a professor of law and director of training at the Law Society of Ireland. He specialised in negotiations and travelled to law schools all over the world lecturing on it. One day, when I was about sixteen years old, he brought me to work and let me sit in on one of his lectures. The young law students were bright and keen, eager to prove themselves in a cut-throat business. There was a role-playing exercise during the session where the students were paired up and given the details of an opposing pair of clients. What their clients wanted were poles apart from each other. The exercise was to see how good a deal you could get for your client. Many went in hard, wanting it all. They wanted to win and they wanted to win big. By the end of the session, inevitably, no deal had been struck and both solicitors had failed to get a resolution for their clients. The few that had gone in with moderate offers and a little compromise had, within the allocated time, met somewhere in the middle and struck a deal that was fair for both clients. And there endeth that day's lecture.

It always stuck with me, that lesson. Negotiation is about seeing the other person's side of things and coming up with an agreement where nobody feels totally ripped off, where nobody has totally 'won' or 'lost'. It's only by meeting somewhere close to the middle that issues get resolved. And getting a resolution makes the deal, and everything that goes with it, better for you. And your kids. And your family. And your friends. And your bank balance.

So when conflicts arise I try to adopt this lesson, hard as it is at times.

Shopping

When I first arrive home in Ireland my older sister, Siobhán, is back in London after spending Christmas at our family home. She had helped sort out the rental house for me, but now feels useless. She wants to be there for me. Do something to help. She is always the helper.

She sends money to my PayPal account without discussion. It comes with strict instructions. It is to be spent on 'nice things only' – cosy accessories for the house and new clothes for me. Of course I do as I'm told.

After buying some 'must haves' for the house, I fill my online basket in Topshop and clear out the rest of the money. Stupidly, I select the wrong payment method, so it is charged not to my PayPal balance but to the credit card saved to my computer. Kristian's credit card.

An incredulous email from Spain arrives.

PAYPAL. TOPSHOP. – 226.67€

'You have tipped the credit card over its limit! Why are you using it?!'

I cringe. I know how bad it looks. He is barely holding it together, alone in Spain, and here I am waltzing around Topshop buying new outfits for myself. Neither of us have any money to spare and we are both holding our cards very close to our chest, fearful of the next hand we may get.

I tell him that I've changed the card details on the PayPal account and that I'll return the money immediately. I have also loaned him some money from my small savings to pay for additional costs on our rental villa, and his move home. Are these his costs or ours? Who paid for my move back? Does it matter?

I have always been better than Kristian at saving money, putting some aside for broken boilers and unexpected medical fees. I am mindful never to dip into this fund for my own personal use, but I'm conflicted now as to whether it is mine – I saved it when I could have frittered it away on myself – or ours – because everything up to now is jointly owned and he has been paying the majority of the costs of running the family. I decide not to think about it for now. The waters are dark and murky down there.

Spreadsheets begin to get filled out and sent back and forth. Your expenses. My payments. Our holidays. Christmas. Moving. Spain. Ireland. Who owes how much to whom? It is exhausting and draining and the anger builds in my chest with each ping into my mailbox.

'I will stress again that I am perfectly happy to pay my fair share in terms of supporting the children, but it needs to be done based on actual detailed expense plans', his email reads.

I immediately write back. 'Perhaps you could tell me what you think is your fair share in supporting the children and when you might start paying it?'

It is a low dig written in anger, but a little weight is briefly lifted from my chest.

His response comes back within ten minutes. It's not pretty.

My stomach feels sick. Is it going to be this bad? Are we going to have to fight each penny out in court? Are we going to be one of those awful statistics? Are our children going to be caught in the middle and damaged for life?

The more we go into lockdown the worse we both feel. We are both stressed and confused and frightened. I remember my dad and think about what he would have advised. My next email gives a little. I outline all my expenses. Pull back on some things. Offer others. He replies graciously, explaining where he is coming from and what he thinks might be fair.

Relief floods through me. We can do this. It might be a bit bumpy but we can – we must – make it work. The emails go back and forth until we reach a figure based on our monthly incomes and expenses. 'What do you think?' he asks.

'I think you're being a pain in the arse but it's a good start ;)', I reply.

Weekend Away

Months later another email pops into my mailbox. He has booked a weekend away. It's not that I mind; I absolutely don't. But I know that there would have been a huge deal made if it had been me that had gone ahead and booked a trip without checking with him first. So I set out to make a point. To draw a line for the future.

'You should have cleared it with me first before just going ahead and booking', I reply.

'I don't think you are in a position to tell me that anymore', he fires back.

'I would never book a weekend away without asking you first', I say.

Within seconds he is back, apologising. 'You're right. I should have cleared it with you.'

I'm pleased. We are still tussling out details at every turn and when one goes as easily as this does it's a relief. Any trips away need to be checked and cleared first. Now we both know where we stand. Another box checked.

Money, Money, Money

After four months of delicate balance, money lurks its ugly head again. My earnings are down, expenses are up. I'm feeling hard done by that Kristian has booked breaks to see friends in England while I am exhausted and barely keeping my head above water. He is feeling hard done by being in

Ireland when he needs to see his friends in England. He is stuck in the outskirts of my life, unable to leave because of his love for his children. The emails begin again, as they do whenever something weighty needs to be discussed. The first is simply titled Money. My stomach knots before I even open it.

'Does my aversion at the idea of having to make up the shortfall for your continually sliding income make me such a bad person?' he asks.

Does it? I wonder. In truth I am torn. I want to be self-sufficient, not depend on coming to Kristian with a begging bowl when money is tight. But at the same time I am supporting our children, feeding them, clothing them, caring for them, keeping a roof over them. My mothering duties cancel out my ability to get a full-time job, and the very thought of the stress that a full-time job would put on each and every one of us makes me discount it as an option – unless things get really desperate. Part-time working works for all of us but limits my income so that I am in a vulnerable position. So where does Kristian's responsibility to us begin and end? There's no easy answer. I am doing all I can and he is giving all he can. We're stuck. And when you are stuck the fear sets in, and with it the anger.

We both lash out, sniping about how unfair the other one is being, martyring ourselves to the cause. The delicate net we have woven around ourselves begins to unravel and I see firsthand how quickly things can spiral out of control. Courts and lawyers are waiting in the wings. My stomach is in knots and a heavy weight sits on my chest, baring down, making it hard to breathe. I spend my days and nights wondering how we can figure it all out between us. The mass and minutiae of everything that needs to be agreed swirls around my head like a swarm of bees, my mind buzzing even when it should be at rest. The house, the shared car that gets delivered to whoever has the kids that day, the drop-off and collection times, pensions, school costs, birthday party presents, Christmas arrangements, parenting decisions, rent, mortgage, salaries, childcare. It is exhausting. I guess Kristian must feel the same as I receive another long, long email.

> I would like to believe we have the trust, integrity and maturity to deal with this in the right manner. I am never going to cheat my kids (or you) of anything. At the same time I don't for a minute forget that you have the kids for the vast majority of the time and what it takes out of you to deal with that on your own. These financial discussions are the only things that have periodically knocked us off sync since getting back, everything else has been great. I feel like you think I am not giving as much as I should (financially) and questioning my integrity and this makes me respond with emotions I am trying hard to get rid of. I know you. I know you are not manipulative nor selfish nor deceitful or any of those things. Our kids are a beautiful testament to both of us being honest, loving, loyal and all round beautiful people! I want us to remain great friends, not because of our kids, but because of all the great experiences we have encountered together and the growth through them. When we come to our kids there is nothing to think about. They are our babies. We love them and we will do everything we can both do in our lives to make them happy. That will never cease until we die.

I take a deep, full breath for the first time in weeks, and the knot in my stomach unravels. Communication. Cooperation. Compromise. And the love of our children. They are the four pillars we need to come back to every time there is a bump in the road. And of course there are plenty.

Trapped

Kristian is stuck. Trapped on an island he doesn't call home. Despite spending twelve years of his adult life in Ireland, he is English through and through. He is a Portsmouthsupporting, pork-pie-eating, London-calling, real-ale-drinking Brit. He misses friends he grew up with and family who worry about him. He yearns for that feeling of home, that sense of belonging, that popping out to the pub for a pint where everybody knows your name. Cheers.

Everything that I have, he doesn't. Somehow I am to blame. Or at least I feel that way.

Every few months the issue rises again and he rages against the injustice, ties himself in knots that become tighter and tighter the more he talks. When he has exhausted his mind and set the demons free he hangs his head, suddenly tired of it all again. But his feet are still stuck. Planted on Irish soil. He doesn't belong here, but his kids do, and he belongs with his kids. It's a circle that has no exit.

I have no answers, other than to make the best of what he has. We live in a gorgeous town. He works from home. There are friends he can go out for a drink with if he just picks up the phone. Join a football team. Take a class. Go out and meet people. But it's hard to make new friends when you're a 40-year-old fish out of water.

I ask him what he wants me to do about it. But I think he just needs someone to let the words hit, to get them out of his head when it gets too full. It's the least I can do. But the more I do it the more my eyes peer heavenward each time. Exasperated, I nod in silence. I know. I know. I know.

Things We Don't Argue About

The children. Housework. Nights out. Hangovers. Relationships. Breaking up. Travel. Phone calls. Debts. Savings.

Kristian inherits some money. It is two years after we have broken up and we have no legal agreement in place. I am happy for him. It will take the pressure off day-to-day living. Could I be entitled to half of it? I honestly don't know, and I don't intend to find out. Our debts or assets up to when we split up I consider 50/50. Everything after that point is our own. I ask for nothing. He buys me a car.

'What about when one of you meets someone?' everybody asks. I don't know. How would I feel if Kristian fell in love while I was still drinking my way to freedom? I think it would depend on the person. Occasionally he shows me a picture of someone he has a date with. I like her kind face and smiling eyes. I am totally fine with this. Or. There's something about her I don't trust. I don't want her around my kids. My muscles tighten. Not fine.

When I meet Aodhán, Kristian is nothing but open and supportive. Though he wonders aloud why any guy would want to take on a woman with three kids. In fairness I've pondered the same thing myself. Even my sister looks at me in wonder: 'I mean, you're good, but you're not *that* good.' Thanks sis.

But there is no conflict. It is honoured and accepted from the very start. The one thing that everyone warned us about sails past us without drama.

LOOKING BACK

Experts

Seeking expert advice can sometimes knock things off course. But it can also give peace of mind and determination to fix the issue at hand. Whenever we had a major problem arise that looked like it might turn everything on its head I always knew I had another card to play if I needed it. When I had my one-hour chat with a solicitor I ignored all of his advice. I should get more money. We should sell the negative equity house or Kristian should be forced to move there. I knew if it came down to courts and lawyers I could end up with increased maintenance (though I would then be kissing goodbye to a good separation). Just having the knowledge of legal advice, entitlements, and how the law viewed everything made it easier to not push back in fear and anger. I kept the card in my pocket, knowing that if things got really bad that I could play it.

Mediation helped too, although we dropped out before the end. But it forced us to put everything on the table – all our bank accounts, debts, savings, assets, expenditure. We were completely open and honest with our figures and, by keeping our outgoings lean, we managed to just about balance the books. The mediator told us it doesn't happen very often.

Communication

It's the key to a happy marriage, but also an easier divorce. It's so easy to slip back into old arguments when meeting in person, and often at those times the children are around – not a recipe for success. We found email good for sorting out the heavier issues. It gives us time to think about what we want to say. The only times it failed us was when we lashed back immediately to something we didn't want to hear. At those times it was better to walk away, digest the contents and reply (or not) later when the dust had settled. We sorted out a lot over email.

Kristian is an only child. He is organised and methodical and tidy. I am one of five. I like to blame my chaotic house and life on my creative mind. Though more likely it's just not a top priority for me. Perhaps I'm just not wired that way. It used to be the source of endless arguments: the state of the house, the unpaid bills and lost paperwork. He couldn't understand how someone could live this way. He would rage about keeping things in order and I would roar about him helping me more. To and fro, tug-of-war on a daily basis. Now when he enters my house he looks around and shakes his head. I know what he's thinking. I laugh out loud; the dismay on his face doesn't touch me now. I no longer have to live up to his expectations. So many potential arguments filter off into the air and get caught in the waiting cobwebs.

Most of our face-to-face meetings are at handovers, but we still go out for drinks or coffee together. Sometimes we are all invited to a family dinner. These times are not for airing issues. They are kept light – checking in with each other, seeing friends, keeping the children happy. I'd like to think that we both still enjoy each other's company.

We text daily, mostly about kids' stuff. Occasionally, on a bad day, the texts get heavy and frequent, weighing us both down. It's the downside to being in constant contact. No escape.

We keep all lines of communication open, but sometimes I just want to hide away in a dark and silent room. Ping. Ping. Ping.

The Four Pillars

Communication. Cooperation. Compromise.* And the love of our children.

Everything comes back to these. When we are stuck, or angry, or hurt, or can't see a way forward – we bring ourselves back to these. We open the door a little, see if they will meet halfway. Give them time. We put ourselves in each other's shoes. Ask ourselves what is best for the children. We dig deep. Find the answers. Or the courage. Or the acceptance.

Nicola, a woman I know only slightly, asks me to go for coffee. She has just split up with her husband but they are still living in the same house. He is being unreasonable. He won't sell the house and he won't move out. She is exhausted. 'What do I do? What did you do?' she asks. I tell her what I tell others. 'Play the long game.' Don't look for the small wins that will make this day, or this week, or even this year easier. Look at the long-term goal. Give in to smaller asks, accept what he is saying, let him lash out his anger. When you have nothing to fight against, the fire quickly dies out. Once you both come to a point of acceptance, you can then move forward, using the four pillars as your yardstick.

If that acceptance doesn't come mediation could be the next stop.

---

* Deirdre Burke, 'Secrets for a Successful Divorce – The Three C's', *Burke Legal*, 14 October 2015, https://burkelegal.ie/secrets-for-a-successful-divorce-the-three-cs.

I also recount Professor L.G. Sweeney's negotiation skills training – meeting halfway gets you further quicker.

KRISTIAN'S WORLD

Even though we are separated for over four years and getting along fine, the occasional flare-up still occurs. Less and less so about money as we have worked to a plan and are now in the process of selling our house. We'll have another discussion around increased monthly maintenance payments once I don't have to cover the deep, cash-consuming black hole of a mortgage on top of my own rent anymore. It still feels like Katie holds all the cards though. She certainly won't tell me if she has a new work contract with more pay, which could impact the budget I work to, but then nor should she have to after this length of separation either. I still pretty much run to zero every month; I have no expensive hobbies; my car is twelve years old, I hate clothes shopping and I travel back to the UK to see friends no more than twice a year. So, when I hear anecdotally people have said this or that about our finances and how much Katie receives, my gut reaction is anger and then despair. Why is Katie exposing such details to other people and do I need to outline all of my expenses to the whole world to justify hard-laboured decisions that have been made? It seems unfair that any prospects of looking after myself or improving my own financial position is so far down the list of priorities. Even my own!

It's nice to still be invited to family occasions such as Sunday lunch over the Easter holiday and at Christmas, but even these events are totally out of my control. I have no possibility of choosing other Christmas plans with the kids - we go to Katie's mother's house each year. Our three kids have their six cousins to mingle and play with and they love the chaos of so many people and all the noise. Christmas with just me and my parents (who are now back in the UK) wouldn't be half as much fun for them anyway. I guess it's just not having any decision-making power in what are significant landmarks in any family's annual calendar that still occasionally irks me. Just as whenever I hear second-hand that the kids are doing this or that or are going here and there at the weekend and nobody has bothered to consult me or check first to see if I had anything planned. Happens all the time; I just accept it these days. I understand that the plans have been made in the kids' best interests and put my personal feelings at being ignored to the side.

EXPERT ADVICE

...ON DEALING WITH CONFLICT

Erica McKinney is a psychotherapist and counsellor (MIACP) with a special interest in the area of relationships and communication.

Relationship breakdown and separation give rise to many areas where difficult conversations need to take place. These include the 'big conversations' where both parties may have very different opinions, e.g. whether a separation should happen at all, who should move out of the family home, how to co-parent, how to live together as a non-couple until full separation occurs and how assets will be split or future financials agreed.

Separation causes emotions to run high, with both parties under tremendous stress dealing with the loss of the relationship and all that this encompasses, emotionally, mentally, physically and practically. This leads to an environment where emotional reactivity is prevalent, defences are up, and hearts may close as individuals start acting from their inner pain rather than from a logical, grown-up or loving place.

Tricky subjects in this landscape are like landmines, ready to explode the minute they are broached, but the more successfully they can be navigated the less pain for all involved. This advice will help you to approach and manage these conversations in a way that is more likely to have a positive outcome and be easier on both parties.

Focus on One Problem or Goal at a Time

Don't try to tackle multiple problems at once. It becomes overwhelming and confusing for both parties. Decide which issue is most important and concentrate on this alone. When it's resolved you can move on to the next problem.

Plan for the Conversation

Get clear on the specific issue, your concerns and the outcome you would like from the conversation.

Use 'I' Statements When Communicating

'I' statements focus on what you have observed, feel, need and request. They avoid blame and criticism and help you to raise a problem in a non-confrontational manner. Marshall Rosenberg's nonviolent communication model, which focuses on communicating honestly, authentically and compassionately in difficult situations, suggests breaking communication into four components:

1. What I have observed
2. What I feel in relation to my observations
3. What I need
4. What I request

Example: 'I notice we are fighting more often in the last few months (what I have observed). I feel really upset about this (what I feel). I'd like to find a way to communicate without fighting *(what I need)*. Would you be willing to work with me on this *(what I request)?'*

While your ex-partner may act in a difficult, unreasonable or downright mean manner, at heart we are all compassionate by nature. We just get hijacked by our own emotional pain and this can sometimes turn us into toddlers or monsters. Structuring your communication around the four components and 'I' statements will help you to bypass emotional defences and connect with the compassionate human inside.

Stick to Facts

When raising an issue, stick to the facts. Do not embellish, add or generalise. If you are addressing a behaviour that is problematic, use specific examples of the behaviour.

Example: 'Yesterday when you took the children and didn't tell me you were keeping them overnight (factual observation) I felt very worried (what I felt). This has happened three times in the last month (factual observation).'

Not: 'I can't believe you kept the children overnight again without telling me (accusatory). You are always doing this (not specific and probably not factual).'

Roll with Pushbacks

Roll with, instead of arguing with, any attempts to challenge or derail you, to postpone or change the focus of the conversation.

Example 1:

You: 'We need to talk about our disagreement yesterday.'

Ex: 'I'm busy.'

You: 'Ok I understand, but it's important that we talk about this so when would be a good time for you?'

Example 2:
You: 'When you said X I felt disrespected.'
Ex: 'I didn't disrespect you.'
You: 'I hear that you see the situation differently but it is important that we discuss this because it is affecting how we are with each other. Can we talk some more about it?'

Collaborate on Finding Solutions

Don't assume that your answer to the problem is the only right answer. Trying to force a solution on another person rarely works. Be willing to openly discuss and listen to your ex's ideas, or brainstorm together when your solution does not suit them.

Genuine Open Listening Is Your Superpower

When we listen openly to someone, i.e. without judgement or preconceived ideas of what they are or will say, it automatically lowers their defences. They no longer have to argue their point and instead can explain and hopefully be understood. Once they feel heard, it is also more likely they will be willing to listen to you. Do not underestimate the power of genuine open listening. It can achieve amazing things.

Be a 'Broken Record' about the Problem that Needs to Be Solved

Hold the 'problem that needs to be solved' as a central focus for the conversation. No matter what pushback or reaction you get, continue to repeat the problem that needs to be solved and the reason that solving it is important.

Example: 'I appreciate that you don't agree that moving out of the house is the solution but <u>the tension between us is continuing to grow and is causing us both</u>

<u>a great deal of stress</u> *so we need to find a solution. Can we discuss how best to resolve this?'*

Use the Goal of Finding a Resolution as an 'Anchor' for Your Own Emotional Reactivity

It is important that problems are discussed in a way that will lead toward resolution. Reacting emotionally, getting angry, blaming, criticising or point-scoring will have a negative effect on any conversation. Hold the aim of finding a resolution to the problem central in your mind and use it to manage or 'anchor' your own emotional reactions. Use a calm tone when communicating and use deep breaths and pauses before responding to keep your emotional reactions under wraps.

Review the Solution

When a solution is agreed, review it so that it is clear that you are both on the same page and understand the same thing.

8

The Changing Emotional Needs of the Children

MY STORY

A Pain in My Heart

Those early days of eight-armed lullabies were hard on the kids. Probably harder than I realised. Emotions too big for their little hearts and souls spilled out in hot tears or got pushed down deep for another time.

'Mummy, I have a pain in my heart', Kaya says as she lies in bed in the darkness. Oh darling. I know you do. We all do. I can do no more than sit on the edge of her bed and stroke her pain away. There are no right words to say. No answers to give. Nothing I can do to make her feel better. My smart, sensitive, beautiful girl is hurting, and I fear the damage being done will be irreparable. Gone are the carefree days of childhood. She left them behind when she was forced to leave Ireland. Confidence has been lost on her travels overseas. She left her safety net of friends and was thrown into a new school with a new language. With a brand-new curriculum to learn in a foreign tongue, our top-of-the-class student plummeted to the bottom. She was a newborn foal learning to walk, stumbling blindly, spindly foundations trying to keep her upright. Now she was back in Ireland, negotiating a return to her old life as a different person. So much for her little shoulders to carry.

She misses me when she stays at her dad's house. But misses him when she is with me. All she wants is a normal family. Some Fridays, after school, she goes to Ali's house. Ali lives in a nice house on a nice street, and her home is filled with siblings, parents and love. It's one of those houses that you walk into and a feeling of comfort settles around you. Smiling faces and a sense of calm. Homeliness, happiness, shrieking laughter and a wet dog. Ali's parents drift around the house, rolling eyes and smiling at spilt drinks. They are lovely. Their home is lovely. All of it is filled with a love that radiates from it like a Ready Brek advert. It's everything that Kaya wants but will never have. She comes home subdued and silent.

'Are you ok darling?' I ask, but I know already what the problem is.

'Ali's family is just so nice', she sighs, head hanging.

I know exactly what she means, and how deeply that injustice runs. 'Why couldn't I have had that?' her slumped shoulders silently ask the ungiving gods.

She never blames though. She never, ever tries to make us feel guilty. Sometimes I wonder if she should. Perhaps she should shout and cry and stamp her foot. It's not fair! But she doesn't. I worry about her.

As the months go on she settles into her new routine, finds her feet again. But Dad's house is small and cramped. Perfect for one; a squash and a squeeze for four. There are not enough beds and loud voices bounce off confined walls, hurting her quiet soul. She wants her special markers and purple fluffy cushion, and the book she forgot to bring with her again.

It's just not working for her.

So we try out a new arrangement. While the weekend plan remains the same – with all of them staying at their dad's house – during the week she begins to stay with my mother instead. It is quiet and calm and it allows her to relax into her daydreams. She sits cuddled up with blankets on the big sofa, staring out the window with a cup of tea in hand. Her cat, Bo, lies contentedly beside her, warm furry stomach quietly moving up and down.

Bo had been left behind in the move abroad, adopted by my reluctant mother on the condition that we take her back at some stage. That stage never came as we realised too late in the day that, in fact, Marley is allergic to cats. Marley will never be forgiven by his sister for this failing.

Not only did Kaya lose her cat in the move, we lost our new dog, Mazzy, too. Mazzy was a cute and crazy miniature Schnauzer puppy whose yapping sent me over the edge in the stress-filled days of packing boxes and preparing a failing family for an international move abroad. Mazzy was simply one step too far for me. She was the first casualty of the breaking apart of the family home. We spoke to her original owner, explained the situation. He agreed to take her back and rehome her. The children were devastated. They never wanted to make this stupid move and now we were giving away their dog? It's not fair. It wasn't. It isn't. It never will be. The guilt bears down hard on me and finding photos on old hard drives bring a physical pain to my heart. Torture. But at the time I pushed it away, didn't dwell on it. I couldn't. I was operating in survival mode. Only so much anguish one mother can bear.

Before long Grandma is referring to 'Kaya's room' and buying her favourite cereal for breakfast.

Kaya's week is broken into staying at home, at Dad's, and at Grandma's house. She carries an extra bag with her, slung over her shoulder like the Littlest Hobo. Sometimes she hates it, trying to work out where she is for the next two days, going through what she needs to bring where. PE kits, homework books, riding boots – she is always thinking ahead, always making sure she is organised for what's to come. It's not ideal. But then none of this is. It's the best we can come up with and most of the time it works. I tell myself that in the long run it will be the making of her. Independent, organised, resilient. In darker moments, deep at night, I worry that she will become neurotic, stressed and damaged instead.

Peak Moments

An email arrives. I've been offered a free holiday – a trip to England's beautiful Peak District. There are luxury cabins in the woods with hot tubs, and a swimming pool and play parks onsite. All I have to do is write up my experience and tell others what I think. I hit reply before I even finish reading, the thoughts of misty mornings and hot bubbling water already soothing my chaotic mind.

I send it on to Kristian. It's eighteen months since we broke up and I am yet to meet Aodhán.

'Can I come?!!' he fires back. 'I promise to behave.'

'Yes. But don't take over', I reply, glad to have a navigator. We could easily get lost for life in the picturesque mountains with my sense of direction.

I'm a little nervous though. Life with Kristian can often be like tip-toeing on eggshells. Don't poke the bear. Other times it can be fun and interesting and joyous. And then there are the kids. I think it will be good for them. Add moments to their happy family memory bank. But I don't want to give them false hope. I don't want them thinking we are going to get back together, or miss even more than before all that they have lost. I'm not sure if we are doing the right thing. We tell the kids to whoops of delight.

Blue skies abound and the sun is shining hard as we drive through the park to our holiday home. Tall trees and a gentle breeze carry our cares away, and a peaceful calm settles in our hearts. Woodland walks, secret ponds, bird boxes, flower-strewn meadows and surprise obstacle courses surround us. Country pubs, hilltop hikes and cycle paths are all on our doorstep. We laze in the hot tub and march up mountains. We play cards and kick footballs. We read books and meet up with friends. It is perfect. A week of harmony where the kids thrive and their parents relax. Together. When it is time to go we all feel a sadness descend. It has been a little peek into what could have been. As soon as we get home and part once more, the children fall into the gloom. They miss their dad desperately. Their happy family time in the sun has come to an end and the grey reality of normal life returns. I worry that we have confused them. Made things worse.

But the memories live on much longer than the melancholy.

Conversations in the Bath

Baxter is sad. Two years after his parents break up he finally understands what has happened. He was only five years old at the time of the break and we misread his understanding. Now he is seven and the conversation in the bath has just happened. He feels stupid. 'You and Daddy aren't together anymore?!' he asks incredulously, before the full realisation dawns on him. After his bath he is quiet, head down, deep in thought.

'Can I sleep with you tonight Mummy?' he asks, his big green eyes pleading with pain.

We snuggle up in bed together and he tells me he feels sad. He knew, but he didn't *know*. Now he does and it hurts.

'I miss Dada', he says quietly.

'Do you want to call him?' I ask. Desperate for something that might make him feel better. Anything that will make those big, troubled eyes clear again. He nods his head and I reach for the phone. It's hard listening to him talk to Kristian, his brave face covering a broken heart as his head nods silently. I'm sure it's even harder for Kristian, who has to spend the night worrying when he hangs up the call. We arrange for Baxter to stay with him on his own the next night. Special Daddy time. They all need it and we regularly make it happen. Over the next few weeks we talk about the situation as much as Baxter will allow us to, telling him how loved he is, that we'll always be his mum and dad, teasing out questions we don't have answers to. The sadness lifts and normal life returns for a while.

Cheap Therapy

The door to our house has magical powers. Every day, on entering through it after a school run, or a football match, or a shopping trip, or an outing, the magic dust descends and the fighting begins. It's a most tiresome trick.

Baxter stands just inside the door, unmoving and in the way of us all. Marley pushes into him and he pushes back.

'Get out of the way!' Marley spits through gritted teeth.

'Baxter. Can you move out of the way please?' I ask calmly. We are all tired and I can't face another argument yet. I have come straight from work to school to home and I just want to shut my own front door before the next battle begins.

Baxter stands his ground, his back to us. I'd bet money that he has a smile on his face as he waits for us all to kick off, knowing where this is going, waiting for the fireworks to explode.

'Baxter!' I push through and Marley follows. They shove each other on the way past. Marley does a Ronaldo, diving to the floor in agony, clutching a random limb. He kicks out at passing legs. Baxter smirks down at him as if to say 'What are you doing down there Stupid?'

'He's smiling at me! Mum! Mum! He's smiling at me!' Marley yells with deep rage, tears of frustration already pricking at his eyes.

I'm too tired for this. At least let me have a cup of tea before I have to don my referee hat. I glide into the kitchen in a bubble, hoping the trail of destruction behind me stops exploding.

Of course it doesn't.

Marley jumps up and pushes Baxter against the wall. Baxter pushes back. Anger rising. 'Muuuum! Muuum!' they call. Then Baxter drops the grenade. 'Marley's got anger issues', he taunts.

Boom!

And it all kicks off.

They both have anger issues at the moment. I think I do too. Baxter toys with Marley until he explodes, and then lets his own aggression out in the wrestling that follows. My own anger comes spilling out on top until the whole house operates in a cloud of outrage that can be seen from space.

Everyone is cross and shouty. All. The. Time. It's exhausting and frustrating and upsetting.

I decide we need a catalyst for change. We need to replace the hate with positivity. Flowers in gun barrels. I buy a huge piece of blue cardboard and some pink love heart post-it notes and call the children around the kitchen table. They watch me as I write in big letters on the top of the card – 'THE GUNN LOVE BOMB'.

They roll their eyes as I stick it to the wall. Whatever. Another of Mum's crazy ideas.

'Ok. Take a love heart and write something nice about the person next to you', I instruct. 'I'll start.'

Baxter, I am very PROUD of you I write.

The others begin to take the notes, silently writing.

To Mum. I appreciate all you do for me. Love Marley.

Baxter you are very cuddly. From Kaya.

Marley. You are grate at football. From Baxter.

Kaya. You are sweet and kind. Love Mum.

Every day we all write one love bomb for someone in the family. Before long the blue sky is filled with pink love hearts declaring us all wondrous. We sit next to it at dinner and read them out. It's like a tiny hole in a big balloon, slowly releasing the pressure. €2.50 therapy for the whole family.

Wild Things

One of the children is struggling. Behaviour is getting out of control. He picks fights and hits out. Toddler tantrums and angry outbursts not in keeping with his age. He has big emotions bursting from him and it scares and pains me to see it. I've used up all my parenting skills and patience. I am at the end of my very frayed tether. I shout back and say terrible things in the heat of terrible arguments.

'Why do you have to try to annoy everyone all the time?'

'Why do you have to make everyone unhappy?'

I am a Wild Thing, gnashing my terrible teeth and showing my terrible claws.

I need some outside help.

I seek out a play therapist who begins to sees him once a week. It's his time, his space. I cannot enter and I cannot ask questions. He tells me they just play and I look at my bank statement wondering how expensive a 45-minute sword fight can be possibly be. But after a couple of months we gain insights into his mind and feelings that we might never have figured out on our own. It makes parenting the meltdowns easier. A small ray of light blinks from the back of the cave and we move towards it.

LOOKING BACK

All You Need Is Love

Taking on our children's emotions when our own are so heightened is hard. How can I comfort when I need to be comforted? I'm not sure I realised that it was ok to tell them that I felt sad; sometimes they need to know that. Sometimes I needed a hug as much as they did. I gave whatever I could in those early days, it hurt but it helped me too.

Others further down the track counselled me: Lean on others. Ask for help. Take it when it is offered. Keep a close eye on the children; they will need you and your unconditional love more than ever.

Throughout the past four years whenever I have had a wobble, wondering whether we have damaged our children for life, wondering if they will need therapy when they get older (who doesn't?), wondering if their future relationships are doomed, I always go back to one simple piece of advice my sister gave me. Children will be ok as long as they know that they are fully loved – unconditionally, unboundedly, unmistakably. If love is at the heart of everything they will get through anything. Our children have love from us both in spades – buckets and spades of love. I can only trust that this will balance out the upheaval and heartbreak they have suffered along the way. Smother them with love.

The Blame Game

I read countless online articles about how to manage children's emotions when divorcing. Many of them told me to tell them, again and again, 'This is not your fault', 'None of this is your fault.' But I could never bring myself to say it to them. It wasn't of course that they were in any way to blame at all; it was just that I didn't want to put that seed of thought into their head in the first place. I didn't believe that they *did* think it was their fault. And by saying 'It's not your fault', would they begin to wonder if it actually was? I still think I did the right thing for my kids in my circumstance, and it raises the importance of not blindly following expert advice. We are often the greatest experts on our children. Sometimes we just need to quieten the noise and listen to our own advice. Sometimes we just need to go with our gut.

Special Occasions

We've been on a few family trips together since the break-up. Forty-eight hours in Lapland with Kristian's parents eased us in. In the Peak District we hit our peak. Festivals in England and Ireland were a mix of 'this is great' and 'I'm never doing this again'. It's funny how we revert to past selves despite how far we've come. Is going away together when you're not together the right thing to do? I don't honestly know. But even now, after trips of a lifetime to Italy, Disney World, Lapland and more, many of which were funded by Kristian's ever-generous parents, the Peak District holiday stands out in their mind as their favourite. That's got to stand for something right?

Christmas and birthdays are sacred. Neither of us is missing them for anything. When it all comes down to it having both their mum and dad there smiling on their special day is the best present we can give them. So we make it happen. The relationship we've built since breaking up allows us to. Of course this isn't always possible in every relationship. Now that the children are older birthdays usually consist of a cake at Grandma's house and a family meal. We split costs as much as possible and it works for us.

Christmas is a little more complicated, and expensive. For the first few years we bought our own 'big' presents for the kids and split the cost of everything else. We both ended up crippled by the costs. Last year their main present was from both Mum and Dad. They didn't seem to notice the fact that they were each one present down, but the bank balance certainly did.

'What's happening with Christmas?' Kaya asks. Ever organised, she wants to know who will be staying where and what exactly will be happening. The first year forms a routine that remains. Kristian comes over on Christmas Eve and stays the night with us. We have carols and mince pies and smoked salmon and a real fire; it is everything it should be. When the children finally make their way to bed we watch a movie and then rummage around in the dark for Santa sacks. We say goodnight on the landing and he climbs into one of the children's beds. In the morning the joy of Christmas is brought into my bedroom with cups of tea and we all pile onto the bed together. The children are overjoyed. No stain on their memories.

What's Normal?

One of the hardest matters I've found when it comes to children's emotions is siphoning through what is normal six-, seven-, eight- or nine-year-old behaviour and what is down to their circumstances. It's easy to blame every outburst, every mood, every bad day on the break-up – but *all* kids have outbursts and moods and bad days. How do I stop feeling guilty for every tantrum? How do I work out what needs to be worked out and what's just part of childhood and growing up? I spend nights worrying that Kaya's high expectations of herself are because she feels the need to please everyone around her to keep them happy. I fret that Marley's slamming doors mean that his anger at us is unresolved. I agonise that Baxter's tantrums over homework are because he doesn't feel good enough. It's virtually impossible to work out what behaviour is caused by broken dreams and what just by hormones, so I stop trying. I go back to my sister's advice. Keep loving as hard as you can.

Within a year Marley's 'over' anger is gone. He is steady, kind, happy, with occasional outbursts that I'd be worried if he didn't have. One day Baxter wakes up as a different child. Considerate, thoughtful, in control. He still has his moments, but the extreme emotions that leave us all reeling have left, for now at least. Ages and stages and changes. Keep loving.

We both check in with them all constantly still. Giving them an opportunity to open up about any feelings they may be struggling with. Sometimes I forget about the super-powers of one-on-one time. Such a simple thing, but there is so much to gain from it. Our arrangement means that all three have special Daddy time frequently. But one-on-one Mum time is harder to steal. I'm still working on that. When Baxter was going through a particularly difficult time and I was tearing my hair out with frustration I looked for advice from an online parenting group (everyone should have one of these). 'Have you tried one-on-one time?' someone asked. Of course I hadn't. Silly me. I was so desperate for something to help that I farmed the other two out and arranged a hot chocolate date that very day. I was worried that big, scary feelings were raging into the home from past memories resurfacing. We had recently looked through old photos and I was sure this had caused a shift in his unsteady foundations. I tried to draw it out of him, asking questions, telling stories. But he wouldn't budge. Until we were about to leave and he told me that actually there was something that had been on his mind. I leaned in close, praying that it wouldn't be something out of my control, hoping he wasn't going to say he wanted us to get back together or he cried himself to sleep every night.

'I think Robert is better at football than me', he said, head down.

I melted onto the floor with relief. We talked out the problem together, then walked merrily home holding hands.

A huge lesson that sometimes the big things troubling them aren't my big things at all.

Thankfully, so far, any behavioural issues are contained within the house. They are house devils and street angels, charming everyone left in their wake. They save their worst for me. Doesn't every child? Sometimes it gets to me, but mostly it's ok.

I do now understand why single mothers feel that their child needs to be better behaved than everyone else's – because we feel society will judge the child otherwise. 'He comes from a broken home, that's why he's always rude.' 'Poor girl, her home life is difficult; no wonder she's acting up.' We question it ourselves when behaviour is bad, so it's no wonder we predict that other people will.

My children have been through so much in their short lives, coped with the changes, rolled with the upheaval. They are strong and compassionate and polite and caring and I couldn't be prouder of the people they have become.

KRISTIAN'S WORLD

The first few nights in my new one-bedroom abode had my daughter in with me in my double bed, and the boys top-to-toeing on a single mattress on the floor down the side of my bed. It wasn't ideal. Nor was trying to get up to go to the toilet in the middle of the night without stepping on one of them. I used to joke around, playing 'silly daddy' and trying to keep their minds from wandering off anywhere too deep. I wasn't ready for their questions, as I wasn't sure I had answers. I was still in a state of confusion as to what was happening in my life. However, looking at their little faces fast asleep used to fill me with immense joy and an extremely strong will to protect them. No matter what, they were my babies.

I would often look back to my erratic behaviour and hope and pray it wouldn't leave a lasting impact. This has always been my biggest fear as a parent, that any of my negative traits would eventually be reflected in my own kids' behaviours. Don't be like that, be more like this. 'We become our parents', they say. Anyone who has met my parents would say I am really lucky. I hope that in the future people will say the same thing to my children – that they were lucky to have me as a dad.

Physical and verbal displays of love and affection play a massive part in my life. I think that would sound normal to most people. Maybe not. I do think kids are overly pampered in today's society and that parents' whole 'raison d'être' in the modern world appears to be about becoming the ultimate perfect parents, but then maybe it's a generational reaction to our more conservative upbringings. Regardless, looking my kids in the eyes and telling them I love them, as well as smothering them in endless kisses and cuddles, is the happiest part of my week. They're getting older now, so I am learning to rein it in, especially on the school drop-offs or in front of friends – but knowing that I truly love them, am always here for them and that they are the most important part of my life is hopefully all they need to grow up stable, confident and prepared to take some risks.

EXPERT ADVICE

...ON CHILDREN'S CHANGING EMOTIONAL NEEDS

Peadar Maxwell is a chartered psychologist who has worked with children, adolescents and their families for twenty years in Ireland and the United States. Peadar has a keen interest in attachment and relationships as well as how children cope with anxiety. Peadar is a well-respected public speaker and media contributor and has developed and delivered training to parents and professionals as well as speaking at conferences

We are all wired for attachment, to experience love, security and togetherness. Our children require our love, attention and guidance from birth and all through life to help them form the basis of independence and healthy interdependence in future relationships. Children assume that their parents and their family will be together always. Parental separation interrupts this part of relational development and can impact children, adversely affecting their mental health and ability to experience trust in new relationships. Separation and divorce can lead to profound feelings of loss, for which children require the time and space to grieve. It is not divorce itself that is the problem developmentally but how parents manage this challenging situation. At the time of separating partners may be enmeshed in conflict. Their child needs them to continue to parent in a loving, mindful and grounded way. Those needs are surprisingly similar across ages and developmental stages.

Parents must keep in mind that while they are divorcing one another their commitment and responsibility to their child will continue into the future and encompass birthdays, significant life events and maybe grandparenting. Parents are needed to nurture their child's development well into adulthood. While some parents might disappear after separation others can learn how to parent in ways they did not do in the marriage. Either way, separation can offer ex-partners the opportunity to grow as parents, take on new roles and protect their child from the disruption caused by divorce. The most important task for parents in the process and aftermath of divorce is to reduce and manage conflict. If the divorce happened because of conflict then why would adults continue to live a life of conflict that wears them down and damages their child's emotional health and sense of well-being?

To help your growing child stay healthy emotionally try to remember these five points:

- Resolve conflict. Let go of the pre-separation angst and allow yourself and your ex-partner to move on. You are no longer together so accept the other person for who they are. It is time to transfer your needs as an adult to other adults. Your ex-partner is no longer responsible for your needs and neither are your children. Try to be the best parent you can be by focusing where you have influence rather than on what you cannot change.
- Do not undermine your child's other parent just as you would not speak badly to someone else's child about what you think of their parents. Undermining your ex is tempting but petty and undermines one of your child's primary relationships. If you harbour judgements share those with a close friend or a professional.
- Facilitate good and frequent access between parents and get professional advice where there has been abuse or if danger exists. Parents can feel lonely when their children are away but it's not our children's job to mind us. They need time with both of their parents; show love for your child by facilitating this where there is no risk.
- Never use your child as a pawn to hurt or punish their other parent. Many parents inadvertently use their child as a way to get at the other parent. This is unhealthy and is not in the best interests of your child. Cooperating with your ex is not giving in; it is doing what is right for your child.
- Keep safe boundaries in your parenting relationships. While the best approach for your child's positive mental health is to smile, speak respectfully and co-parent, blurred boundaries such as fighting one day and being intimate the next confuses children and creates false hope. Let your child know that you have ceased to be a couple but will always be their parents.

Separation and divorce bring up lots of feelings for children. By letting your child know that you are available to answer their questions, to facilitate their relationship with their other parent and to keep their world as safe and consistent as you can you are minding their mental health and building their resiliency.

For children of all ages change can cause them to feel unsafe. This can turn into a sense of panic or anger at the world. Try your best to keep as many things in your child's life the same as they were, such as school, activities, friends, extended family, and time with each parent. Validate your child's feelings even if you disagree with their take on the situation. Do this by listening, using comforting body language and touch if possible, waiting for them to finish their story and, only then, prompting problem-solving.

Older children and teenagers can be surly, impatient and unkind at the best of times. When their world is radically changed they may express their hurt or confusion by shutting down or through anger. Make sure your door remains open to chat when they are willing to, answer their questions as truthfully as you can, and if their feelings overwhelm them keep your mind open to the fact that this is your child. Use pictures and memories to remind yourself that this angry, maybe belligerent, teenager is your baby. Your older child or teenager, even your young adult, does not have the years of experience of dealing with relationship changes that you might have and can't be expected to handle it as maturely as a grown adult.

Tell yourself, emotions are a source of information; they come but they do pass. Ask yourself, what am I feeling when my older child is expressing disappointment in me or their other parent? Manage your feelings by finding another adult or professional to talk to. When you as a parent become angry or hyper-aroused emotionally when faced with blame or accusations intervene in the spiral of feelings by taking a break, going for a walk, leaving the room, splashing cold water on your face or taking a deep breath. Allow those feelings to be but don't allow them to take over and cause hurt. Get support during separation and divorce so that you can be the resourced parent you wish to be.

9

Going Legal

How long is long enough between separation and divorce? Irish law says it's four years. I suspect it's more complicated than that. It depends on the circumstances of the break-up. Four years of waiting to break free from an abusive relationship or a controlling partner seems like much too long. For me though, four years seems just about right.

When I first became pregnant I was at times terrified of our baby's arrival – the fear of the unknown. As the weeks passed I went through a whole heap of thoughts and emotions. I read up on pregnancy and birth and babies, and armed myself with as much knowledge as possible. As the end of the nine months came into view I realised that the perfect amount of time had passed and I was now ready for my baby to arrive. I had dealt with my demons, learned what I needed to, and was now prepared to take on the next phase of my life.

That's how I feel about my own impending divorce. I'm now ready to give birth to the next chapter of my life.

But where to start?

DESTINATION: DIVORCE

I know that it's time to start divorce proceedings. I'm not really sure how though. There seems to be lots of different options with hugely varying price tags attached. Solicitors, barristers, courts, mediation, do-it-yourself. Lots and lots of different highways, railroads and tiny slipways – all leading to the same destination. Tickets please.

I do some research online and talk to others who have taken this journey before me. How was it for you? What did you do? What should I do?

Do-It-Yourself (DIY) Divorce

You do not in fact need a solicitor or barrister for a divorce I am told.

In a full DIY divorce you source the forms, fill them out and represent yourself. If you're feeling a bit daunted by the process but still don't want to involve a solicitor, there are a number of different companies that will help fill out the forms and tick the right boxes. The cost is still very low – approximately €600 for a managed divorce. Usually they will recommend their service if most of the big issues are in agreement already. Are there disagreements about maintenance? Custody? Pensions? The family home? Do you both live in the same country?

A legal or judicial separation is not needed to begin the DIY divorce process; you simply need to have been separated for four years, with one of you living in Ireland. Proof of separation is not required; however, you will be asked under oath in court to confirm your month and year of separation.

But is it really that straightforward?

'Couples should ensure that the terms agreed are in their interest, and at a minimum try to get legal advice before signing', says Deirdre M. Burke, solicitor. 'My own view is that DIY divorce is only useful to save costs if you are literally copper-fastening a previously agreed separation, or if there are no children, and the issues are clear cut. I have borne witness to some problems that have arisen post DIY divorce.'

Each person will have responsibilities when it comes to the paperwork, such as consenting to the divorce, and filling out a financial Affidavit of Means. In fact, there are a number of different forms that need to be filled out in a DIY divorce, some fairly detailed. My friend Eva, the only person in the entire world I knew who had had a divorce when I first separated, sent a copy of hers through to me shortly after the split.

'Don't pay a solicitor', her email began. 'The family law courts are so fabulous and normal. Some of this is funny – they *do* want to know how many times a year you cut your hair!'

Four years down the track I can see the funny side. Four months was too soon. I didn't look at the actual forms again until now.

Eva Gold – friend, divorcee and superwoman:

I did it myself as I wasn't in a position to pay fees. I had just started a business nine months previously and was totally strapped for cash. A friend had gone through a divorce a year prior. She too had no kids and she told me to call her solicitor and ask for the same separation document that he had drawn up for her. All it meant was a control/alt, insert name admin job for the solicitor's practice. I told him – 'listen I am skint, and I can give you 400 Euro for this official letter', and he said 'fine, come in and see me.' He was a nice solicitor from a really big practice (one of the top five), so my lesson was don't be scared of the big names. He gave me some facetime and I got the standard separation document from him. That way I had the comfort of that element of the paperwork being correct. The rest I pieced together from a DIY website and the Citizens' Information group and I went down to the family law courts in Dublin and asked the staff behind the counter. They were so, so nice and helped with the order of the paperwork, as in 'no, no not that, first you need this ….' They told me to go off and get this bit done and then come back to me with this signed. It was slow going and I felt drowned in paper but got there in the end. It saved me €6,000 at the time. So, as dull as it was schlepping through it I did it. I felt doing it gave me power back in a way. I drove the process as my ex had zero interest in helping. You can divorce if the other person is silent; all you have to do is prove at each step that your correct paperwork was issued. So the tracked mail receipts were important. However, without the staff in the courts, I would have been lost; they were really, really kind to me.

I represented myself in court. The scary bit is not having a solicitor there on the day of the court appearance to tell you what to do. I felt alone there just by myself standing in the lobby area on the day waiting. They usher you into the larger courtroom like a herd of cattle with all the other couples. It's weird. You can see some couples ready to kill each other from across the room and some being civil and standing together. Everyone is called by initial, for example I was E.G. and my husband was W.H., and that's how the cases were called. My ex had returned to Australia so he wasn't there in court and he hadn't hired a solicitor to represent him in Ireland. I had a letter from him with the appropriate bit of paperwork needed for the last leg, stamped that it was sufficient for the judge.

It was a weird day. It's very sombre and you are sworn in so it almost felt like I was taking the stand in a trial. I guess I was in a way. I wasn't expecting to have to answer questions. The female judge was really nice. She asked me was the marriage not reconcilable (I am paraphrasing) and I said no and I nearly burst out crying as she was the first person to actually ask me that. Anyway, she was very empathetic. There was something missing from my file on the day so I had to wait and leave the room while they went back to the file store and retrieve something. So I waited outside in the lobby. Another case went in. I was called back in 30 minutes later and told all was in order and a formal separation was granted. I would get the paperwork in the mail a few weeks later verifying that. I left the court, headed out the door and jumped on my bike.

I remember cycling up to Christchurch and getting off the bike to have a good cry. I did it on my own and didn't want a pal there but looking back I should have had a friend with me. I was making the day a transactional day, but actually it was a really significant event I wasn't willing to give credence to.

In saying all of that, I loved the process as it taught me a lot. I understand the system and have given my set of paperwork out to a bunch of people who have been in the same situation as me. I would recommend doing it yourself if you don't have property or kids which we didn't at the time. If we had I would have had to have used a solicitor as it's a more complicated process.

Eva is amazing.

Mediation

Mediation is used to work out all those tricky, and not to tricky, aspects of a divorce that may prevent taking the DIY option. It's making sure you both know what you're agreeing to before papers are issued. Mediation gives you a working document, free of legal jargon, to go forward into the necessary legal part of your divorce. Depending on how much you have already worked out between yourselves over the four years, the mediation process can take between one and six sessions.

When Kristian and I went to a free mediation service it was with a view to working out our financial arrangements in light of our newly separated status, not a full divorce. We went to three sessions via the state-run Family Mediation Service, and drew up an agreement to refer back to. It wasn't legalised, but it was there if we needed it. I dig it out and read through – four years later and a lot of it still stands. It's a good starting point for us. I think about how far we've come since walking up those cold grey steps in Dublin and can't help but feel a little proud, but mostly just hugely thankful.

In the case of initiating divorce proceedings, Mediation Ireland advises that the mediation process can take as little as one day with everyone together in a room (if most of the issues have been agreed already). It recommends that divorcing couples each have their own legal counsel/solicitor with them for the day when this is being done. The legal representative then uses this agreement to draw up the terms for which a divorce can then be granted in a court of law.

Once a working agreement is in place then it's time to jump to the next stage of the divorce process – either via DIY divorce or through a solicitor.

Solicitors

If communication has broken down, or you just can't work out the details of the split between yourselves or with the help of a mediator, then it's probably best to get some legal advice. In fact I would say that it's a good idea to get legal advice regardless – it's so important to make sure things are as they should be before legalising matters.

However, I am reminded time and time again that the legal process can be frustrating and costly. If one party decides not to engage or to drag out the process it can be difficult to hurry them along. Letters fly back and forth as it all inches forward, slowly, slowly, slowly.

A friend tells me about her spouse who walked out after having an affair. Four years later after paying nothing towards the mortgage costs he's back – wanting half the house that was in negative equity when he left. He's dragging his heels as the house prices shoot up, waiting for the best deal he can get. It's beyond frustrating for her. Her solicitor sends another letter and the wait continues.

But it's not all bad news. Many solicitors recommend getting to a point where couples can all meet together – with legal counsel present – to thrash out the details so that a court date can then be set. Not all solicitors are out for legal costs – often they genuinely want to do the best for their client, in as cost-effective a way as possible.

I also discover that alongside the free Family Mediation Service provided by the Legal Aid Board there is an (almost free) legal aid service also available. The aid is income-dependent, so only those earning less than €18,000 a year are eligible. Waiting lists depend where you are in the country, but it is well worth looking into if you (a) need legal counsel and (b) can't afford one.

Paying a solicitor can cost from about €5,000 for a straight-forward divorce, but costs can run into tens of thousands of Euro if issues can't be resolved. In bigger cases, where more is at stake, costs can be increased much further by expert reports such as from valuers, accountants and child psychologists.

Anya Harris – divorcee, mum of two, human lifeline:

For some of us, the hardest step of all is the separation one and by the time it comes to an actual divorce, it's more or less a formality.

I was one of those who went to a solicitor during their busiest week of the year – the first few working days in January.

We had been separated for some time and had two very young children. I'd been in no hurry to proceed any further than was absolutely necessary. I was happy we were living apart and my ex was paying as much child support as he was supposed to. Even though the sum was dire, my solicitor had advised this was all that would be possible.

Plus, the arrangements for the children to see him every other weekend were working out because he worked away.

These are two entirely different matters in the eyes of the law. You can't withhold access to the children if your ex-partner is not doing their bit financially or vice versa. My solicitor would even go to the extent of writing out two separate letters – one for each aspect – even though they went into the same envelope for posting.

I was lucky in that I had been granted legal aid, but not so lucky in that this was because my husband had been abusive – clever and controlling as opposed to violent, but nevertheless qualities that constituted qualification for help.

The paperwork was enough to put off anyone less determined (or desperate, depending on how you viewed it) and this alone nearly broke me.

I don't know what I would have done without this support though. I certainly couldn't have afforded proceedings on my own, but I had to get out, formally, once and for all for the sake of my own sanity.

My solicitor taught me how important it was to always be decent. My emotional ramblings to her would be cut to a legal paragraph to him. He actually didn't even employ a legal representative of his own. He would just phone her – which kind of says it all.

She was more like a counsellor most of the time – very kind, empathetic, knowledgeable and fair, and I discovered it's not actually that hard to divorce someone for unreasonable behaviour. I'd been keeping notes of various incidents behind my husband's back for a few years – as previously advised to when first making enquiries about separating – and these were enormously useful.

It's quite a scary thing to do, but it's surprising how much you can forget when you live day in and day out with someone who undermines everything you say and do, exploiting your vulnerability because you have young children to consider. You're kind of trapped and it takes strength and help – or, ideally, expertise – to extricate yourself.

I remember her saying that she had enough information to proceed after the first four or five things I'd read out, but I'd insisted on keeping on going. This stuff had been a long time building up and the secrets I'd never told a soul came pouring out. Getting them all off my chest in such an understanding and experienced environment worked wonders for my self-esteem and it turned out to be quite a cathartic hour or so, because the perpetrator holds the power until you tell, and once you start it's best not to stop.

My then-husband could not and did not contest one thing; however he had complicated things for us all by his frequent threats to commit suicide whilst we were still together. This is chronic emotional blackmail – typical domestic abuse I would later learn – and it meant I put up with a lot more than I should have for much longer than I could cope with, so by the time I finally managed to enforce a formal separation I was already exhausted and was grateful for the buffer that my solicitor provided.

He was only allowed supervised contact with the children for a long time as a result and I swear it saved my life to be able to consistently tell him, 'My solicitor says ...' rather than have the repeated arguments he would have delighted in and whereby he would attempt to mercilessly bully me into doing what he wanted. With my solicitor's support, I never gave into him once and, to this day, many years later, I can still quote her and keep him at bay.

I will forever be grateful for that and for her making our divorce as smooth as was possible, considering the otherwise fractious nature to it.

See You in Court

If an agreement just can't be reached it means going to court to sort out the details – and that's when it can get nasty, and *very* expensive. However, sometimes just the threat of court will encourage the other party to engage with proceedings, and agreements can be reached at any point along the way.

A case running for just two days could come to at least €15,000 – and that's before barrister costs. So that's at least fifteen thousand reasons to try to avoid it.

Regina Hinds – two-times divorcee and office style icon:

It was when I realised that my husband was clearing out our accounts and hiding money that I knew things were going to get nasty.

For eighteen months we lived in the same house as solicitors' letters were sent back and forth. At night I used to lock myself in my bedroom, and every weekend I would go home to my mother's or else stay with a friend. Anything to get away from the crushing atmosphere.

He wanted the house. 'No problem', I said. I never liked it anyway, and I didn't want to be left with the unhappy reminders. But he wasn't willing to give me anything for it. Or anything else for that matter.

It soon became clear that court was the only option. I should have known sooner; he was an aggressive bully who had shown his true colours when he started throwing things at me.

When the day came I had my solicitor and a barrister with me, as did my ex. My brother had also agreed to come; I was feeling vulnerable and deeply emotional and needed that support.

We had arranged to use the private rooms in the chamber of the courthouse to try to resolve the negotiations. He sat with his team in one room and I sat with mine in another. They moved back and forth, inching arguments forward bit by bit.

Barristers want concrete evidence of why you deserve what you are looking for, so you need the facts and proof to back up any claims.

Seven hours passed. It was the most stressful day of my life.

In the end we agreed a figure. He thought it was far too much, but the alternative was forensic accountants who would dig over his considerable business figures, so he signed the documents.

Our agreement was reached on the steps of the courthouse. Little did I know that ten years down the track I would be back again. This time defending my home from an unscrupulous second husband who lied and cheated his way through my money and my heart. This one ended up inside the court, but lasted just 30 minutes. 'I've heard enough!' the judge declared as he sent him on his way, tail between his legs.

I ended up with post-traumatic stress from the ordeal, but can say with 100 per cent certainty that my legal teams, on both occasions, saw me through the worst. Without them who knows where I would have ended up. I fought for my rights and nothing more. And I'm proud that I stood up for myself when I could have run away and hidden.

Divorce is an expensive and deeply stressful life event, and I know for sure that I will never, ever go through it again.

Each of these different options is about going through exactly the same steps to get the same piece of paper at the end:

1. Agree the split
2. Agree the terms (children, maintenance, assets/debts, pensions/insurance)
3. Go to court to finalise the divorce

As for Us ...

As for us, I'd like to think we have made it this far amicably, compassionately and fairly. We are currently in the process of getting our house ready for sale, which is another step down separate roads. It's been unexpectedly emotional going back there – clearing out cupboards and cleaning rooms. A couple of lone plates that made up part of our first dining set sit chipped and dusty at the back of a press. I wipe a cloth across the fireplace and it snags on something. As I run my finger along the wood I realise that it is the small nail we tapped in to hang Kaya's first Christmas stocking on. A lump forms in my throat and I use the dusty cloth to wipe my eyes. Memories, guilt and sadness are all stirred up, like a big bucket of dirty water with specks of glitter in it.

Once the house is finally sold we will split the profits or losses in half and then apply for a divorce, with legal advice. Hopefully the only aspect we'll need additional legal input on is the pensions aspect, as this is complex and is normally dealt with by specific pension experts.

I'm looking forward to having the i's dotted and the t's crossed. To knowing exactly where I stand for the future and what I have to do to make sure I have my long-term security sorted. To drawing a line under things, and then stepping forward once again into my next scene.

But I'm not looking forward to the emotional aspect of that concluding break. The finality of it saddens me. Not that I'm not sure. I am. It's just the sorrow that the relationship didn't work out for us, despite our best efforts and our wonderful children. That our happily ever after didn't ever happen. And even though it won't be a final severing of ties – because we will always be a part of each other's lives – it is a forceful cutting of bonds and breaking of promises made in hope and earnestness. I'll carry the bloody gash across my heart always, a part of me forever wounded.

KRISTIAN'S WORLD

Katie knows very well how I feel about this subject. Legal fees, insurance, mortgages - in my view it's all an absolute racket. Rules rubber-stamped by government into law to make all of the relevant 'service providers' and their associated crony 'board members' very rich.

Insurance was my first painful experience. Within two weeks of moving into our first home and our beautiful first child being born, I was diagnosed with testicular cancer. I had been to my local GP prior to the mortgage agreement being settled with a concern over an unexplained swelling. The GP gave his assessment that it was nothing to worry about. It happens in lots of older men he said (I was 30) and if it gets too uncomfortable,

I could come in and get it drained. A standard procedure I was reassured. I was not convinced. A few weeks
later I went for a job interview at the same place where
Katie was working. I was successful pending a standard
medical procedure at the IFSC in Dublin. There was
no problem with the medical, but when the doctor
asked if there were any concerns or questions, I felt the
strong impulse to tell him. 'Yes, I have a very enlarged,
uncomfortable testicle which is constantly on my
mind', I said. 'Hop up on the bed and let's check you
out.' Within about five seconds he referred me directly
back to my GP for a review and a suggested specialist
referral. This happened that very same day. The speed
was concerning. I went to another GP in the same
practice, and I was referred to a specialist at the Black-
rock Clinic. Katie and I sat at the consultant's desk in
the clinic. Kaya, our six-week-old baby, was in her rock-
a-tot car seat balanced on another chair beside us. I was
quickly, but formally, diagnosed with cancer. Within a
two-month period we had bought a house, had a baby
and I had started a new job. And now I had cancer. But
surely our insurance would see us through? To cut a
long story short, we had signed the mortgage papers
after the initial GP visit but before my IFSC medical. Our
subsequent mortgage protection claim was therefore
declared void on the grounds of a 'non-declaration of a
previous medical condition'.

Subsequently, my view on having to pay any form of
insurance is begrudging. Insurance is a business; they
want to take your monthly premiums, and should you
make a claim their natural position is how do we avoid
paying out on this claim in order to remain profitable?

My limited experience with legal affairs didn't exactly
bowl me over with positivity either. Katie and I had
talked about getting a formal separation agreement in
place and my parents thought it would be a good idea
to cover my own circumstances too. I made an appoint-
ment with a local solicitor, went to see him armed with

all the details that Katie and I had naturally come to agreement on as a rational couple of human beings with similar values, and proceeded to run through the details with the man. He was overwhelmed at how little acrimony there was to resolve and was happy that formalising all of the details I had provided him with into a legally binding agreement would be simple enough. When I asked him whether he would simply plug in the details I had provided him into a standard template, he confirmed this would be the case. I was with him for approximately 30 minutes and the secretary charged me €110 on my way out. I received the solicitor's quote the following week and burst out laughing. Two and a half grand! Mind-blowing and unjustifiable.

Wouldn't it be nice for people who have managed to agree their own separation details themselves to just book into the same church they were married in, sign the 'marriage annulment register', have the relevant certificates issued and move on?

My hope is that Katie and I will just print off our own divorce template from the internet, outline an agreed, fair monthly maintenance amount (and payment end date?), agree to split my pension pot value in half as of when we separated and finally sell the house and split the debt or profit 50/50. If we have both signed the agreement, why should we be obliged to anything more? I do still need to draw up a will (always on the long-finger to-do list) and I hope to do this in a DIY fashion also. Naturally, any estate of mine will be split equally between the three children.

EXPERT ADVICE

...ON GETTING A DIVORCE

Deirdre Burke is a trained family law mediator, qualified barrister and practising solicitor. She is a member of the board of the Legal Aid Board, and of the Family and Child Law Committee of the Law Society. She was also the founder of the Guardian Children's Project, a charity which provided essential support services to children and young people coping with the effects of separation and marital breakdown in their families.

There is no real way to avoid legalities if you want to secure a binding and solid agreement.

It is, in my view, essential that anyone on the threshold of a formal separation attends at least one comprehensive advice consultation with a family law solicitor. This will outline the rights, entitlements and responsibilities of all parties, and should ideally provide a roadmap or pathway to follow. Information is vital to enable informed choice.

Separations can be resolved in one of two ways: by agreement or by court order where a judge decides the outcome. With a divorce, the terms of the divorce itself can be agreed; however it must go to court to be approved by a judge. Therefore there is no way to avoid court at some stage with divorce.

As a practising family lawyer, it has always been my advice to clients that they should try to resolve their dispute outside of court if at all possible. Settling a family law dispute by agreement outside of court:

- Provides greater flexibility in problem-solving
- Retains control of the separation with the couple
- Is better for children
- Reduces levels of conflict and therefore improves future communication
- Saves time
- Saves money
- Is less stressful

There are a number of ways to achieve agreement, including mediation, collaborative law and also negotiation with the assistance of solicitors. The latter two processes involve direct legal advice at all points; however it is equally important if you choose to go through mediation to achieve agreement that you obtain legal advice as necessary as you proceed.

Mediation

Mediation, in summary, is a voluntary process which involves both parties attending with a trained mediator for joint meetings over a number of sessions. This can take on average one to six meetings, but can be shorter or longer depending on the complexity of the dispute. The mediator will help the couple to reach agreement and, if successful, a mediated agreement will be signed. This is not, however, legally binding until legalised by your solicitors or the court.

Collaborative Law

Collaborative law is similar to mediation in the sense that it involves joint meetings over a period of time. However, in this process your solicitors are also present with you and there is a commitment made to avoid court if at all possible. The additional cost of solicitors can be beneficial if the issues are more complex.

Traditional Legal Negotiation with Solicitors

This involves each person appointing a solicitor to act for them. The solicitors will communicate with each other, either in person or by letter, setting out proposals, until an agreement is reached. The solicitors can often suggest that a settlement meeting is held where everyone comes together for a couple of hours to try to agree matters.

Whichever process you choose, your final separation agreement should always be completed with the benefit of legal advice.

Unfortunately, there will always be situations where agreement is simply not possible. In this event, there is no other option but to proceed via the court route. At this point, it is essential that you obtain legal advice as the process and the documentation needed can be very detailed and often confusing. This is particularly the case where many issues have to be decided, such as custody and access, maintenance, the family home and the division of other assets and liabilities.

The process of applying to court involves the preparation of the following key documents:

- A Civil Bill – the application which is made to the court, setting out the facts and the various orders needed
- An Affidavit of Means – setting out assets, liabilities, income and expenditure
- An Affidavit of Welfare – only needed where there are dependent children, setting out their circumstances

A solicitor will advise you about the correct court to choose, and about the detail of your application to suit your particular circumstances.

Epilogue

Love Letters

To my beautiful children,

How strong you are.

All those years ago, when I first held you in my arms as babies, I was breathless with love for you. I couldn't believe this overwhelming depth of love was possible. Kaya, my heart swelled and grew so much when I looked into your wide blue eyes that I didn't think I could possibly have room for any more love in there. But then your brothers joined us, and my heart kept growing. Expanding to fill my body and spill out into the world.

It was frightening. This all-encompassing and terrifying love. I worried day and night about you all, and swore to protect you always.

Like all mothers, I weathered so many sleepless nights and terrible tantrums. I pushed prams up and down roads until the wheels wore thin. I mixed up homemade playdough, baked cakes, planted seeds, painted pictures, kissed cuts, soothed, bathed, tickled and loved you for all I was worth. But I couldn't keep that promise of always protecting you.

I wonder now whether you will remember that mum. Or will your memories be filled with arguments and broken hearts instead?

I'd like to think that when you are older, maybe even reading this, that you will understand how hard we tried. That we didn't just give up on each other. That we were once in love, but that somewhere our happiness was lost and we couldn't find it no matter how hard we searched. And we did search.

I hope you know how loved you are.

I hope you know that we always have you in our hearts and minds.

I hope you know that we did our best.

I hope you know that we do not expect to be applauded for our brilliance, or condemned for our failings. We are simply two parents trying to do our best. Not perfect, not awful, just human.

I still love you all with that heart-bursting, soul-lifting love, even when I'm yelling at you with a wooden spoon in one hand and my ever-present phone in the other. I juggle ideals of perfection and fear of failure on a daily basis, but usually end up somewhere in the middle. Another 'World's Okayest Mum'.

Kaya. You are sweet and kind and clever and responsible. I hope this life lesson you never signed up for has taught you empathy, compassion and strength.

Marley. You are caring, calm and cool. A leader who takes his troops on the good fight, returning for injured soldiers when they fall. I hope this life lesson has taught you that you can help others through troubled waters because you know how it feels.

Baxter. You are funny and bright and charming. You light up the room, sprinkling your magic everywhere you go. I hope this life lesson has taught you that the world is not always black and white, and that sometimes greatness lies in failure.

I hope you all know that –

It's ok to be sad.

It's ok to be happy.

It's ok to love.

And it's ok to give up.

We will both continue to smother you with buckets and spades full of love forevermore.

Kissing the cuts on your heart until they heal.

Love,

Mum.

To my three beautiful babies,

You three have given my life meaning when I didn't think it had any. I love you more than words can possibly explain. Love can cause pain, that's how we understand how important it is. I know that pain. I feel it whenever I am away for over three days. I've found out three nights away is my limit. Three is the magic number. My heart hurts after three nights away because I miss the three of you too much.

I stayed in Greystones to be near you, to be part of your lives and so you can feel as much part of a normal family as possible. Whatever normal means. I stayed because you are all part of me and to live too far from you would leave me feeling broken.

I know I'm far from perfect, I'm impatient and I get frustrated, but I hope you feel swathed in the love I have for you constantly. I love all three of you equally and without condition. I am enormously proud to look at you all from afar and see how you grew from babies into beautiful, charming and independent young people. I know this will always continue to be the case. I look forward to all of the future memories where you make me laugh. And cry. It means we have love and love is the most important thing in life.

I will be here for you until my final breath. May that not be for many, many years yet.

Love, always,

Dad.

读 客®

全球顶级畅销小说文库

全球文化，尽收眼底；
顶级经典，尽入囊中！

岛 上 书 店

THE
STORIED
LIFE OF
A.J.FiKRY

江苏凤凰文艺出版社
JIANGSU PHOENIX LITERATURE AND
ART PUBLISHING LTD

THE
STORIED LIFE OF
A.J. FIKRY

献给我的父母，

他们用书本丰富了我的成长历程；

还要献给那个男孩，

他在多年前的冬日送给了我一本

《弗拉基米尔·纳博科夫短篇集》。

来吧，亲爱的，

且让我们来相爱，

趁你我

尚在人世。

——鲁米[1]

① 莫拉维·贾拉鲁丁·鲁米（Jalalud-din Rumi, 1207-1273），波斯苏菲派学者、诗人。

目 录

第一部

第二部

第一部

《待宰的羔羊》

1953/罗尔德·达尔[1]

妻子用冻羊腿打死了丈夫，然后让警察吃了这条羊腿，以此处理这件"凶器"。达尔所写的很说得过去，但是兰比亚斯质疑一位职业家庭主妇是否真的会以小说中描述的方式烹制一条羊腿，即不化冻、不放调料，也不用腌泡。这样难道不会导致肉硬、肉熟的程度不均匀？我做的这行不是烹饪（也不是犯罪），但是如果你对这一细节有怀疑，整个故事就开始散架了。尽管这一点有待商榷，但它还是给我留下了印象，那是因为一个女孩的缘故，很久以前她喜欢《詹姆斯与巨桃》。

——A.J.F.

---

[1] 罗尔德·达尔（Roald Dahl, 1916-1990），英国作家，以童书创作最为著名，包括《詹姆斯与巨桃》以及《查理与巧克力工厂》。另，本书中的章节标题均为短篇小说题目。

在从海恩尼斯[1]到艾丽丝岛的渡轮上，阿米莉娅·洛曼把自己的手指甲涂成黄色，等指甲油干透的间隙，她浏览了一下她的前任所做的笔记。"小岛书店，年销售额约三十五万美元，夏季几个月的销售额所占比重较大，是卖给来度假的人。"哈维·罗兹写道，"书店有六百平方英尺大，除了老板没有全职雇员，童书很少。网上宣传有待发展。主要服务于本社区。存货偏重文学方面，这对我们有利，但是费克里的品位很特殊，没有妮可，靠他难以卖出去书。对他来说幸运的是，小岛书店经营着岛上的独家生意。"阿米莉娅打了个呵欠——她还在消解轻微的宿醉——琢磨着一家提出百般要求的小书店值不值得长途跋涉来一趟。等到她的指甲油干了后，她性格中坚定不移的乐观一面又发挥了作用：当然值得！她就擅长跟那些要求挺多的小书店和经营那种

---

① 海恩尼斯（Hyannis），美国马萨诸塞州东南部的一个镇。

书店的挑剔人打交道。她的才能还包括一心几用，晚餐时挑选合适的葡萄酒（以及协调能力、照顾喝太多酒的朋友），养室内盆栽，寻找走失的猫或狗，以及其他一些注定会失败的事。

下渡轮时，她的手机响了。她不认识那个号码——因为她的朋友们都不太习惯用手机打电话了。不过，她对能够转移一下注意力而高兴。有种人认为好消息只能通过期待中的电话传来，打电话的还得是你已经认识的人，她不想成为那种人。打电话的原来是博伊德·弗拉纳根——是她通过网络认识的第三位约会对象，但是这三次全都失败了——大概半年前，他曾经带她去看马戏表演。

"几个星期前，我试过给你留言。"他说，"你收到了吗？"

她告诉他自己最近换了工作，所以各种设备都乱了套。"另外，我在重新考虑网上约会这个主意，不确定是否真的适合我。"

博伊德似乎没有听到最后那句话。"你还想一起出去吗？"他问。

关于：他们的约会。有好一会儿，去看马戏的新奇劲儿让她不再去多想他们毫无共同点这一事实。等到快吃完晚饭时，他们俩格格不入的事实就更为突出地显现出来。也许在点开胃菜时他们未能达成一致，或者吃主菜时他承认自己不喜欢"老的东西"（古玩、房子、狗、人）时，这一事实就显而易见了。然而，阿米莉娅并未让自己妄下定论，直到吃甜点时，她问对他的人生影响最大的书是什么，他回答是《会计学原理》（第二部）。

她语气柔和地告诉他，不，她想他们两个人还是不要再约会了。

她能听到博伊德的呼吸声，焦躁而不规律。她担心他可能会哭。"你没事吧？"她问。

"别一副屈尊俯就的样子。"

阿米莉娅知道自己应该挂了电话，但是她没有。她有点想知道是怎么回事。如果没有好玩的轶事可以讲给朋友们听，那些糟糕的约会还有什么意义呢？"你说什么？"

"你要注意到我当时没有马上打电话给你，阿米莉娅，"他说，"我没有给你打电话，是因为我遇到了一个更好的，等到那个没戏时，我决定再给你一次机会。所以别以为自己高人一等。你的笑容还不赖，我得承认这一点，但是你的牙齿太大，你的屁股也是，而且你也不再是二十五岁了，即使你喝起酒来还像是二十五岁的样子。别人送的马，你就别往马的嘴里看了[①]。"这匹别人送的马哭了起来，"对不起，我真的很抱歉。"

"没关系，博伊德。"

"我这是怎么啦？看马戏挺好玩的，对吧？而且我也没那么糟糕。"

[①] 此处涉及一句英语中的俗语（look a gift horse in the mouth），因为能从马齿看出马的年龄，往别人送的马的嘴里看，指对礼物吹毛求疵。

"你很棒，去看马戏这个主意很有创意。"

"可是你不喜欢我，这肯定是有原因的，说实话吧。"

此时此刻，有很多原因不喜欢他，她选了一个："你还记得当我说我在出版界工作时，你说你不怎么读书吗？"

"你是个势利鬼。"他总结道。

"在某些事情上，我想我是。听我说，博伊德，我在工作。我得挂了。"阿米莉娅挂了电话。她并没有为自己的长相感到自负，当然也不会重视博伊德·弗拉纳根的意见，反正他也并不是真的在跟她聊天。他不过是在抱怨她新增了自己的失望，而她也有自己的失望之事。

她三十一岁了，觉得自己到现在应该已经遇到某个人了。

然而……

阿米莉娅乐观的一面相信，跟一个情不投意不合的人过日子倒不如一个人过得好。（的确是，不是吗？）

她妈妈喜欢讲，是小说害得阿米莉娅找不到真正的男人。这种话侮辱了阿米莉娅，因为这暗示她只读主人公是典型浪漫主义者的作品。她并不介意偶尔读一本有位浪漫主义主人公的小说，只是她的阅读品位要比这宽泛得多。再者，她虽然很喜欢作为书中角色的亨伯特·亨伯特[1]，但又接受这一事实，即她不会真正想让他成为自己的生活伴侣、男朋友甚或只是泛泛之交。对于霍尔顿·考菲尔

---

[1] 指小说《洛丽塔》中的主人公。

德、罗彻斯特先生和达西①，她也持同样观感。

那块招牌挂在一幢维多利亚风格的紫色小屋的前廊上，已经褪色，阿米莉娅差点错过。

> 小岛书店
> 1999年迄今艾丽丝岛唯一一家优质文学内容提供者
> 无人为孤岛；一书一世界

书店里，一个十几岁的孩子一边留心着收银台，一边在读艾丽丝·门罗②的最新短篇小说集。"噢，这书如何？"阿米莉娅问。阿米莉娅很喜欢门罗，可除了度假，她很少有时间读自家出版社书目之外的图书。

"这是学校的作业。"那个女孩回答，似乎这就回答了问题。

阿米莉娅介绍自己是奈特利出版社的销售代表，那个十几岁的女孩眼睛都没有从书本上抬起来，含糊地往后一指："A.J.在办公室。"

沿着走廊不稳当地排列着一摞摞抢读本和样书，阿米莉娅脑海里闪过常常出现的绝望感。挂于肩头的大手提包里有几本会添到A.J.的那一摞样书上，另外还有份书目，上面是她要推销的其

---

① 霍尔顿·考菲尔德、罗彻斯特先生和达西分别为小说《麦田里的守望者》《简·爱》和《傲慢与偏见》中的人物。
② 艾丽丝·门罗（Alice Munro, 1931–　），加拿大作家，2013年获诺贝尔文学奖。

他书。她对自己书目上的书从来不撒谎，不爱的书，她从来不会说爱。对于一本书，她通常能找到肯定它的话，不行就说封面，还不行就说作者，再不行就说作者的网站。所以他们才付我大把的钱，阿米莉娅偶尔跟自己开玩笑。她每年挣三万七千美元，另外可能有奖金，不过干她这行的人很少能拿到奖金。

A.J.费克里的办公室关着门，阿米莉娅走到半路，她羊毛衫的袖子勾到那几摞书中的一摞，有一百本书——也许更多——轰隆隆地砸倒在地板上，令她窘迫不堪。门开了，A.J.费克里看了看那堆乱摊子，又看了看那个脏兮兮的金发女巨人，她正手忙脚乱地想重新摞好那些书。"你究竟是谁？"

"阿米莉娅·洛曼。"她再摞上十本书，又有一半倒了下来。

"由它去吧，"A.J.命令道，"这些书是按顺序摆的。你这不是在帮忙。请走吧。"

阿米莉娅站直身子。她比A.J.至少高四英寸。"可我们还有事要谈呢。"

"我们没什么好谈的。"A.J.说。

"有的，"阿米莉娅坚持道，"我上星期就冬季书目的事给您发过邮件。您说我星期四或星期五下午过来都行，我说我会星期四过来。"来往邮件很简短，但她知道此言非虚。

"你是销售代表？"

阿米莉娅点点头，她松了一口气。

"哪家出版社，再说一遍？"

"奈特利。"

"奈特利出版社的销售代表是哈维·罗兹，"A.J.回答，"你上星期给我发邮件时，我以为你是哈维的助手什么的。"

"我接替了哈维。"

A.J.重重地叹了口气。"哈维去了哪家公司？"

哈维死了，有那么一瞬，阿米莉娅考虑说句蹩脚的玩笑话，把来生说成一种公司，哈维是其中的员工。"他死了，"阿米莉娅直截了当地说，"我以为您已经听说了。"她的大多数客户都已经听说了。哈维是个传奇，销售代表中最大的传奇。"美国书商协会的简讯发了讣告，《出版人周刊》或许也发了。"她语带歉疚地说。

"我不怎么留意出版新闻。"A.J.说。他摘下厚厚的黑框眼镜，擦了半天眼镜框。

"如果这让您感到震惊，我很抱歉。"阿米莉娅把手放在A.J.的胳膊上，他甩开了她的手。

"我有什么所谓？我几乎不认识那个人。我每年见他三次，还不够称他是朋友。而每次见到他，他都是想卖什么东西给我。这不是友谊。"

阿米莉娅看得出A.J.没心情听她推销冬季书目。她应该主动提出改天再来，可她转念想到这一路开车到海恩尼斯的两个小时、坐船到艾丽丝岛的八十分钟以及渡轮十月之后更不定时的班次。"既然我都来了，"阿米莉娅说，"我们过一遍奈特利出版社的冬季书目，您不介意吧？"

A.J.的办公室就是个小储藏间，没有窗户，墙上没挂画，办公桌上没有家人照片，没有小摆设，没有逃生通道。里面有书、车库里用的那种廉价的金属架、文件柜和一台可能来自上世纪的老古董台式电脑。A.J.没有问阿米莉娅要喝点什么，尽管阿米莉娅口渴，她也没有开口要喝的。她把一张椅子上的书搬开，坐了下来。

阿米莉娅开始介绍冬季书目，这份书目是一年中最小的书目，内容最少，期望值最低。有几本重要的（至少是有前途的）处女作，但其余的都是些出版商只抱最低商业期望值的图书。尽管如此，阿米莉娅通常最喜欢"冬季书目"。这些书不被看好，可能爆冷门，风险也大。（如果说她也是这样看待自己的，倒不算太牵强。）她把自己最喜欢的书放到最后来介绍，这是一位八十岁的老人所写的回忆录，他单身了大半辈子，七十八岁时结婚。婚后两年，新娘因癌症去世，享年八十三岁。根据简介，作者在中西部好多家报纸当过科学报道方面的记者。书中的文字精确、滑稽，一点都不过于伤感。阿米莉娅在从纽约到普罗维登斯[①]的火车上因这本书不可自抑地哭过。她知道《迟暮花开》是本小书，描述听上去挺缺乏新意，但是她有把握如果别人给它一个机会，他们也会喜欢上的。按照阿米莉娅的经验，大多数人如果能给更多事情一个机会的话，他们的问题都能解决。

① 普罗维登斯（Providence），美国罗得岛州的首府。

阿米莉娅刚把《迟暮花开》介绍到一半，A.J.就把头趴在了桌子上。

"怎么了？"阿米莉娅问。

"这本书不适合我。"A.J.说。

"就试读下第一章吧，"阿米莉娅把样书往他手里塞，"我知道这个主题特别没有新意，但是等您看到它的文——"

他打断了她的话："这本不适合我。"

"好吧，那我给您介绍别的。"

A.J.长叹了一声。"你看上去是个很不错的年轻人，可是你的前任……问题是，哈维知道我的品味，他跟我趣味相投。"

阿米莉娅把那本样书放到办公桌上。"我希望能有机会了解一下您的品位。"她说，感觉自己有点像色情片中的角色。

他压着嗓子嘟囔了一句什么。她觉得听着像是"有什么意义呢？"，却又拿不准。

阿米莉娅合上奈特利出版社的书目。"费克里先生，请您还是跟我说说您喜欢什么吧。"

"喜欢。"他厌恶地重复了一遍这个词。"我跟你说说我不喜欢什么好吗？我不喜欢后现代主义、后世界末日的背景、已亡故的讲述者以及魔幻现实主义。对那些按说是机巧形式的设置、多种字体、在不应该出现的地方出现的照片——根本说来，任何一种花招——我都几乎没有共鸣。我觉得关于大屠杀或者世界上任何一种大悲剧的虚构文学作品都令人反感——拜托，这些只能用非虚构写法。我不喜欢按侦探文学或者幻想文学的路子来写类型小说。文学就是文学，类型小说就是类型小说，混搭很少能有令人满意的结果。我不喜欢童书，特别是有写到孤儿的，我也不想让我的书架上有很多给青少年读者看的书。我不喜欢任何超过四百页或者低于一百五十页的书。我厌恶电视真人秀明星请人捉刀的小说、名人的图文书、体坛人物的回忆录、搭电影顺风车的版本、新奇玩意儿以及——我想这不用说——关于吸血鬼的书。我几乎不进处女作、鸡仔文学①、诗集和翻译作品。我也宁愿不进系列书，可是钱包的需要让我不得不进。至于你，你不用跟我说什么'下一部畅销系列书'，等它上了《纽约时报》畅销书榜再跟我讲也不迟。最重要的是，洛曼女士，我觉得一个小老头儿的薄薄一本回忆录，写他的老婆死于癌症，这样的书绝对让人难以忍受。不论销售代表声称写得有多好，也不管你向我保证母亲节那天我能卖出多少本。"

阿米莉娅脸红了，不过她更多是生气，而非尴尬。她同意A.J.的有些话，但是他没必要说得那么侮辱人。不管怎样，他提到的内容有一半奈特利出版社根本就没出过。她仔细看他。他比她大，但也大不了很多，不超过十岁。他还挺年轻，不该喜好如此狭窄。"您喜欢什么？"她问。

"除此之外的一切，"他说，"我承认我还挺喜欢短篇小说集，可是顾客从来都不想买。"

---

① 指由女性撰写并且主要面向二三十岁的单身职场女性的文学作品。

阿米莉娅的书目上只有一本短篇小说集，是本处女作。阿米莉娅还没有把整本书读完，时间关系，她也很可能不会读完，但是她喜欢其中第一个短篇。一个美国的六年级某班跟一个印度的六年级某班参加了一个国际笔友活动，叙述者是美国班级里的印度小孩，他一直给美国人提供关于印度文化的滑稽的错误信息。她清了清仍然特别干的喉咙。"《孟买改名的那年》。我觉得它特别有意——"

"别说了。"他说。

"我根本还没跟您说它是关于什么的书呢。"

"就是别说了。"

"可是为什么呢？"

"如果你够坦诚，就会承认你之所以跟我提这本书，只是因为我有部分印度血统，你觉得这本书会合乎我的独特趣味。我说得对吗？"

阿米莉娅想象着把那台古董台式电脑砸到他头上。"我之所以跟您说这本书是因为您说您喜欢短篇小说集！我的书目上只有这一本。请记住——"她在这里撒了个谎，"——它从第一篇到最后一篇都无比精彩，即使它是本处女作。

"还有一点您知道吗？我喜欢处女作，我喜欢发现新东西。我做这份工作，部分就是因为这一点。"阿米莉娅站起来。她的头咚咚跳着疼，也许她真的喝得太多了？她的头咚咚跳，她的心脏也是。"您想听听我的想法吗？"

"不是特别想，"他说，"你多大啦，二十五岁？"

"费克里先生，这是一家可爱的书店，但是如果您在经营上继续采用这种这种这种——"她小时候口吃过，现在生气时还会犯；她清清喉咙"——这种落后的思维方式，很快就不会有什么小岛书店了。"

阿米莉娅把《迟暮花开》和冬季书目放到他的办公桌上。她离开时，又被走廊上的书堆绊了一下。

下一班渡轮一小时后才开，于是她不急不忙地从镇上走回去。一家美国银行外墙上有块铜制铭牌，纪念赫尔曼·麦尔维尔[1]曾在那里过了一个夏天，当时那幢建筑是艾丽丝旅馆。她拿出手机给自己和那块铭牌照了一张相。艾丽丝岛这个地方挺不错，但她猜测自己近期没有理由再来一趟。

她给在纽约的老板发了条短信："小岛书店应该不会订什么书。☹"

老板回复："不用烦恼。只是个小客户，小岛书店的大部分订货都在夏季来临前，到时候那里有游客。那位书店老板是个怪人，哈维总是在推销春夏季书目时运气好一点。你也会的。"

六点，A.J.让莫莉·克洛克下班。"门罗那本新作怎么样？"

---

① 赫尔曼·麦尔维尔（Herman Melville，1819-1891），十九世纪美国最伟大的小说家、散文家和诗人之一。

她叹息了一声。"为什么今天每个人都要问我这个问题？"她只是指阿米莉娅，不过莫莉说话爱走极端。

"我想是因为你在读它。"

莫莉又叹息了一声。"好吧。人物，我说不好，有时候太人性了吧。"

"我觉得那更应该说是门罗的优点。"他说。

"不知道。更喜欢老式的那种。周一见。"

得对莫莉采取点措施了，A.J.把牌子翻到"结束营业"时想。除了喜欢看书，莫莉真的是个非常糟糕的书店店员。但她只是兼职，而且培训新手很费事，另外，至少她不偷东西。妮可请她，肯定是看中了莽撞无礼的克洛克小姐身上的什么优点。也许明年夏天，A.J.就能下决心炒了莫莉。

A.J.把剩下的顾客都撵了出去（他对一个有机化学学习小组特别恼火，他们什么都不买，但是从四点钟起，就在杂志区那边安营扎寨——他还相当肯定其中有一位把厕所给堵了），然后他开始处理收据，这项任务跟听起来一样令人沮丧。最后他上楼到了所住的阁楼房间。他取出一盒冷冻的咖喱肉放进微波炉，按照盒子上的说明，要加热九分钟。他站在那里时，想起了奈特利出版社的那个女孩。她看上去像一位来自上世纪九十年代西雅图的时间旅行者，穿着上面印着锚形图案的橡胶套鞋、老奶奶穿的那种花裙子和毛绒绒的米色羊毛衫，留着齐肩发，似乎是她男朋友在厨房里给她剪的。或是女朋友？还是男朋友，他认为。他想到了嫁给科特·柯本①时的科特妮·洛芙②。那张硬朗的粉红嘴巴说着"没人能够伤害我"，但是那双温柔的蓝眼睛却在说"对，你能，你也很可能会"。他把那个就像一大朵蒲公英似的女孩弄哭了。干得不错啊，A.J.。

咖喱肉的味道越来越浓，但计时器上还有七分半钟。

他想找件事做做，体力活方面的，但又不能太辛苦。

他拿了把割纸箱的刀来到地下室，去把装书的箱子折叠起来。用刀割，压平，摞起来。用刀割，压平，摞起来。

A.J.为自己对待那位销售代表的行为感到后悔。那不是她的错。总得有人告诉他哈维·罗兹已经去世。

用刀割，压平，摞起来。

很可能已经有人告诉过他，A.J.只浏览电子邮件，从来不接电话。举办过葬礼吗？倒不是说A.J.知道的话就会参加，他几乎不怎么了解哈维·罗兹。这显而易见。

用刀割，压平，摞起来。

然而……在过去的五六年里，他跟那个人共度了好多时光，他们只讨论过书，然而在他的一生中，还有什么比书更亲近？

用刀割，压平，摞起来。

找到一个跟你阅读兴趣相同的人又何其难得啊？他们唯一一

---

① 科特·柯本（Kurt Cobain，1967–1994），美国著名摇滚歌手，涅槃乐队主唱。
② 科特妮·洛芙（Courtney Love，1964– ），科特·柯本的遗孀，美国著名摇滚女歌手，演员。

次真正的争执，是关于大卫·福斯特·华莱士[①]，那是在华莱士自杀后的那段时间。A.J.觉得讣告中那种尊崇的语气令人难以忍受。那个人写了一本虽然无节制、篇幅过长，但是还不错的长篇小说，几篇有一定深度的随笔，其他就没什么了。

"《无尽的玩笑》是杰作。"哈维说过。

"《无尽的玩笑》是在比赛忍耐力。你好不容易读完了，你别无选择，只能说你喜欢这本书。否则，你就得面对浪费了自己生命中几个星期的事实，"A.J.反驳道，"有风格，无实质，我的朋友。"

哈维的身子探过办公桌，他的脸变得通红。"跟你同年代出生的每位作家，你都这么说！"

用刀割，压平，摞起来。捆好。

等他回到楼上，咖喱肉又凉了。要是再用那个塑料盘子加热那块咖喱肉，他很可能最后会患上癌症。

他把那个塑料盘子端到桌上，第一口烫嘴，第二口还没有解冻。分别像是熊爸爸的咖喱肉和熊宝宝的咖喱肉。他把那盘东西朝墙上扔去。他在哈维眼里多么微不足道，而哈维对他又是多么重要啊。

独自生活的难处，在于不管弄出什么样的烂摊子，都不得不自己清理。

---

① 大卫·福斯特·华莱士（David Foster Wallace，1962-2008），美国作家，后文中提到的《无尽的玩笑》为他的代表作。

不，独自生活的真正难处在于没人在乎你是否心烦意乱。没人在乎为什么一个三十九岁的老男人会像个蹒跚学步的小孩子那样，把一盘咖喱肉扔到房间那头。他给自己倒了杯梅洛红葡萄酒，往桌子上铺了一张桌布，然后走进客厅，打开一个恒温的玻璃盒，拿出了《帖木儿》[①]。回到厨房后，他把《帖木儿》放在桌子对面，把它靠在妮可以前坐的椅子上。

"干杯，你这个破玩意儿。"他对那本薄薄的册子说。

喝完那杯，他又给自己倒了一杯。他跟自己保证这杯之后他要读本书。也许是一本喜欢的旧书，例如托拜厄斯·沃尔夫[②]的《老学校》，不过当然，他把时间花在某本新书上更好。那个傻乎乎的销售代表喋喋不休说的是什么？《迟暮花开》——呃。他说的话句句当真。最糟糕的莫过于鳏夫矫揉造作的回忆录，特别是如果你自己就是一个鳏夫，就像A.J.在过去二十一个月的时间里那样。那位销售代表是个新人——她不知晓他那乏味的个人悲剧，那不是她的错。天哪，他想念妮可，想念她的声音，她的脖子，甚至她的腋窝。她的腋窝就像猫舌头一样拉里拉碴的，一天过完后，气味就像马上要坏掉的牛奶一样。

三杯酒之后，他醉倒在桌前。他只有五英尺七英寸高，体重一百四十磅，甚至没有吃冷冻咖喱肉来补充能量。今晚，他的读书计划不会有丝毫进展。

---

① 美国作家埃德加·爱伦·坡（Edgar Allan Poe，1809–1849）的第一本诗集。
② 托拜厄斯·沃尔夫（Tobias Wolff，1945– ），美国作家，尤擅长创作短篇小说。

"A.J.，"妮可悄声说，"上床睡觉吧。"

终于，他在做梦了。喝了那么多酒，就是为了这个目的。

妮可——他醉后梦中的鬼妻——扶他站了起来。

"你很丢人，傻子。你知道吗？"

他点点头。

"冷冻咖喱肉和五美元一瓶的红酒。"

"我这是尊重我继承的悠久可敬的传统。"

他跟那个鬼魂拖着脚步进了卧室。

"恭喜，费克里先生，你正在变成一个货真价实的酒鬼。"

"对不起。"他说。她让他躺到床上。

她的褐色头发短短的，像个假小子。"你剪了头发，"他说，"怪怪的。"

"你今天对那个女孩很糟糕。"

"都是因为哈维。"

"显然如此。"她说。

"以前认识你的人死了，我不喜欢这样。"

"所以你也没有炒掉莫莉·克洛克？"

他点点头。

"你不能继续这样下去了。"

"我能的，"A.J.说，"我一直是这样，以后还会这样。"

她吻吻他的前额。"我想我的意思是我不想你这样。"

她不见了。

那次事故不怨任何人。下午的一个活动后，她开车送作者回家。她大概在超速驾驶，想要赶上回艾丽丝岛的最后一班汽车轮渡；她或许突然急转，想避免撞上一头鹿；可能只是因为马萨诸塞州冬季的道路状况。这些都已无法获悉。有位警察在医院询问她是否有自杀倾向。"没有，"A.J.说，"完全没有。"她已经怀孕两个月，他们还没有跟任何人说。因为以前他们经历过失望。他站在太平间外面的等候室，非常希望他们已经告诉过大家了。至少在这个更为漫长的——他还不知道该怎么称呼这个时期——之前，还会有短暂的幸福时光。"不，她没有自杀倾向。"A.J.犹豫了一下，"她只是个很糟糕的司机，而她自以为还不错。"

"对，"那位警察说，"这不是任何人的错。"

"人们喜欢这么说，"A.J.回答道，"可这的确是某个人的错，是她的错。她那样做可真是傻啊，傻得离谱。真是个丹尼尔·斯蒂尔①式的情节发展，妮可！如果这是本小说，我现在就不往下读了。我会把它扔到房间那头。"

那位警察（很少读书，休假时才会偶尔读一本杰弗里·迪弗②的大众市场版平装本）想把谈话转回现实。"没错，你是书店老板。"

---

① 丹尼尔·斯蒂尔（Danielle Steel, 1949- ），当今美国通俗文坛最具代表性的畅销书作家之一。

② 杰弗里·迪弗（Jeffery Deaver, 1950- ），美国当代著名的侦探小说家。下文中林肯·莱姆（Lincoln Rhyme）是其笔下的侦探。林肯·莱姆系列小说是杰弗里·迪弗的代表作品。

"我和我妻子，"A.J.想也没想地脱口而出，"噢，天哪，我刚才做了件蠢事，就像书中的人物忘记他妻子已死，不经意地使用了'我们'一词。真是废话连篇啊——"他顿了一下去看那位警官的徽章——"兰比亚斯警官，你跟我都是一部糟糕的长篇小说中的人物。你知道吗？我们他妈的怎么到了这里？你很可能自个儿在想，真是个倒霉蛋，然后今天夜里你拥抱自己的孩子时会抱得格外紧，因为那种长篇小说中的人物就是那样做的。你知道我所说的那种书，对吗？那种热门文学小说嘛，会略微着笔于几个不重要的配角，好显得很有福克纳[1]的风范，无所不包。看看作者多么关心小人物！普通人！作者的胸怀多么宽广！甚至还有你的名字。对于一个形象陈腐的马萨诸塞州警官来说，兰比亚斯警官是个完美的名字。你是个种族主义者吗，兰比亚斯？因为你那种角色，应该是个种族主义者。"

　　"费克里先生，"兰比亚斯警官说，"我可以帮你给什么人打电话吗？"他是位好警察，习惯了看到悲痛的人以各种方式垮掉。他把手搭到A.J.的肩膀上。

　　"没错！对极了，兰比亚斯警官，此时此刻，你一点没错，就应该这样做！你把自己的角色扮演得很出色。你是不是也刚好知道鳏夫接下来要做什么？"

　　"给某个人打电话。"兰比亚斯警官说。

---

[1] 威廉·福克纳（William Faulkner, 1897-1962），美国小说家，获1949年诺贝尔文学奖。

"对，很可能是那样。不过我已经给我妻子的姐姐家打过电话了。"A.J.点头，"如果这是短篇小说，我跟你到现在已经被写完了。一个小小的讽刺性转折，然后就结束了。所以在散文以外的文字世界里，最雅致的就属短篇小说，兰比亚斯警官。

"如果这是一篇雷蒙德·卡佛[①]的短篇，你会给我些许安慰，然后黑暗降临，这一切就会结束。可是这个……我还是感觉更像是一部长篇小说，我是指从感情上来说。要过上一阵子才能经历完，你知道吗？"

"我说不好我是不是知道。我没读过雷蒙德·卡佛，"兰比亚斯警官说，"我喜欢林肯·莱姆。你知道他吗？"

"那位四肢瘫痪的犯罪学家。作为类型写作还不错。但是你有没有读过什么短篇小说？"A.J.问。

"也许上学时读过。童话。或者，嗯，《小红马》[②]？我觉得我当时应该读过《小红马》的。"

"那是个中篇。"A.J.说。

"嗯，对不起。我……等一下，我记得上中学时，读过里面有位警察的一篇，有点类似于一桩完美的罪案，所以我记得那篇。这位警察被他老婆杀了，凶器是一块冻牛肉，然后她做好了给另外——"

---

① 雷蒙德·卡佛（Raymond Carver，1939-1988），美国20世纪下半叶最重要的小说家，小说界"简约主义"的大师，是继海明威之后美国最具影响力的短篇小说作家。
② 美国作家约翰·斯坦贝克（John Steinbeck，1902-1968）的早期作品。

"《待宰的羔羊》，"A.J.说，"那个短篇叫《待宰的羔羊》，凶器是一条羊腿。"

"对，没错！"那位警察高兴起来，"你真是懂行。"

"这一篇很有名，"A.J.说，"我妻子的家人应该随时会到。我很抱歉，我刚才把你比作一位'不重要的配角'。那很无礼，而且你我心知肚明，在兰比亚斯警官更为辉煌的传奇中，我才是'不重要的配角'呢。跟一个书店老板比起来，警察才更有可能成为主角。您，警官，自成一类。"

"嗯嗯，"兰比亚斯警官说，"你这话说得不无道理。再回到我们刚才所说的。作为一名警察，我对那个短篇的时间安排有疑问。比如，她把牛——"

"羊。"

"羊。这么说她是用那块冻羊腿杀人，然后没有解冻，就把它放进烤炉烹制。我不是什么蕾切尔·雷[1]，但是……"

等他们把妮可的车从水里吊上来的时候，她已经开始冻住了，在太平间的抽屉里，她的嘴唇是青色的，让A.J.想到她为最新一本吸血鬼什么的举办图书派对时用的黑色唇膏。对于让傻不拉几的十几岁女孩穿着舞会裙来小岛书店闹腾，A.J.不感兴趣，但是妮可——她居然会真的喜欢那本关于吸血鬼的破书和写那本书的女人——坚持认为开一次吸血鬼主题的舞会对生意有帮助，而且也好玩。"你知道什么是乐趣，对吧？"

---

[1] 蕾切尔·雷（Rachael Ray，1968- ），美国电视烹饪女王。

"模模糊糊。"他说，"很久以前，在我还没卖书之前，当时周末以及晚上都是我自己的，我读书是为了愉悦，我记得当时有乐趣。所以，模模糊糊地知道，没错。"

"让我来刷新一下你的记忆吧。乐趣就是有个聪明、漂亮、随和的老婆，每一个工作日你都跟她一起度过。"

他仍然能想起她穿着那件可笑的黑色缎子裙的样子，她的右臂懒散地抱着前廊上的一根柱子，她的嘴唇漂亮地涂成一道黑。"可悲的是，我的老婆被变成了一个吸血鬼。"

"你这个可怜的人儿啊。"她穿过前廊，过来吻了他一下，留下一道淤伤般的唇膏印迹，"你唯一能做的，就是也变成一个吸血鬼。不要试图反抗，你那样做可就再糟糕不过了。你一定要酷起来，傻子。邀请我进去吧。"

《像里兹饭店那样大的钻石》

1922/F.司各特·菲茨杰拉德[1]

　　从技术角度说来，这是一部中篇，但是话说回来，中篇属于灰色地带。然而，如果你置身于那种不怕麻烦、想要进行这类区分的人群中——我以前就是那种人——你最好还是知道有什么不一样。（如果你最后进了一所常春藤联盟大学★，很可能会遇到这种人。用知识来武装自己以对付这帮傲慢的家伙。不过我扯远了。）埃德加·爱伦·坡把短篇小说定义为一口气能读完的小说。我想象在他那时，"一口气"持续的时间更长。不过我又扯远了。

　　这个故事写作手法巧妙、剑走偏锋，写的是用钻石建造的一个镇所遇到的挑战，还写到富人们为了保卫自己的生活方式极尽所能，展现了菲茨杰拉德的精湛写作技巧。《了不起的盖茨比》无疑令人眩目，但

是在我看来，那部长篇小说有些地方写得过于雕琢，就像花园里修剪过的灌木。对他来说，短篇小说发挥空间更大，可以写得更凌乱一点。《像里兹饭店那样大的钻石》就像一个被施了魔法的花园侏儒那样，富有生气。

关于：何以列入此篇。我应不应该做这件显而易见的事，告诉你就在我遇到你之前，我也丢失了一件——若估价的话——价值不菲的东西？

——A.J.F.

★对此，我有自己的看法。要记着，除了通常那些地方，也可以在别的地方获得不错的教育。

尽管他想不起来自己是怎样上床的，也想不起来是怎样脱掉衣服的，A.J.却是在床上醒来，身上只穿着内衣。他记得哈维·罗兹死了，记得自己在奈特利出版社那位漂亮的销售代表面前表现恶劣，记得在房间里扔过咖喱肉，记得喝下的第一杯葡萄酒以及向《帖木儿》祝酒。在那之后，他什么都不记得了。从他的角度看，这个晚上过得成功。

　　他的头在咚咚跳着疼。他走到大房间那里，想着会发现咖喱肉的残迹。但地板和墙面都一尘不染。A.J.从药柜里找出一片阿司匹林，一边暗自庆幸自己有这样的远见，居然把咖喱肉都清理干净了。他坐在餐厅的餐桌前，注意到葡萄酒瓶已经拿出去扔掉了。他做事这么一丝不苟倒是奇怪了，但也并非前所未有。若喝醉后能保持整洁不算一项本领，那他真的一无是处了。他往餐桌对面看去，他本来把《帖木儿》放在那里的。现在书不在了，也许他只是以为他从盒子里拿出了那本书？

走过房间时，A.J.的心脏跟他的头比赛着咚咚直跳。走到半道上，他就看到用来保护《帖木儿》不受外界侵害的、用密码锁锁着的恒温玻璃棺材敞开着，里面空空如也。

他披上一件浴袍，穿上最近没怎么穿过的那双跑步鞋。

A.J.沿着威金斯船长街慢跑，他破破烂烂的格子浴袍在他身后飞舞拍打。他看上去像是位意志消沉、营养不良的超级英雄。他拐上主街，径直跑进睡意未消的艾丽丝岛警察局。"我被偷了！"A.J.叫道。他没有跑多远，却在大喘气，"拜托，谁来帮帮我！"他努力不让自己感觉像个被偷了钱包的老太太。

兰比亚斯放下咖啡，打量这个穿着浴袍的狂乱男人。他认出他是书店老板，也是他，一年多之前，他年轻漂亮的妻子开车冲进湖里。和上次见面时相比，A.J.显得苍老许多，虽然兰比亚斯觉得变老是一定的。

"好吧，费克里先生，"兰比亚斯说，"告诉我出什么事了。"

"有人偷了《帖木儿》。"A.J.说。

"什么是'帖木儿'？"

"是一本书，一本很值钱的书。"

"说清楚点。你指的是有人没付钱拿走了店里的一本书。"

"不，是我个人收藏的书，是一本十分稀有的埃德加·爱伦·坡的诗集。"

"所以，这好像是你很喜欢的一本书？"兰比亚斯说。

"不，我根本不喜欢它。它是本垃圾，不成熟的垃圾作品。只不过……"A.J.喘不过气来，"操。"

"别激动，费克里先生。我只是想弄明白。你不喜欢这本书，但是它具有感情价值？"

"不！操它的感情价值。它有很高的商业价值。《帖木儿》就像珍本书中的霍纳斯·瓦格纳[①]。你知道我在说什么吗？"

"当然，我老爹收集棒球卡。"兰比亚斯点头，"这么值钱？"

A.J.的嘴巴跟不上脑子的速度。"这是埃德加·爱伦·坡最早的作品，当时他十八岁。这本书数量极少，因为首印只印了五十本，还是匿名出版的。封面上没有印'埃德加·爱伦·坡著'，而是'一位波士顿人著'。依据品相和珍本书的行情，每本能卖到四十万美元以上。我本来打算过段时间等经济有点起色后，就把这本书拍卖了。我本来打算关掉书店，靠那笔收入过退休生活。"

"如果你不介意我问，"兰比亚斯说，"你干吗把那种东西放在自己家里，而不是银行的保险库里呢？"

A.J.摇摇头。"我不知道，我蠢，喜欢它在身边，我想。

---

① 霍纳斯·瓦格纳（Honus Wagner，1874-1955），美国棒球运动员，1936年首批入选棒球名人堂的五人之一。他被公认为棒球史上最优秀的游击手，也有人认为他是美国棒球联盟史上最佳全能运动员。他的球星卡现在的拍卖价或达一百五十万美元。

我喜欢看到它，让它提醒我什么时候我不想干了，什么时候就可以不干。我把它放在一个配组合密码锁的玻璃盒里。我本来想着那够安全的了。"确实，除了旅游季节，艾丽丝岛上极少有盗窃案。而此时是十月。

"这么说，有人打破了玻璃盒子还是破解了密码？"兰比亚斯问。

"都不是。昨天晚上我想一醉方休。真他妈蠢，可是我把那本书拿出来，好让自己能看着它。就是让它跟我做个伴吧，我知道这借口很糟糕。"

"费克里先生，你为《帖木儿》投过保吗？"

A.J.把头埋进双手当中。兰比亚斯把那理解为书没有投保。"我大约一年前才发现那本书，是我妻子去世后两三个月的事。我不想多花钱，就一直没去办。我不知道，有上百万个白痴理由，主要的一条是，我是个白痴。兰比亚斯警官。"

兰比亚斯没有费事去纠正他应该是兰比亚斯警长。"我准备这样做。首先，我会跟你做一份笔录。然后，等我的探员来上班后——淡季她只上半天班——我会派她去你那里寻找指纹和别的证据。也许会有所发现。我们还可以做一件事，就是给所有拍卖行和经营这类物品的其他人打电话。如果它像你说的那样，是本珍本书，那这样一本来路不明的书出现在市场上，大家会注意到的。像那种东西不是需要有份记录，说明谁曾经拥有过，一份叫什么的那个吗？"

"来源证明。"A.J.说。

"对，一点没错！我妻子曾经爱看电视上的鉴宝节目。你看过那个节目吗？"

A.J.没有回答。

"最后一件事，我想知道还有谁知道这本书。"

A.J.哼了一声。"谁都知道。我妻子的姐姐，伊斯梅，她在中学教书。她一直担心我，自从妮可……她总在劝说我走出书店，去岛外走走。大约一年前，她拉我去密尔顿参加了一次乏味的资产拍卖会。这本书跟五十本左右其他的书放在一个箱子里，除了《帖木儿》，别的全都一文不值。我付了五美元。那些人根本不知道自己手里有什么东西。如果你想听实话，这件事让我感觉挺不自在，倒不是说现在还有什么所谓。不管怎么样，伊斯梅觉得如果我把它放在书店展览，会对生意有帮助，有教育意义和别的狗屁好处。所以去年整个夏天我都把那个玻璃盒放在书店里。你从没来过书店，我想。"

兰比亚斯看着自己的鞋子，上千节中学英语课上他没能完成老师所要求的最低阅读作业量时那种熟悉的羞愧感又一下子回来了。"我算不上个读书人。"

"不过你读一些罪案作品，对吧？"

"好记性。"兰比亚斯说。事实上，A.J.对人们的阅读品位记性绝佳。

"迪弗，是吗？你要是喜欢那类，有这么一位新作家，来自——"

"没问题，我什么时候会过去一下。我能帮你给谁打个电话吗？你的妻姐是伊斯梅·埃文斯-帕里什，对吗？"

"伊斯梅在——"就在这时，A.J.突然呆住了，像是有人按了他身上的暂停键。他眼神茫然，嘴巴张着。

"费克里先生？"

有将近半分钟的时间，A.J.就待在那里，然后他接着说话，似乎什么都没发生过。"伊斯梅在工作，我没事。不需要给她打电话。"

"你刚才有一会儿失去了意识。"兰比亚斯说。

"什么？"

"你昏过去了。"

"噢，天哪。那只是一时走神，我小时候经常那样，成年后很少再犯，除了在压力特别大的时候。"

"你应该去看看医生。"

"不，没事，真的。我只想找到我的书。"

"你去的话，我会感觉好一点。"兰比亚斯坚持道，"你今天早上受到很大的打击，我也知道你是一个人住。我要送你去医院，然后我要让你的妻姐、姐夫去那里找你。同时，我会让我的人看看能不能找到关于你那本书的什么线索。"

在医院里，A.J.等待，填表，等待，脱衣服，等待，接受检查，等待，穿上衣服，等待，接受更多的检查，等待，再脱衣服。最后，一位中年的全科医生为他看病。女医生并不特别担心他这样的突然发作。然而各项检查表明对于他这样三十九岁的男性来说，他的血压和胆固醇水平正好处于偏高这一区间。她询问A.J.的生活方式。他实话实说地回答道："我不是您所称的那种酒鬼，不过我的确喜欢至少每星期一次把自己灌醉。偶尔抽烟，吃的全都是冷冻食品。我很少用牙线。我曾是个长跑运动员，但是现在根本不锻炼。我一个人住，也没有值得维系的人际关系。自从我妻子去世后，我也讨厌起自己的工作。"

"哦，就这些吗？"医生问，"您还是个年轻人，费克里先生，可是一个人的身体只能承受那么多。如果您想自杀，我当然能想到更快、更容易的方式。您想死吗？"

A.J.一时答不上来。

"因为要是您真的想死，我可以安排对您进行精神方面的观察。"

"我不想死，"过了一会儿A.J.说，"我只是觉得很难一直待在这里。您觉得我疯了吗？"

"不。我能明白您为什么有那种感觉。你正在经历一段艰难时期。先从锻炼开始吧，"她说，"您会感觉好些的。"

"好吧。"

"您妻子挺可爱的，"医生说，"我以前参加过您妻子在书店组织的母女读书会。我的女儿现在还在您那里做兼职。"

"莫莉·克洛克？"

"克洛克是我先生的姓。我是罗森医生。"她敲敲自己的名牌。

在医院大厅里，A.J.看到了熟悉的一幕。"您会介意吗？"一位穿着粉红色实习服的护士拿着一本破旧的大众市场平装本，递给一个穿着肘部有补丁的灯芯绒西装上衣的男人。

"我很乐意，"丹尼尔·帕里什说，"你叫什么名字？"

"吉尔，就是'杰克和吉尔去爬山①'里面的吉尔。梅西，就是那家百货公司的名字。我读过您所有的书，但我最喜欢这一本。嗯，到目前为止吧。"

"那可是普遍的看法，山上的吉尔。"丹尼尔不是开玩笑。他的其他书都不如第一本畅销。

"我根本表达不出它对我有多么大的意义。嗯，我一想到它就会流泪。"她低头垂目，像位艺妓那样恭敬，"是这本书让我想当一名护士！我才来这里上班。自从我得知您住在这个镇后，就一直希望您哪天会来这儿。"

"你是说，你希望我生病？"丹尼尔微笑着说。

"不，当然不是！"她脸红了，然后捣了一下他的胳膊，"你！你真坏！"

"我是坏，"丹尼尔回答，"我的确坏得要命。"

---

① 这是一首广为流传的英语童谣的第一句。

妮可第一次见到丹尼尔·帕里什时，曾评论他长得帅，可以在本地新闻台当新闻节目主持人了。等开车回到家时，她修改了她的看法："他的眼睛太小，不适合做新闻节目主持人。他可以当天气预报员。"

"他的确声音洪亮。"A.J.当时说。

"如果那个人告诉你暴风雨已经过去，你绝对会相信他的话。哪怕你正在被风吹雨打，你还是很可能会相信他的话的。"她说。

A.J.打断了那番调情。"丹，"他说，"我还以为他们给你的妻子打电话了呢。"A.J.可不会拐弯抹角。

丹尼尔清清嗓子。"她身体有点不舒服，所以我来了。你怎么样，老兄？"丹尼尔喜欢叫A.J."老兄"，尽管事实上，丹尼尔比A.J.大五岁。

"我破了大财，医生说我快死了，不过除此之外，我状态奇佳。"镇静剂让他看问题别具慧眼。

"好极了。我们去喝一杯吧。"丹尼尔转向吉尔护士，在她耳畔低语了几句。丹尼尔把她那本书还给她时，A.J.看到他写下了自己的电话号码。"来吧，你这主管葡萄园的大君！①"丹尼尔说着朝门口走去。

尽管A.J.爱书，还拥有一家书店，但他不是特别喜欢作家。他觉得他们不修边幅、自恋、傻乎乎的，通常也不讨人喜欢。他

---

① 出自莎士比亚戏剧《安东尼与克莉奥佩特拉》第二幕第七景。

尽量避免认识那些写了他很喜欢的书的作家，担心作家本人会破坏他对那些书的感觉。幸好，他不是很喜欢丹尼尔的书，就连他那本受欢迎的第一部长篇也不是很喜欢。至于丹尼尔其人呢？嗯，他一定程度上让A.J.感到开心。换句话说，丹尼尔·帕里什是A.J.最亲密的朋友之一。

"这要怪我自己。"第二杯啤酒下肚，A.J.说，"本来应该买保险的，本来应该放进保险柜的，本来不应该在喝酒时把它拿出来的。不管是谁偷的，我不能说自己完全没有过失。"镇静剂加上酒精，让A.J.放松下来，把他变得像位哲学家。丹尼尔拿起酒壶又给他倒了一杯。

"别那样了，A.J.，别自责了。"丹尼尔说。

"这对我就是当头棒喝啊，"A.J.说，"我绝对要少喝点酒了。"

"喝完这杯再说。"丹尼尔打趣道。他们碰了杯。一个女高中生走进酒吧，她穿着粗斜纹布毛边短裤，短得底边那里露出了一点屁股。丹尼尔朝她举起酒杯。"衣服不错！"那个女生对他竖起了中指。"你得戒酒了，我也不能再背着伊斯梅偷情了，"丹尼尔说。"可是紧接着我就看到了那样的短裤，我的决心遭遇严峻考验。今天晚上真可笑。那个护士！那条短裤！"

A.J.呷了口啤酒。"书写得怎么样？"

丹尼尔耸耸肩。"是一本书，就会有内页、有封面，就会有情节、人物、枝枝叶叶。它会反映出我多年来在创作上研究、推敲和实践的成果。尽管如此，它还是肯定不会像我在二十五岁时写的第一本书那样受欢迎。"

"倒霉蛋。" A.J.说。

"我挺有把握你会赢得本年度倒霉蛋大奖的，老兄。"

"我可真是走运啊。"

"坡是个差劲的作家，你知道吗？《帖木儿》是最差劲的，是模仿拜伦的无聊作品。如果它是那种他妈的还像样一点的第一版，还算好。你没了它应该感到高兴啊。反正我讨厌可以收藏的书。人们对某些故纸堆可真是如痴如醉的。重要的是思想，伙计。里面的字句。"丹尼尔·帕里什说。

A.J.喝完杯中酒。"这位先生，你是个白痴。"

调查持续了一个月，在艾丽丝岛警察局的时间观念里，那就像是一年。兰比亚斯和他那一组人在事发现场未能找到相关的实物证据。除了扔掉酒瓶、清理咖喱肉，罪犯显然还把自己留在那套住宅里的指纹全都抹掉了。调查人员询问了A.J.的雇员以及他在艾丽丝岛上为数不多的几位朋友和亲戚。这些面谈都没取得特别能将某人定罪的结果。也没有书本经销商和拍卖行报告有什么《帖木儿》出现在市场上。（当然，拍卖行在这种事情上是出了名的低调。）调查无果。那本书不见了，A.J.知道自己再也不会见到它了。

那个玻璃盒现在是没用了，A.J.拿不准该拿它怎么办。他没有别的珍本书。然而玻璃盒挺贵的，将近五百美元。他内心残留的乐观一面想去相信会遇到更好的东西，可以放进玻璃盒。购买时，人家告诉他也可以用来存放雪茄。

鉴于一时退休无望，A.J.就读样书、回邮件、接电话，甚至还写了一两张货架卡。夜里，书店打烊后，他又开始跑步。长跑中有很多难题，但是最大的难题之一，是把钥匙放在哪里。到最后，A.J.决定不锁前门。照他估计，店里没有一样东西值得偷。

《咆哮营的幸运儿》
1868/布赖特·哈特[1]

　　发生在一个采矿营地的极为感伤的故事。那个营地收养了一个"印第安宝宝",他们起名为"幸运儿"。我第一次读到它,是在普林斯顿大学参加一个名叫"美国西部文学"的讨论会上,当时一点都没有感动。在我的读后感(写作日期为1992年11月14日)中,我觉得这篇小说唯一值得称道之处,是其中有趣的角色名字:"矮墩墩""肯塔克""法国佬皮特""切罗基人萨尔"等等。几年前我碰巧又读到了《咆哮营的幸运儿》,我哭得很厉害,你会发现我那本多佛超值版上有泪渍。依我看是人到中年变得更多愁善感了。不过我觉得我后来的反应也说明了读小说需要在适合它的人生阶段去读。记住,玛雅:我们在

---

[1] 布赖特·哈特(Bret Harte, 1836-1902),美国作家,因其关于加利福尼亚矿业城镇的小说而著名。

二十岁有共鸣的东西到了四十岁的时候不一定能产生共鸣，反之亦然。书本如此，生活亦如此。

——A.J.F.

失窃案发生后的几个星期里，小岛书店的销售额略有增长，从以往统计来看，这让人难以置信。A.J.把增长归因于一项鲜为人知的经济指标，名为"好奇的镇民"。

一位心怀善意的镇民（以下简称"心善镇民"）会悄悄走到办公桌那里。"《帖木儿》有消息吗？"（意为：你个人遭受了重大损失这件事，我可以拿它消遣一下吗？）

A.J.会回答道："一点儿也没有。"（意为：生活还是被毁了。）

心善镇民：哦，肯定会有线索的。（意为：既然这种情况的结果对我而言没有什么损失，乐观点也花不了我一分钱。）有什么我没读过的吗？

A.J.：我们有几种新书。（意为：几乎全是。你有几个月，甚至可能几年没来过这里了。）

心善镇民：我在《纽约时报书评周刊》上读到过一本书。也许是红色封面的？

A.J.：哎，听着挺熟。（意为：那可不是一般的模糊。作者、书名、情节梗概——这些信息对找到书更有用。那本书封面也许是红色的，它上了《纽约时报书评周刊》，这两条信息给我的帮助，比你以为的要少得多。）你还记得什么别的吗？（用你自己的话。）

这时A.J.会把那位心善镇民领到新书那面墙，在那里，他确保能卖给他或她一本精装书。

很奇怪的是，妮可去世对生意却有着相反的影响。尽管他像一位纳粹党卫军军官一样没什么感情色彩地定时开门、打烊，妮可去世后那三个月，书店的销售额是史上最低的。当然，人们那时同情他，但人们是过于同情他了。妮可是本地人，是他们中的一分子。当这位普林斯顿大学的毕业生（也是艾丽丝岛中学的致辞学生代表）和她眼神严肃的丈夫回到艾丽丝岛开了一家书店时，他们被感动了。看到总算有年轻人回到家乡寻求改变，这令人振奋。而她一死，他们觉得自己跟A.J.再无共同之处，除了跟他一样，都失去了妮可。他们怪他吗？有些人的确有点怪他。那天晚上为什么不是他开车送作者回家？他们安慰自己，悄声说他一直有些怪怪的，还有点异类（他们发誓这么说丝毫没有种族歧视的意味）；但显然这个家伙不是附近这儿的，你要知道。（他出生在新泽西。）那时他们走过那家书店时会屏住呼吸，仿佛那是处墓地。

A.J.看了一遍他们的赊账卡，得出结论：失窃是种可被接受并能促进社交的损失，而死亡却会让人们被孤立。到了十二月，销售额跌回失窃之前的通常水平。

星期五——离圣诞节刚好还有两星期——就在打烊前，A.J.把最后的顾客撵走，收好书款。一个穿着鼓鼓囊囊的外套的男人正对着亚历克斯·克罗斯系列小说[1]中的最新一部叽叽歪歪："二十六美元好像太贵了，你知道我在网上买会便宜一点，对吧？"A.J.说他确实知道，同时把那人送到门口。"要想有竞争力，你真的应该降价。"那个人说。

"降价？降低。我的。价格。我以前从未考虑过呢。"A.J.语气温和地说。

"你这是在耍赖吗，年轻人？"

"不是，我很感谢。下一次小岛书店的股东开会，我绝对要把你这个革新性建议提出来。我知道我们要保有竞争力。咱们俩私下说吧，本世纪初的一段时间内，我们放弃了竞争。我觉得那是个错误，但是我的董事会认为最好把竞争留给参加奥运会的运动员、拼词比赛中的孩子和麦片制造商。如今，我要高兴地报告小岛书店绝对又开始参与竞争了。顺便说一句，书店打烊了。"A.J.指向门口。

---

① 美国惊悚小说大师詹姆斯·帕特森（James Patterson, 1947– ）的代表作之一。

当鼓鼓囊囊的外套男人咕哝着走出门口时，一位老太太嘎吱一声又推开门。她是位常客，所以A.J.尽量不让自己对她在营业时间过后登门感到不快。"啊，坎伯巴奇太太，"他说，"不幸的是，我们现在要打烊了。"

"费克里先生，别用你那双奥玛尔·沙里夫[1]式的眼睛瞪着我。我对你很恼火。"坎伯巴奇太太强行走过他身旁，把一本厚厚的平装书"砰"的一声甩在柜台上，"你昨天推荐给我的这本书，是我活到八十二岁读过的最糟糕的书，我要退款。"

A.J.看看那本书又看看老太太。"您对这本书有什么意见？"

"很多意见，费克里先生。首先，它是由死神讲述的！我是个八十二岁的老太太，我觉得读一本由死神讲述的五百五十二页的大部头一点儿都不愉快。我觉得选择这本书特别不体贴。"

A.J.道了歉，心里却毫无歉意。这些人算老几，凭什么觉得拿到一本书时，还得获得保证他们会喜欢这本书？他办理了退款。书脊有破损，他没法再卖出去了。"坎伯巴奇太太，"他忍不住说，"看起来你读了这本书。我想知道您读了多少。"

"对，我读了，"她回答道，"我千真万确读了它，让我一夜都没有睡觉。我对它太恼火了。在我这把年纪，我很不愿意一夜不睡，也不想再像这本小说不时刺激我猛流眼泪那样落泪了。

---

[1] 奥玛尔·沙里夫（Omar Sharif，1932- ），埃及著名电影演员，出演过《阿拉伯的劳伦斯》和《日瓦戈医生》等电影。

你下次再推荐什么书给我，我希望你能记住这一点，费克里先生。"

"我会的，"他说，"我诚心向您道歉，坎伯巴奇太太。我们的大多数顾客都很喜欢这本《偷书贼》[②]。"

书店一关门，A.J.就上楼换上跑步的衣服。他从书店的前门出去，习惯性地没有锁门。

A.J.跑过越野跑，先是在高中校队，然后在普林斯顿大学。他选择这项运动，主要是因为除了读书认真，别的他都不擅长。他从来没有真正把越野跑看作是多么大的本事。他高中时的教练夸张地称他为"可靠的中间人"，指的是A.J.不管跟任何一群人比赛，总可以指望他取得中等偏上的名次。现在他有段时间没有跑步了，他得承认那是种本事。以他现在的状态，他做不到一口气跑两英里。他很少跑得超过五英里，他的背部、腿——基本上是全身每个地方都痛。后来发现疼痛是好事。他以前经常边跑边想事情，而疼痛让他可以不去做那种徒劳无益的事。

跑到最后开始下雪了。他不想把泥巴带进室内，就在前廊脱下跑步鞋。他倚在前门上，门一下子开了。他知道自己没锁门，但他确信自己没有就这样把门开着。他打开灯，好像全都挺正常，收款机也不像有人动过。大概是风把门吹开了。他关了灯，

---

① 当代澳大利亚小说界获奖最多、著作最丰、读者群最广的作家马克斯·苏萨克（Markus Zusak，1975- ）的代表作。

快上楼梯时听到一声哭声，就像鸟叫那么尖锐。哭声又响了起来，这次持续的时间更长。

A.J.再次把灯打开，走回门口那里，然后把书店里的每条过道都来回走了一遍。他来到最后一排，那里是存书很少的儿童及青少年图书区。一个小孩坐在地板上，把书店里唯一一本《野兽家园》[①]（这是小岛书店肯屈尊进货的少数几本绘本之一）放在腿上，翻开到一半的地方。这是个大宝宝了，A.J.想。不是个新生儿。A.J.无法准确估出年龄，因为除了他自己，他私底下从不认识任何小孩。他在家里排行最小，也不用说他跟妮可一直没有自己的孩子。那个小孩穿着一件粉红色的滑雪衫，一头淡褐色头发非常卷曲，眼睛是深蓝色的，皮肤是棕褐色，比A.J.自己的皮肤颜色要浅一点。小家伙长得相当漂亮。

"你到底是谁？"A.J.问那个小孩。

不知何故，她不再哭了，而是对他微笑。"玛雅。"她回答。

这个问题容易，A.J.想。"你几岁了？"他问。

玛雅伸出两个手指。

"你两岁？"

玛雅又露出微笑，然后朝他伸出胳膊。

"你的妈咪呢？"

玛雅哭了起来。她一直朝A.J.伸着胳膊。因为看不到自己

[①] 美国著名儿童文学图画书作家及插画家莫里斯·桑达克（Maurice Sendak，1928-2012）自写自画的代表作品。

还有别的什么选择，A.J.把她抱了起来。她至少有一箱二十四本精装书那样重，重得能让他闪了腰。那个小孩搂着他的脖子，A.J.注意到她身上很好闻，像是爽身粉和婴儿油的气味。显然，这不是个被疏于照顾或者受虐待的幼儿。她对人友好，穿得漂亮，期待——不，是要求——关爱。当然，这个包裹的主人随时会回来，还会作出一番完全站得住脚的解释。比如说车坏了，要么那位妈妈突然食物中毒。他以后要重新考虑自己不锁门的做法。他只想到可能会有人偷东西，却没想到可能会有人留下什么东西。

她把他搂得更紧了。越过她的肩膀，A.J.注意到地板上有个艾摩娃娃[①]，它乱蓬蓬的红色前胸上用一枚安全别针别着一张纸条。他把孩子放下，拿起了艾摩，A.J.一直讨厌这个角色，因为它显得太穷了。

"艾摩！"玛雅说。

"对，"A.J.说，"艾摩。"他取下纸条，把娃娃递给那个小孩。纸条上写着：

> 致这家书店的店主：
>
>   这是玛雅，她两岁零一个月大。她很聪明，对于她的岁数来说，特别会讲话，是个可爱的好女孩。我想让她长大后爱读书，想让她在一个有书本的地方长大，周

---

① 儿童电视节目《芝麻街》中的玩偶主人公。

围是关心这些事物的人。我很爱她，但是我没法再照顾她。她的父亲无法出现在她的生活中，我也没有一个可以帮上忙的家庭。我实在走投无路了。

玛雅的妈妈

见鬼，A.J.想。

玛雅又哭了。

他抱起那个孩子。她的尿布湿透了。A.J.这辈子还从没换过尿布，不过他在包装礼品方面还算熟练。妮可还在世时，小岛书店圣诞节时会为顾客免费包装礼物，他想换尿布和礼物包装肯定具有相通之道。孩子身旁有个袋子，A.J.真心希望那里面装的是尿布。谢天谢地，还真是。他在书店地板上为那个小孩换尿布，同时尽量不把地毯弄脏，也不去多看她的私处。整个过程花了二十分钟。小孩比书本好动，形状也不像书那么方便。玛雅仰着头、噘着嘴、皱着鼻子看着他。

A.J.道歉："对不起，玛雅，可是说实在的，这对我也不算是件多愉快的事。你早点别拉在身上，我们就可以早点结束。"

"对不起。"她说。A.J.马上感觉有点糟糕。

"不，是我对不起。我对这种事一窍不通。我是个笨蛋。"

"笨蛋！"她重复了一遍，接着咯咯笑了。

A.J.又穿上跑步鞋，然后抱起那个小孩，带上那个袋子还有纸条，朝警察局走去。

当然，兰比亚斯警长那天夜里值班。此人似乎命中注定要见证A.J.生活中所有的重要时刻。A.J.把孩子给这位警官看。"有人把这留在书店里。"A.J.悄声说，好不吵醒已经在他怀里睡着了的玛雅。

兰比亚斯的甜甜圈正吃到一半，他尽量掩饰这个动作，因为再一次撞见A.J.，让他感到尴尬。兰比亚斯咀嚼完后，极不专业地对A.J.说："噢，长得像你。"

"这不是我的孩子。"A.J.继续悄声说。

"是谁的？"

"一位顾客的，我想。"A.J.从口袋里掏出那张纸条递给兰比亚斯。

"哦，哇，"兰比亚斯说，"那位妈妈把她留给你了。"玛雅睁开眼对兰比亚斯微笑。"可爱的小家伙，不是吗？"兰比亚斯朝她俯下身，她抓住了他的胡子。"谁抓住了我的胡子？"兰比亚斯用可笑的童稚声音说，"谁偷了我的胡子？"

"兰比亚斯警长，我觉得你对此事没有表现出足够的关心。"

兰比亚斯清清喉咙，站直了身子。"好吧，这么说吧。现在是星期五晚上九点钟，我会给儿童与家庭服务局打个电话，可是现在下雪，又是周末，再考虑到渡轮的班次，恐怕没有谁能赶过来，最早也得到星期一吧。我们会努力去找孩子的妈妈，还有她的爸爸，万一有人在找这个小淘气鬼呢。"

"玛雅。"玛雅说。

"你叫这个名字吗？"兰比亚斯用童稚的声音说，"这是个好名字。"兰比亚斯又清清喉咙，"得有人周末带这个孩子。我，以及另外几个警察可以轮流在这儿照看，要么——"

"不，没事，"A.J.说，"让小孩一直待在警察局好像不太合适。"

"你知道怎么带孩子吗？"兰比亚斯问。

"只是一个周末而已，能有多难？我会打电话给我的妻姐。有什么她也不知道的，我会上谷歌搜索。"

"谷歌。"孩子说。

"谷歌！那可是个很大的词，嗯哼。"兰比亚斯说，"好吧，我星期一会去你那里看看情况如何。世界真有趣，对吧？有人偷了你一本书，还有人给你留了一个孩子。"

"哈。"A.J.说。

他们一回到住处，玛雅就扯开嗓门纵情大哭，哭声介于除夕夜派对喇叭和火警报警器之间。A.J.估摸着她是饿了，但是对于该喂两岁零一个月的小孩吃什么，他毫无头绪。他把她的嘴唇拉开，看她有没有长牙。她有，而且想用牙咬他。他在谷歌上搜索了这个问题："我该喂两岁零一个月大的孩子吃什么？"搜出的答案大多是这么大的孩子应该是父母吃什么，他们就能吃什么。谷歌所不知道的是，A.J.吃的食物大部分都让人恶心。他的冰箱里放着各种各样冷冻食品，很多还是辣的。他打电话向伊斯梅求助。

"对不起，打扰你了，"他说，"可是我想知道，该喂两岁零一个月大的小孩吃什么东西？"

"你为什么想知道这个呢？"伊斯梅语气紧张地问。

他解释了有人把一个小孩留在书店的事，伊斯梅沉默了一会儿，然后说她马上过来。

"你确定可以吗？"A.J.问。伊斯梅已经怀孕六个月，他不想麻烦她。

"我确定。我挺高兴你打电话来。反正丹尼尔这位伟大的美国小说家去外地了，而且我最近两三个星期失眠。"

不到半个小时，伊斯梅就到了，从她家厨房里带来了一袋食品：够做一份色拉的原料、一份意式豆腐千层面和半份烤苹果奶酥。"我临时只能找到这些了。"她说。

"不，这已经太好了，"A.J.说，"我的厨房里那叫没法看。"

"你的厨房就是个犯罪现场。"她说。

看到伊斯梅，那个小孩大哭起来。"她肯定是想她妈妈了，"伊斯梅说，"也许我让她想起了她的妈妈？"A.J.点点头，不过他觉得真正的原因，是他妻子的姐姐把孩子吓坏了。伊斯梅的头发剪得时髦，红色头发支楞着，皮肤和眼睛都是浅色的，四肢又长又瘦。她的五官都有点太大，她的动作有点太过生动，怀孕的她像是个很漂亮的咕噜[1]。就连她说话的声音都有可能吓到一个小孩。她的声音清晰准确、训练有素，总是调整得能让室内的人都能听到。在他认识她的十五年左右的时间里，A.J.觉得伊斯梅像个女演员一样年龄渐长：从饰演朱丽叶到奥菲莉娅到格特鲁德到赫卡特[2]。

伊斯梅把食物加热。"你想让我喂她吗？"伊斯梅问。

玛雅怀疑地看着伊斯梅。"不，我想试一试。"A.J.说。他转而对玛雅说："你用勺子什么的吗？"

玛雅没有回答。

"你没有宝宝椅。你需要临时堆个什么出来，好不让她翻倒。"伊斯梅说。

他让玛雅坐在地板上，用一堆样书垒成三面墙，然后在样书堡垒的里面再垫上床上用的枕头。

他喂的第一勺烤宽面条毫不费事地进了玛雅的嘴里。"容易。"他说。

喂第二勺时，玛雅在最后一刻头一扭，把调味汁弄得到处都是——A.J.身上、枕头上、样书堡垒的侧面。玛雅扭回头对他露出满面的笑容，似乎她开了个聪明绝顶的玩笑。

"我希望这些不是你要读的书。"伊斯梅说。

---

[1] 英国作家托尔金（J. R. R. Tolkien, 1892-1973）小说中的虚构角色，他在《霍比特人》里首次登场，并且是续作《魔戒》的主要角色。
[2] 这四个人分别为莎士比亚戏剧《罗密欧与朱丽叶》《哈姆雷特》和《麦克白》中的人物。

晚饭后，他们把孩子放到第二间卧室里的蒲团上让她睡觉。

"你干吗不索性把孩子留在警察局？"伊斯梅问。

"感觉那样做不合适。"A.J.说。

"你没想留下她，对吧？"伊斯梅摩挲着自己的腹部。

"当然没有。我只照看她到星期一。"

"我想那位妈妈到时候也会出现，改变主意的。"伊斯梅说。

A.J.把那张纸递给伊斯梅看。

"可怜的人。"伊斯梅说。

"我看也是，可是我做不到，我做不到就那样把自己的孩子遗弃在一家书店里。"

伊斯梅耸耸肩。"那个女孩很可能有自己的理由。"

"你怎么知道是个女孩？"A.J.问，"有可能是个实在山穷水尽的中年妇女。"

"我觉得那封信的语气听着年轻，我想。或许笔迹也是。"伊斯梅说。她的手指在自己的短头发中划拉了一下，"你别的方面怎么样？"

"我还行。"A.J.说。他意识到自己有几个小时没有想到《帖木儿》或者妮可了。

伊斯梅洗了碗，尽管A.J.让她别管了。"我不会留着她的，"A.J.又说了一遍，"我一个人住，又没存下多少钱，而且生意也不算红火。"

"当然不会，"伊斯梅说，"你这样的过法要养个孩子太说不过去了。"她把盘子擦干后放好，"不过，你开始偶尔吃点新鲜蔬菜也没有坏处。"

伊斯梅吻了一下他的脸。A.J.觉得她跟妮可很像又很不像。有时，她们俩像的那些方面（脸、身材）让他很难忍受；有时，她们俩不像的方面（头脑、心）又让他很难忍受。"你还需要帮助的话就告诉我。"伊斯梅说。

尽管妮可是妹妹，她却一直担心伊斯梅。妮可认为，她姐姐在怎么安排自己的生活方面没有多少经验。伊斯梅选择上一所大学，是因为她喜欢宣传册上的照片；嫁给一个男人，是因为他穿着燕尾服特别帅气；去教书，则是因为她看了一部关于某位能激励人的老师的电影。"可怜的伊斯梅，"妮可说过，"到头来她总是失望。"

妮可会希望我对她姐姐好一点的，他想。"戏剧排得怎么样了？"A.J.问。

伊斯梅笑了，这让她看起来像个小女孩。"我的天，A.J.，我不晓得你竟然知道排戏的事。"

"《萨勒姆的女巫》[1]，"A.J.说，"孩子们来店里买这本书。"

"对，那就说得通了。事实上这部戏很糟糕。可在戏里那些女生可以尖叫、大喊，她们喜欢，我可没那么喜欢。我总是带一

_____

① 美国剧作家阿瑟·米勒（Arthur Miller，1915–2005）的作品。

瓶泰诺①去参加排练。也许吧，在一片尖叫和大喊中，他们也能顺便学点美国历史。当然，我选择这出戏的真正原因，是里面有很多女性角色——你知道，在公布入选名单时，会少些孩子流眼泪。但是现在，我的孩子快要出生了，这一切开始显得像是有，嗯，很多戏剧性的时刻。"

因为她带了食物过来，A.J.感觉自己欠她人情，就主动提出帮忙。"也许我可以帮忙刷油漆或者印制节目单什么的？"

她想说"这真不像你"，但忍住了。除了自己的丈夫，她认为自己的妹夫是她见过的最自私、最以自我为中心的人之一。如果跟一个小孩子待了一下午，就能让A.J.有这样的改观，那么等到宝宝出生后，丹尼尔会怎么样呢？她妹夫小小的举动给了她希望。她摩挲着自己的腹部。是个男孩，他们已经选好了一个名字，还有一个备选名字，以防之前的名字不合适。

第二天下午，雪刚停，才刚开始融化进泥泞里时，一具尸体被冲到灯塔附近的一小溜陆地上。她口袋里的身份证说明她叫玛丽安·华莱士，没费多长时间，兰比亚斯就推断出这具尸体跟那个小孩有血缘关系。

玛丽安·华莱士在艾丽丝岛上没有亲人，谁都不知道她为什么来到这里，不知道她来找谁，也不知道她为什么决定自杀，游进了艾丽丝岛海峡十二月的冰冷海水中。也就是说，没人知道具

---

① 有治头痛及退烧的功效。

体原因。他们知道玛丽安·华莱士是黑人，二十二岁，她有个两岁零一个月大的孩子。除了这些事实，他们还可以再加上她给A.J.的纸条中所说的。一个虽有漏洞，但已经成形的故事浮出水面。警方断定玛丽安·华莱士为自杀，其他的就没什么了。

周末，随着时间的推进，出现了更多关于玛丽安·华莱士的信息。她靠奖学金上哈佛大学。她获得过马萨诸塞州的游泳冠军，是位热心的创意写作者。她是罗克斯伯里人，她的母亲在她十三岁时死于癌症。一年后，她的外婆死于同一种病。她的父亲是个瘾君子。上中学时，她时断时续在寄养家庭生活。她的养母之一记得小玛丽安总是在埋头看书。没人知道她孩子的父亲是谁，甚至没人记得她有过男朋友。她被勒令休学，因为之前的那个学期，她每门功课都不及格——一方面是当妈妈，一方面是高强度的学业课程，这让她不堪忍受。她漂亮、聪明，这让她的死成为悲剧。她贫穷，还是个黑人，这意味着人们会说他们早就预见到这种事。

星期天晚上，兰比亚斯顺道来了趟书店，想看看玛雅，也跟A.J.交待一下最新情况。他有几个弟弟妹妹，他提出A.J.忙书店的生意时，他可以照看玛雅。"你不介意吗？"A.J.问，"你不用去哪里吗？"

兰比亚斯最近离了婚。他的前妻是他高中时的甜心爱人，所以他过了很久，才意识到事实上她并不是个甜心爱人，也根本不是个很好的人。吵架时，她喜欢说他又蠢又胖。顺便说一句，他不蠢，尽管他读的书不多，去的地方不多。他也不胖，尽管体型像斗牛犬——脖子上肌肉粗壮，腿短，鼻子又宽又平。这是一条结实的美国斗牛犬，不是英国的。

兰比亚斯并不想念自己的妻子，不过他的确怀念下班后有地方可去。

他坐在地板上，把玛雅抱到自己的大腿上。玛雅睡着后，兰比亚斯告诉了A.J.他所了解的玛雅妈妈的事。

"我感到奇怪的是，"A.J.说，"首先她为什么来到艾丽丝岛。你知道，到这儿来可非易事。我住在这里的这么多年里，我自己的妈妈只来过一次。你真的觉得她来不是为了见某个特别的人？"

兰比亚斯调整了一下玛雅睡在他腿上的位置。"我一直在考虑那一点。也许她对去哪里没有计划，也许她只是坐上第一列火车，然后是第一趟大巴，然后是第一班渡轮，最终到了这里。"

A.J.出于礼貌点了点头，但他不相信有什么无缘无故的行为。他爱读书，他认为该有个解释。如果第一幕中出现了一把枪，那把枪最好在第三幕中开火。

"也许她想死在一个风景不错的地方，"兰比亚斯补充道，"哎，儿童与家庭服务局的那位女士星期一会来取这个开心的小包裹。既然那位母亲没有家人，孩子的父亲又不知道是谁，他们就得给她找个寄养家庭。"

A.J.数着抽屉里的现金。"如此安排，对孩子来说挺不容易的，不是吗？"

"有可能，"兰比亚斯说，"可是她这么小，大概会一切顺利吧。"

A.J.又数了一遍抽屉中的现金。"你说那位母亲就被安排过寄养？"

兰比亚斯点点头。

"我想她认为这个孩子在书店里会有更好的生活。"

"谁说得准呢？"

"我没有宗教信仰，兰比亚斯警长。我不相信命运。我的妻子，她相信命运。"

就在这时，玛雅醒了，她朝A.J.伸出胳膊。A.J.合上收款机的抽屉，从兰比亚斯那里把她接过来。兰比亚斯觉得自己听到那个小女孩叫A.J."爸爸"。

"呃，我一直让她别那么叫我，"A.J.说，"可她就是不听。"

"孩子有自己的想法。"兰比亚斯说。

"你想喝杯什么吗？"

"当然。干吗不呢？"

A.J.锁好书店的大门，然后上楼梯。他把玛雅放到垫子上，然后出来进到房子的大房间。

"我没法养小孩儿，"A.J.语气坚定地说，"我两个晚上没睡觉了。她就是个恐怖分子！她醒来的时间很要命，凌晨三点四十五分好像是她一天的开始。我一个人住，又没钱。单靠卖书养不活一个孩子。"

"说得对。"兰比亚斯说。

"我几乎连自己都养活不了，"A.J.接着说，"她比小狗还要难搞，像我这样的人连小狗都不该养。还没有人训练过她上厕所，我根本不知道这样的事情，还有其他相关的事情要怎样办。另外，我从来就没有真正喜欢过小宝宝。我喜欢玛雅，可是……跟她根本没什么好说的。我们谈论艾摩，对了，我受不了艾摩。除此之外，谈话主要是关于她的。她完全以自我为中心。"

"小宝宝都是那个样子的，"兰比亚斯说，"等她知道了更多的词汇，跟她谈话就会好起来。"

"她老是想读同一本书，而且那是最垃圾的图片书。《怪物就在结尾处》？"

兰比亚斯说他没听说过这本书。

"嗯，肯定的。她的阅读品位特别糟糕。"A.J.大笑起来。

兰比亚斯点点头，喝了口他的葡萄酒。"没人说你必须养她。"

"是啊，是啊，当然。可是你不觉得我对她最终到哪里能有点发言权吗？她是个特别聪明的小家伙。比如她已经认识字母表，我甚至让她明白了什么是字母顺序。要是她最后跟一些不能欣赏到这一点的混蛋在一起，我会不乐意的。就像我以前说过的，我不相信命运。可是我的确觉得对她有种责任感。那个年轻的女人的确把她留给我来照顾。"

"那个年轻女人疯了，"兰比亚斯说，"之后不过一个小时，她就投海自尽了。"

"是啊。"A.J.皱起眉头，"你说得对。"从另外一个房间里传来哭声，A.J.欠身走开。"我得去看看她。"他说。

周末快过完时，玛雅需要洗澡了。尽管他宁愿把这项新的亲密活动留给马萨诸塞州的负责人，但是A.J.不想把她交给一个微型郝薇香小姐[1]式的社会福利部门。A.J.在谷歌上搜了又搜，只为确定正确的洗澡方式：两岁孩子洗澡水的适当温度，两岁孩子能否使用成人洗发水，一位父亲怎样清洗一个两岁女孩的私处而不被认为是变态，浴缸里的水放多深——刚学走路的孩子，如何预防一个两岁的孩子在浴缸中遇溺，洗澡安全总则，等等。

他用主要成分是大麻籽油的洗发水给玛雅洗了头发，这瓶洗发水是妮可的。很久以前，A.J.就把妻子的其他一些东西都捐了或者扔了，他还是很不忍心把她的洗浴用品扔掉。

A.J.给玛雅冲洗了头发，她开始唱起来。

"你在唱什么？"

"歌。"她说。

"唱的什么歌？"

---

[1] 英国作家查尔斯·狄更斯（Charles Dickens，1812-1870）的《远大前程》里的人物，一直以别人的恩主自居。

"啦啦，布呀，啦啦。"

A.J.笑了起来。"好吧，我听着是乱唱，玛雅。"

她朝他溅水。

"妈妈？"过了一会儿她问。

"不，我不是你妈妈。"A.J.说。

"走了。"玛雅说。

"对，"A.J.说，"她很可能不会再回来了。"

玛雅想了一会儿，然后点点头。"你唱。"

"我还是别唱了。"

"唱。"她说。

这个丫头失去了妈妈，他觉得至少自己能满足她的愿望。

没时间去谷歌上搜索"适合给小宝宝听的歌曲"。A.J.在认识自己的妻子之前，曾在普林斯顿大学无伴奏男生合唱队"脚注"中唱第二男高音。A.J.爱上妮可后，受损失的是"脚注"，在一个学期错过多次排练后，他被合唱队除名。他回想在"脚注"的最后一场演出，那次是向八十年代的音乐致敬。他在浴缸边的表演跟那次的节目单很接近，从《99只气球》开始，接着是《从我的梦中出来，上我的车》，压轴曲目为《爱在电梯中》。他并没感觉自己特别傻。

他唱完后她鼓了掌。"再唱，"她命令道，"再唱。"

"只演一场。"他把她从浴缸里拎出来，然后用毛巾把她擦干，把她每个完美的脚趾缝也擦干了。

"安气球，"玛雅说，"安你。"

"什么？"

"爱你。"她说。

"你显然是折服于清唱的魅力。"

她点点头。"爱你。"

"爱我？你还根本不了解我呢。"A.J.说，"小姑娘，你不应该如此轻易地到处抛撒你的爱。"他把她拉到自己跟前，"我们处得挺好、挺愉快，至少对我来说，是难忘的七十二小时，但是有些人注定不会永远留在你的生命中。"

她瞪着那双疑虑的蓝色大眼睛看着他。"爱你。"她又说了一遍。

A.J.用毛巾擦干她的头发，然后闻闻香不香。"我担心你。要是你谁都爱，大多时候到头来会受到感情伤害。我想，相对你短短的人生，你觉得似乎已经认识我很久了。你对时间的看法事实上是扭曲的，玛雅。可是我老了，很快你就会忘了你曾认识我。"

莫莉·克洛克敲了敲住处的门。"社会福利部门的那个女人在楼下。我让她上来好吗？"

A.J.点点头。

他把玛雅拉到他的腿上，他们等着，听着社会福利工作人员走上吱嘎作响的楼梯。"别害怕，玛雅。这位女士会为你找到一个完美的家，比这里好。你不能将来一辈子都在一个垫子上睡，你知道的。你不会想去认识那种一辈子都在垫子上睡觉的人。"

那位工作人员叫詹妮。A.J.记不得自己曾碰到过任何叫詹妮的成年女人。如果詹妮是一本书，她会是一本刚从箱子里取出来的平装书——书页没有折角，没有水渍，书脊上没有折痕。A.J.更想看到一位看上去就饱经沧桑的社会福利工作人员。A.J.构思出詹妮之书封底上的故事梗概：当来自康涅狄格州费尔菲尔德的无畏的詹妮在大城市接受一份社会福利工作时，她根本不知道自己在这一行会遇到什么事。

"这是你第一天上班吗？"A.J.问。

"不是，"詹妮说，"我做这份工作有段时间了。"詹妮对着玛雅微笑。"你长得真漂亮啊。"

玛雅把头埋进A.J.的卫衣里。

"你们俩好像很亲啊。"詹妮在她的便笺簿上记了一笔，"好吧，是这样的。我把玛雅从这儿带到波士顿。作为她的个案负责人，我会为她填写一些文件——显然她自己填写不了，哈哈。会有医生和心理专家来对她进行评估。"

"在我看来，她很健康，也很正常。"A.J.说。

"您观察到了这一点很好。医生会看看有没有发育延迟、疾病以及未经训练的人无法一眼看出来的其他问题。之后，玛雅会被安排到诸多我们事先已经核准过的寄养家庭中的一户，然后——"

A.J.打断她的话："一个寄养家庭如何获得事先核准？是不是

就像得到一家百货商店的签账卡那样容易？"

"哈哈，当然不是。比那多了不少流程。要有申请、家访……"

A.J.再次打断她的话："詹妮，我是想说，你怎样确保不会把一个无辜的孩子交到一个十足的精神变态者手里？"

"嗯，费克里先生，我们当然不会预设每个想接受寄养孩子的人都是精神变态者，但是对所有的寄养家庭，我们都会进行全面的审查。"

"我担心是因为……嗯，玛雅很聪明，但是也很容易相信人。"A.J.说。

"聪明，但也很容易相信人。观察得不错。我得把这点记下来。"詹妮记了下来，"好吧，我先把她安排到一个应急的非精神变态……"她朝A.J.微笑，"寄养家庭，我会继续做工作。我会尽量去看看她的旁系亲属里有没有人想接纳她，如果没有，我就开始为玛雅找一种永久性的解决办法。"

"你指的是收养。"

"对，一点没错。很好，费克里先生。"詹妮并不是非得解释所有这些事，但是她想让A.J.这样见义勇为的好人感觉他们付出的时间是值得的。"对了，我真的要感谢您，"她说，"我们需要更多像您这样的人，你们有意愿做好事。"她朝玛雅伸出胳膊，"准备好了吗，小可爱？"

A.J.把玛雅抱得更紧了一点。他做了次深呼吸。他真的要这样做吗？对，我要，亲爱的上帝。"你说玛雅会被安置在一个临时性的寄养家庭？我不可以是那样的家庭吗？"

社会福利工作人员噘起了嘴。"我们所有的寄养家庭都经过了申请程序，费克里先生。"

"问题是……我知道这不合常规，但是她的妈妈给我留了这张纸条。"他把那张纸条递给詹妮。"她想让我养这个孩子，你看。这是她的遗愿。我觉得我养着玛雅才是对的。我不想在这里就有一个特别好的家的情况下，把她送到一个寄养家庭。我昨天晚上在谷歌上搜索了这事。"

"谷歌。"玛雅说。

"她喜欢那个词，我不知道为什么。"

"什么'这事'？"詹妮问道。

"如果她的妈妈是想让我养着她，我不一定非得把她交出去。"A.J.解释道。

"爸爸。"玛雅似乎得到提示，这样叫了一声。

詹妮看看A.J.的眼睛又看看玛雅的，两双眼睛都露出坚定的神色，真叫人头痛。她叹了口气。本来她以为这个下午会过得简单轻松，但现在开始变得复杂了。

詹妮又叹了口气。这不是她上班的第一天，但她一年半前才获得社会福利方面的硕士。她要么是太过热情，要么是经验不足，这使得她想去帮助他们。尽管如此，他是一个住在书店上面的单身汉，文案工作将会繁琐至极，她想。"那请帮我一个忙，费克里先生，跟我说您在教育或者儿童养育方面有经验。"

"呃……我当时是要攻读美国文学的博士学位，可是放弃了，开了这家书店。我的研究方向是埃德加·爱伦·坡。《厄舍古屋的倒塌》[①]是一篇挺好的入门作品，告诉人们不能对儿童做什么。"

"不简单。"詹妮说。她的意思是那完全没有帮助。"你真的有把握你能胜任吗？这需要投入大量的金钱、感情以及时间。"

"没有，"A.J.说，"我没有把握。但是我觉得玛雅跟我在一起和跟别人在一起相比，会有同样不错的人生机会。我工作时可以照看她，我们互相喜欢，我觉得。"

"爱你。"玛雅说。

"对，她老是那么说。"A.J.讲，"要先赢得别人的爱才能付出，我一直这样提醒她，可是说实话，我觉是这是那个狡猾的艾摩带来的影响。它谁都爱，你知道吗？"

"我对艾摩很熟悉。"詹妮说。她想哭，真的会有很多文案工作。这还仅仅是寄养安排这一步，收养手续办起来更是会累死人，而且每次儿童和家庭服务局的人要查核玛雅和A.J.的情况，都得是詹妮花上两个小时来艾丽丝岛一趟。"好吧，两位，我得给我的上司打个电话。"詹妮·伯恩斯坦来自马萨诸塞州梅德福市的一个殷实之家，父母爱她，她从小就很喜欢看像《绿山墙的

---

① 爱伦·坡最著名的心理恐怖小说之一。

安妮》①和《小公主》②之类的孤儿故事。她最近开始怀疑自己之所以选择以社会福利工作为职业，就是一再读那些故事遗留的恶果。总的说来，她发现这种职业并不像她在书中读到的那样浪漫。昨天，她以前的一位同学发现一位寄养母亲把一个十六岁的男孩饿得体重只剩四十二磅。邻居们都以为那是个六岁的孩子。"我还是愿意相信美好的结局，"那位同学说，"但是越来越难了。"詹妮对着玛雅微笑。真是个幸运的小女孩，她想。

那年圣诞节期间以及之后的几个星期，艾丽丝岛上都在热议这条新闻，即那位鳏夫——书店老板A.J.费克里收养了一个被抛弃的孩子。这是一段时间以来——很可能自从《帖木儿》被盗以来——艾丽丝岛上最具八卦价值的新闻。而且特别让人感兴趣的是A.J.费克里这个人。这个镇上的人一直认为他势利、冷漠，似乎让人很难相信就因为一个孩子被遗弃在他的书店里，这样一个人居然就会收养这个小孩。镇上的花店老板讲了件事，说他把一副太阳镜忘在小岛书店，过了不到一天他再去，却发现A.J.把太阳镜扔了。"他说他店里可没地方设置一个失物招领处。那刚好是一副很好的经典款雷朋眼镜！"那位花店老板说，"你能想象出如果涉及到一个活生生的人会怎么样？"此外，有好多年，A.J.都被

---

① 加拿大女作家露西·莫德·蒙哥马利（Lucy Maud Montgomery，1874-1942）的代表作品，被誉为"世界上最甜蜜的少女成长故事"。
② 英语世界家喻户晓的儿童文学作家弗朗西丝·霍奇森·伯内特（Frances Hodgson Burnett，1849-1924）的代表作品。

邀请参与镇上的生活——赞助足球队，参加蛋糕义卖，在中学年鉴上购买广告——他总是一概拒绝，而且并非每次拒绝时都有礼有貌。他们只能总结说自从丢了《帖木儿》，A.J.的心肠变软了。

艾丽丝岛上那些当妈妈的担心那个小孩儿会被疏于照顾，一个单身男人哪懂得什么养育孩子呢？她们把这当成一项事业，尽可能多地顺路去一趟书店，给A.J.提建议，有时候也送小礼物——旧的娃娃家具、衣服、毛毯、玩具。她们惊讶地发现玛雅是个够干净、够快乐、够沉着的小人儿。只是在离开书店后，她们会叽叽喳喳地说玛雅的身世有多么悲惨。

在A.J.这方面，他并不介意她们来看。那些建议他大都当成耳旁风。他收下那些礼物，不过在那些女人走了之后，事实上只是收着并将其消毒。他知道她们来看过之后的闲言碎语，不想自己为那些而恼火。他在柜台上放了一瓶普瑞来免洗洗手液，旁边还有个牌子，要求"在抱小孩之前请先消毒"。另外，那些女人也的确懂得一两样他原先不知道的事：关于训练孩子自己上厕所（贿赂是有用的）、长牙（奇形怪状的制冰盒）和注射疫苗（水痘的打不打都行）。事实证明，在提供养育孩子的建议方面，谷歌搜索出来的结果博而不深。

去看那个孩子时，有很多女人甚至买书和杂志。A.J.开始进一些书，因为他觉得那些女人会喜欢讨论那些书。有一阵子，那个圈子对特别能干的女性被困在不如意的婚姻中那类当代故事感兴趣；她们喜欢看到她有外遇——倒不是她们自己有（有也不会承认）。乐趣在于评判这些女人。女方抛弃自己的孩子就太过火了，但是丈夫遭遇可怕的意外这种安排较受欢迎（他死掉而她又找到爱情，就会额外加分）。有一阵子梅芙·宾奇[1]广受欢迎，直到玛吉妮（她另一个身份是一家投资银行的职员）提出抱怨，说宾奇的作品过于程式化。"在一个气氛压抑的爱尔兰小镇，一个女人太年轻时嫁给了一个长得帅的坏男人，这样的故事我能够读多少次？"A.J.被鼓励去扩充他的书目。"如果我们要成立这个读书小组，"玛吉妮说，"也许我们最好丰富一下图书的品种。"

"这是个读书小组吗？"A.J.说。

"难道不是吗？"玛吉妮说，"你不会以为这么多关于养孩子方面的建议都是免费的吧？"

四月份是《我是海明威的巴黎妻子》[2]，六月份是《可靠的妻子》[3]，八月份是《美国妻子》[4]，九月份是《时间旅行者的妻子》[5]。十二月时，他找不到书名中有"妻子"的好书，她们就读《美声》[6]。

"你给绘本区那里加点书也没什么坏处。"佩内洛普建议道，她总是一副特别累的样子。"孩子们在这里的时候，就也有

---

① 梅芙·宾奇（Maeve Binchy，1940－2012），爱尔兰国宝级畅销书作家。
② 美国作家保拉·麦克莱恩（Paula McLain，1965－ ）的代表作。
③ 美国作家罗伯特·古尔里克（Robert Goolrick，1948－ ）的小说处女作。
④ 美国作家伊莱恩·福特（Elaine Ford，1939－ ）的短篇小说集。
⑤ 美国作家奥德丽·尼芬格（Audrey Niffenegger，1963－ ）的小说处女作。
⑥ 美国作家安·帕契特（Ann Patchett，1963－ ）的畅销小说。

书读了。"那些女人把自己的小孩带来跟玛雅一起玩，所以那样做也说得通。另外也不用说，A.J.也读够了《怪物就在结尾处》，尽管他以前一直对绘本书不是很感兴趣，他决定让自己成为这方面的专家。他想让玛雅读文学绘本书，如果这种书存在的话。最好是现代文学的，而且最好是女性文学方面的，不要什么公主。结果发现这种书千真万确是有的。有天晚上，他忍不住说："在形式上，绘本同样具有短篇小说所具有的雅致。你知道我在说什么吗，玛雅？"

她很严肃地点点头，然后翻动书页。

"这些作者中有些人真是才华横溢，"A.J.说，"我以前真的不知道。"

玛雅轻轻拍了拍那本书。他们在读《小豌豆》①，故事是说一颗豌豆得把他的糖全吃了，然后才能吃作为餐后甜点的蔬菜。

"这叫说反话，玛雅。"A.J.说。

"熨斗②。"她说。她做了个熨衣服的动作。

"反话。"他又说了一遍。

玛雅仰着头，A.J.想还是以后再教她什么是反话。

兰比亚斯警长是书店的常客，为了使自己的到访理由更充分

---

① 美国作家艾米·克劳斯·罗森塔尔（Amy Krouse Rosenthal）作、简·科雷斯（Jen Corace）绘的童书。艾米·克劳斯·罗森塔尔同时还是一位成人书的畅销作家。

② 前面的"反话"原文为"irony"，玛雅不明白，以为跟"熨斗"(iron)有关。

些，他买书。因为兰比亚斯不愿意浪费钱，他也真的阅读那些书。一开始，他主要买大众市场平装版图书——杰弗里·迪弗和詹姆斯·帕特森（或者替他写作的不管什么人）——后来A.J.让他上了个台阶，卖尤·奈斯博[1]和埃尔莫·伦纳德[2]的平装书给他。这两位作家都让兰比亚斯一读钟情，A.J.就又给他提升了一点，让他读沃尔特·莫斯利[3]，然后是科马克·麦卡锡[4]。A.J.最近跟他推荐凯特·阿特金森[5]的《尘封旧案》。

兰比亚斯一进书店就想谈论这本书。"是这样，刚开始我有点讨厌这本书，但是接着它吸引了我，没错。"他靠到柜台上，"因为你知道，它是关于一位侦探的。但是它的故事推进得有点慢，大多数案件到最后都悬而未决。不过我转念一想，那就是生活，这份工作实际上就是这样。"

"还有续集。"A.J.告诉他。

兰比亚斯点点头。"我说不准是不是能继续读下去。有时候，我喜欢一切都解决了。坏人受到惩罚，好人取得胜利。诸如此类。也许再来本埃尔莫·伦纳德吧。嗨，A.J.，我一直在考虑，也许我和你可以为警察成立一个读书会？嗯，我认识的别的

① 尤·奈斯博（Jo Nesbo，1960- ），挪威史上最畅销的作家，素有文坛贵公子、乐界摇滚巨星、欧洲罪案天王之称。
② 埃尔莫·伦纳德（Elmore Leonard，1925-2013），美国最具影响力的畅销书作家之一。
③ 沃尔特·莫斯利（Walter Mosley，1952- ），著名的推理小说作家。
④ 科马克·麦卡锡（Cormac McCarthy，1933- ），美国当代最优秀的作家之一。
⑤ 凯特·阿特金森（Kate Atkinson，1951- ），出生于美国纽约，目前居住在英国爱丁堡，著名畅销小说作家。

警察也许喜欢读点这类书，我是警长，所以我会让他们都来这里买书。也没必要仅仅是警察，也可以是对执法活动很感兴趣的人。"兰比亚斯往手上挤了点洗手液，然后弯腰抱起了玛雅。

"嗨，小美女，你怎么样？"

"被收养了。"她说。

"那可是个很大的词。"兰比亚斯看着A.J.，"嗨，是这样吗？真的有这事？"

办理收养手续的时间跟通常所需的一样，在九月玛雅过三岁生日前完成了。对A.J.的主要不利因素，包括他没有驾驶执照（因为他会突然走神，所以一直没有拿到），另外当然还有他是单身，从来没有养过孩子，甚至没有养过狗或家庭盆栽。最终，A.J.的受教育程度、他跟这个街区（即那家书店）的紧密关系，还有事实上那位母亲想让玛雅跟他一起生活，这些让他克服了不利因素。

"恭喜，我最喜欢的卖书人！"兰比亚斯说。他把玛雅扔到空中再接住她，把她放到地上。他从柜台上探身过来跟A.J.握手。"不不，我得拥抱你一下，老兄。这是个值得拥抱的消息。"这位警察说。兰比亚斯从柜台后边走过来，跟A.J.拥抱了一下。

"我们要干一杯。"A.J.说。

A.J.把玛雅背起来，这两个男人上了楼。A.J.让玛雅上床睡觉，那费时漫长（她要上厕所，还要看两本绘本，曲折复杂），而兰比亚斯开了一瓶酒。

"你现在要为她安排受洗吗？"兰比亚斯问。

"我不是基督徒，也没有任何宗教信仰，"A.J.说，"所以我不会安排。"

兰比亚斯考虑了一下此话，又喝了点葡萄酒。"你没问问我的意见，可是你至少应该办一次派对，把她介绍给大家。她现在叫玛雅·费克里了，对吗？"

A.J.点头。

"大家应该知道这件事。你还应该给她起一个中间名。同时，我想我应该当她的教父。"兰比亚斯说。

"教父到底是干吗的？"

"嗯，这么说吧，这孩子到了十二岁时，她在CVS药店偷东西被抓到了，我很可能会用我的影响力去摆平这件事。"

"玛雅绝对不会干那种事。"

"父母们全是那么想的，"兰比亚斯说，"从根本上说来，我就是你的后援，A.J.。人们都应该有后援。"兰比亚斯喝完了他那杯酒，"我会帮你开派对。"

"一次非受洗的派对要怎么办？"A.J.问。

"没什么大不了的，你就在书店里办。你从飞琳地下商场①给玛雅买一件新裙子。我打赌伊斯梅会来帮忙。你去好市多量贩超市买食物。或许可以买那种大松饼？我妹妹说那种松饼每块就有

①Filene's Basement，美国服装折扣零售商。

一千卡路里的热量。再买点冷冻食品，好的食品。椰味虾。一大块斯蒂尔顿奶酪。既然不是基督教式的——"

A.J.插了句话："话说在前头，也不会是一次非基督教式的。"

"对，我的想法是你可以供应酒。我们邀请你的妻姐、姐夫两口子，你来往的所有那些女士和对小玛雅感兴趣的所有人，我告诉你，A.J.，那差不多是镇上所有的人。我作为教父还要说几句好听的话，如果你同意让我当的话。不是做什么祈祷，因为我知道你不喜欢那样。可是你知道我会祝福这个小女孩在我们称为人生的这一路上顺顺利利的。然后你会感谢大家前来。我们都为玛雅而举杯。每个人都开开心心地回家。"

"所以基本而言，就像是一场图书派对。"

"对，没错。"兰比亚斯从未参加过图书派对。

"我讨厌图书派对。"A.J.说。

"可你是开书店的。"兰比亚斯说。

"这是个问题。"A.J.承认道。

玛雅的非受洗派对在万圣节前一周举行。除了参加派对的几个小孩穿着万圣节服装，这场派对跟洗礼派对或图书派对并无太大区别。A.J.看着穿粉红色礼服的玛雅，心里隐约沸腾着一种熟悉的、略微有点让他难以忍受的欢欣感。他想大笑，想一拳砸在墙上。他觉得自己醉了，或者至少是喝了太多汽水。精神失常了。一开始他觉得这是快乐，而后才知道这就是爱。要命的爱，他想。真是烦人。这完全毁了他打算把自己喝死、把生意做垮的计划。这其中最令人恼火的是，一旦一个人在乎一件事，就发现自己不得不开始在乎一切事。

不，这其中最令人恼火的是，他甚至开始喜欢艾摩了。折叠桌上放着有艾摩形象的纸盘子，盘子里装着椰味虾。这些都是A.J.愉快地从各商店采购回来的。在书店对面畅销书那边，兰比亚斯在高谈阔论，都是些陈词滥调，但都发自内心，恰当得体：A.J.怎样把坏事变成好事，玛雅如何绝处逢生，上帝关上一扇门却又打开一面窗的做法在这里确实如此，等等。他朝A.J.微笑，A.J.举起酒杯，回以微笑。后来，尽管事实上A.J.不信上帝，他却闭上眼睛，全心全意地感谢起所有人，那种更强的力量。

A.J.选了伊斯梅当教母，她抓住他的手。"对不起我要抛下你们了，但是我感觉不舒服。"她说。

"是因为兰比亚斯讲的话吗？"A.J.说。

"我可能感冒了。我要回家了。"

A.J.点点头。"晚一点打电话给我，好吗？"

晚一点打电话过来的是丹尼尔。"伊斯梅在医院，"他口气平淡地说，"又流产了。"

这是过去一年时间里的第二次，总共已经五次了。"她怎么样？"A.J.问。

"她失了点血，也疲劳。不过她像匹强壮的老母马。"

"她的确是。"

"这件事怎么说来都挺糟糕，可偏偏不巧的是，"丹尼尔说，"我得赶早班飞机去洛杉矶。拍电影的人在忙得团团转。"在丹尼尔的描述里，拍电影人的总是忙得团团转，却好像没有一个会伤心。"你不介意去医院看看她，确保她顺利到家吧？"

兰比亚斯开车送A.J.和玛雅到了医院。A.J.让玛雅跟兰比亚斯在等候室等，他进去看伊斯梅。

她的眼睛红红的，脸色苍白。"对不起，"看到A.J.时，她说。

"因为什么，伊斯梅？"

"这是我活该。"她说。

"别这么想，"A.J.说，"你不应该那么说。"

"丹尼尔让你过来，他真是个混蛋。"伊斯梅说。

"我乐意啊。"A.J.说。

"他背着我偷情。你知道吗？他一直背着我偷情。"

A.J.什么都没说，但是他的确知道。丹尼尔在外面拈花惹草并非秘密。

"你当然知道，"伊斯梅嗓音沙哑地说，"谁都知道。"

A.J.一言不发。

"你确实知道，可你不想谈论此事。某种错误的男性准则，我想。"

A.J.看着她。病号服之下，她的肩膀瘦骨嶙峋，但腹部仍然略微鼓起。

"我的样子一团糟，"她说，"你在想着这个。"

"不，我注意到你的头发长长了。那样挺漂亮的。"

"你真好。"她说。此时，伊斯梅坐直身子，想吻A.J.的嘴。

A.J.侧身闪开。"医生说你想回家的话，现在就可以走。"

"我妹妹嫁给你的时候，我认为她是个白痴，可现在我看出来了，你不错。看你对玛雅，看你现在，赶到了这里。赶到这里是重点，A.J.。"

"我觉得今晚我还是待在这里吧，"她说着一下子从A.J.身边挪开，"我家里一个人都没有，我不想那么孤单。我以前说的一点都没错。妮可是个好女孩，是我不好，嫁的也是个坏男人。我知道坏人的下场是罪有应得，但是哦，坏人也真的不想孤独一人。"

《世界的感觉》

1985/理查德·鲍什[1]

胖乎乎的女孩跟爷爷一起住；她参加体操训练，好在小学的汇报演出上表演。

你会对自己有多么关心那个小女孩能否完成那个手撑跳跃感到惊讶，鲍什能把这种似乎是个小插曲的作品写得惊心动魄（不过显然他的目的也在于此）。你应该记住这一点：一次手撑跳跃表演，完全有可能像坠机事件一样戏剧性十足。

我成为一名父亲后才读到这个短篇，所以我无法说在我遇到玛雅之前会不会同样喜欢它。我这辈子经历过一些阶段，那些时期我会更有心情读短篇小说，其中一个阶段刚好也是你蹒跚学步的时候——我哪有时间读长篇小说呢，我的小女孩？

——A.J.F.

---

[1] 理查德·鲍什（Richard Bausch，1945- ），美国作家，尤擅长短篇小说创作，并多次获奖。《世界的感觉》为其短篇小说之一。

玛雅通常在日出前醒来，这时只能听到A.J.在另一个房间里打呼噜的声音。穿着连体睡衣的玛雅轻手轻脚走过客厅，来到A.J.的卧室。她一开始是悄悄地说："爸爸，爸爸。"如果不管用，她就叫他的名字；如果还不管用，她就大声叫他的名字；如果叫也不管用，她就跳上床，不过她宁愿不用这种恶作剧做法。今天，她刚到说话那一步，他就醒了。"醒醒，"她说，"楼下。"

　　楼下是玛雅最爱去的地方，因为楼下是书店，而书店是世界上最好的地方。

　　"裤子，"A.J.嘟囔着说，"咖啡。"他嘴里的气味就像被雪弄湿的袜子味儿。

　　下到书店有十六级台阶。玛雅坐在那里一级一级往下滑，因为她的腿还短得不能自信地一级级走下去。她摇摇晃晃地走过书店，经过那些里面没有画的书本，经过贺卡。她的手滑过杂志，把放书签的旋转货架转了一下。早上好，杂志！早上好，书签！早上好，书本！早上好，书店！

书店的墙上有木质护墙板，刚好到她头顶那么高，但再往上是蓝色墙纸。玛雅的手摸不到墙纸，除非站在椅子上。墙纸上有种表面不平整、旋动的图案，她把脸贴上去摩擦，感觉挺舒服。后来有一天她在书中读到了"锦缎"这个词，她想：对，当然应该叫那个名字。与此形成对比的是，"护壁板"那个词让人极其失望。

书店有十五个玛雅宽，二十个玛雅长。她之所以知道，是因为她有次花了一下午时间，通过在室内一次次躺下而测量出来的。幸好没有超过三十个玛雅长，因为那天她最多只会数到三十。

从她在地板上的有利位置望出去，人们就是鞋子。夏天是凉鞋，冬天是皮靴。莫莉·克洛克有时穿高度到膝部的红色皮靴。A.J.穿的是鞋头为白色的黑色运动鞋。兰比亚斯穿的是圆圆的大头鞋，伊斯梅穿时而像昆虫时而又像珠宝的平根鞋。丹尼尔·帕里什穿棕色的懒汉船鞋，鞋里还装着一便士。

就在书店上午十点钟开门营业之前，她到了她的目的地，绘本书全都在那一排。

玛雅拿到一本书会先去闻。她拆掉书的封套，然后举到脸前，让硬纸板包着自己的耳朵。书本典型的味道有这些：爸爸的香皂，青草，大海，厨房里的餐桌以及奶酪。

她研究那些画，尽量用它们编出故事。这工作挺累人，但即使才三岁，她就了解了一些比喻。例如，绘本里的动物并不总是动物，它们有时代表父母和孩子。一头打着领带的熊可能是爸爸，一头戴着金色假发的熊可能是妈妈。从图画中可以了解挺多故事内容，但有时图画会误导你。她更喜欢认字。

如果没有什么来打岔，她一个上午能看七本书，但是总会有什么来打岔。然而，玛雅大部分时间喜欢顾客，并努力对他们礼貌相待。她明白自己和A.J.所从事的这一行生意。小孩们来到她的这一排时，她一定会往他们手里塞一本书。那些孩子溜达到收款台那里，经常发生的状况是，那位陪着来的监护人会买下这个孩子所拿的那本书。"噢，天哪，你自己选了那本书？"在场的爸爸或者妈妈会问。

有一次，有人问A.J.玛雅是否是他的孩子。"你们俩皮肤都黑，但不是同一种黑。"玛雅记得这句话，因为A.J.用了一种她从未听他对顾客用过的语气回答。

"什么叫同一种黑？"A.J.问。

"我，我没想要冒犯你。"那个人说，然后穿着平底人字拖的那位退往门口，没买书就走掉了。

什么是"同一种黑"？她看着自己的手，疑惑着。

这些是她想知道的另外一些事：

怎样学会阅读？

为什么大人会喜欢没有图片的书？

爸爸会死吗？

午饭吃什么？

午饭在一点钟左右开始，是从三明治店里买来的。她要了烤奶酪，A.J.要了火鸡三明治。她喜欢去三明治店，但她总是抓着A.J.的手，她可不想被留在三明治店。

下午时，她用画画来评论书。一个苹果代表这本书的气味还可以；一块奶酪代表这本书的气味难闻；一幅自画像代表她喜欢里面的画。她在这些读书报告上签了"玛雅"，然后交给A.J.审阅。

她喜欢写自己的名字。

"玛雅"。

她知道自己姓费克里，但是她还不知道怎样写。

有时，顾客和店员都走后，她觉得世界上只有她和A.J.两个人。任何别的人都不如他那样真实，别人只是不同季节所穿的不同鞋子，仅此而已。A.J.不用站在椅子上就能够摸到墙纸，能够边讲电话边操作收款机，能够把重重的一箱箱书举过头顶，能够使用长得让她难以相信的单词，他无所不知，无所不晓。谁能跟A.J.费克里相比？

她几乎从来不会想到自己的妈妈。

她知道她的妈妈死了，她也知道死就是睡着后再也不会醒来。她为她的妈妈感到很可惜，因为不会醒来的人就不能在早上下楼去书店。

玛雅知道她的妈妈把她留在小岛书店，但是也许每个小孩在某个岁数都会遇到这种事。有些孩子被留在鞋店，有些被留在玩具店，还有些被留在三明治店。你的整个人生都取决于你被留在什么店里。她可不想生活在三明治店。

后来，等她再长大一点后，她会更多地想起她的妈妈。

晚上，A.J.换好鞋子，然后把她放进婴儿车。这辆车坐进去有点紧了，不过她喜欢坐车出去，所以她尽量不抱怨。她喜欢听到A.J.的呼吸声，喜欢看到世界从身旁飞速掠过。有时他唱歌，有时他给她讲故事。他告诉她他曾经有本名叫《帖木儿》的书，这本书有书店里所有的书加起来那么值钱。

"《帖木儿》。"她说，她喜欢这个不解之谜和那些音节的音乐性。

"你就是这样有了你的中间名。"

夜里，A.J.让她上床睡觉并给她掖好被子。她虽然很累了，但还不想睡觉。A.J.要想劝她睡觉，最好的做法就是给她讲个故事。"哪个故事？"他问。

他一直在唠叨让她别选《怪物就在结尾处》，所以她为了让他高兴而选了《卖帽子》。

她以前就听过这个故事，但是听不明白。这个故事讲的是有一个人卖五颜六色的帽子，他打了个盹，帽子就都被猴子偷走了。她希望这种事永远不要发生在A.J.身上。

玛雅皱着眉头，紧紧地抓着A.J.的胳膊。

"怎么了？"A.J.问。

猴子要帽子干吗？玛雅纳闷。猴子是动物。也许就像戴假发的熊是妈妈一样，猴子代表别的什么，但是是什么……？她有想法，可说不出来。

"读。"她说。

有时，A.J.请一位女士来书店大声读书给玛雅和其他孩子们听。那个女人做手势，脸上很多表情，为了取得戏剧效果，声音抑扬顿挫的。玛雅想告诉她让她放松。她习惯了A.J.的读书方式——柔和而低沉。她习惯了他。

A.J.读道："……在最上面，是一摞红帽子。"

图画上是一个戴着好多顶色彩鲜艳的帽子的人。

玛雅按住A.J.的手，让他先别翻页。她扫了一眼图画，又看看那页字，然后再看图画。突然她明白了"r-e-d"就是"红色"，就像她知道自己名叫玛雅，A.J.费克里是她的爸爸，世界上最好的地方是小岛书店一样。

"怎么了？"他问。

"红色。"她说。她抓起他的手，把它拉过来指向那个词。

《好人难寻》
1953/弗兰纳里·奥康纳[1]

全家出游出了岔子。这是艾米最喜欢的一篇。（她表面上显得那么可爱，不是吗？）我跟艾米并非总是品位完全一致，但是这一篇呢，我喜欢。

她告诉我她很喜欢这一篇时，我想到之前没有猜到过的她的性格中那些奇怪而精彩的方面，一些隐秘的地方，我也许想去探究一下。

关于政治、上帝和爱，人们都讲些无聊的谎话。想要了解一个人，你只需问一个问题："你最喜欢哪本书？"

——A.J.F.

---

[1] 弗兰纳里·奥康纳（Flannery O'Connor，1925-1964），当代美国南方女作家，美国文学的重要代言人。《好人难寻》为其短篇小说代表作之一。

八月份的第二个星期，就在玛雅开始上幼儿园之前，她戴上了眼镜（红色圆框），还出了水痘（红色圆包），相映成趣，A.J.咒骂那位跟他说水痘疫苗可打可不打的妈妈，因为水痘成了他们家的灾难。玛雅很痛苦，A.J.因为玛雅痛苦而痛苦。她的脸上全是那种点点，空调又坏了，他们家里谁都没法睡。A.J.给她拿来冰冷的毛巾，剥橘子给她吃，把袜子套在她的手上，守护在她的床边。

　　第三天，凌晨四点钟，玛雅睡着了。A.J.筋疲力竭，却放松不下来。他之前让一位店员从地下室给他拿几本样书。不幸的是，那位店员是新来的，她从"待回收"那堆而不是从"待读"那堆拿书。A.J.不想离开玛雅的身边，于是他决定读一本以前没有进过货的样书。那堆书的最上面是一本青少年幻想小说，里面的主角死了。呃，A.J.想。这本书里有他最不喜欢的两样（已亡故的讲述者和青少年长篇小说）。他把那本被他判了死刑的书扔到一旁。那堆书中的第二本是一位八十岁老人写的回忆录，他单身了大半辈子，曾在好多家中西部报纸当过科学报道方面的记者，他七十八岁时结了婚。他的新娘在婚礼后两年去世，享年八十三岁。利昂·弗里德曼所著的《迟暮花开》。这本书A.J.觉得熟悉，但不知道是为什么。他打开那本样书，一张名片掉了出来：奈特利出版社，阿米莉娅·洛曼。对，他现在想起来了。

当然，从尴尬的首次见面以来，他跟阿米莉娅·洛曼这些年一直碰面。他们通过几封友好的电子邮件，她每年来三次，报告奈特利出版社最有希望大卖的图书。在跟她度过了差不多十个下午后，他最近得出结论她工作挺在行。她通晓自己的书目以及比较突出的文学潮流。她乐观积极，但又不会过分吹嘘自己公司的书。她对玛雅也很好——总记着给这个小姑娘带一本奈特利出版社的童书。最重要的是，阿米莉娅·洛曼很专业，那意味着她从未提起过他们刚认识时A.J.差劲的言行。天哪，他曾经对她很糟糕。为了将功补过，他决定给《迟暮花开》一个机会，尽管那仍然不是他所喜欢的类型。

"我八十一岁了，从统计学上说来，我应该四点七年前就死了。"那本书如是开篇。

早上五点，A.J.合上书，轻轻拍了它一下。

玛雅醒了，感觉好了些。"你为什么在哭？"

"我在看书。"A.J.说。

阿米莉娅不认识那个号码，但第一声铃响，她就接了电话。

"阿米莉娅，你好。我是小岛书店的A.J.费克里。我没想到你会接电话。"

"确实，"她笑着说，"我是全世界最后一个还接自己电话的人。"

"对，"他说，"你也许真是。"

"天主教会在考虑封我为圣人。"

"接电话的圣人阿米莉娅。"A.J.说。

A.J.之前从未给她打过电话，她认为这一定是原因。"我们是两周后见面，还是你得取消？"阿米莉娅问。

"哦，不，不是那码事。事实上，我只是想给你留个言。"

阿米莉娅用机械的声音说："嗨，这是阿米莉娅·洛曼的语音信箱。哔。"

"嗯。"

"哔，"阿米莉娅又说了一遍，"说吧。请留言。"

"嗯，嗨，阿米莉娅，我是A.J.费克里。我刚读完了你向我推荐过的一本书——"

"哦，是吗，哪一本？"

"奇怪了，语音信箱好像在跟我说话呢。这一本是几年前的了。利昂·弗里德曼的《迟暮花开》。"

"别来伤我心了，A.J.。那本绝对是四年前那份冬季书目里我最喜欢的一本。没人想读这本书。我爱那本书，我现在还爱！

不过我是一天到晚碰壁啊。"

"也许是因为封面。"A.J.没有说服力地说。

"糟糕的封面。老年人的脚，花，"阿米莉娅同意这一点，"好像谁愿意去想老人有皱纹的脚似的，更别说买一本封面上有这样的脚的书。平装本重新设计了封面，也根本无济于事——黑白风格，更多花。但封面就是图书出版业的出气筒，我们一出错就怪封面。"

"我不知道你是否记得我们第一次见面，你就给了我《迟暮花开》。"

阿米莉娅顿了一下。"是吗？对，那就说得通了。那是我刚开始在奈特利做的时候。"

"嗯，你知道，事实上我并不喜欢读文学性的回忆录，但是这一本尽管格局不算大，却写得很精彩。睿智而且……"在谈到他很喜欢的什么时，他有种赤身裸体的感觉。

"继续啊。"

"每个词都用得恰到好处。基本上这是我所能给的最高赞美了。我遗憾的只是过了这么久我才来读它。"

"这真是我的人生故事。是什么让你最终拿起了这本书？"

"我的小姑娘病了，所以——"

"哦，可怜的玛雅！但愿她病得不重！"

"出水痘。我整夜没睡陪着她，而这本书当时离我手边最近。"

"我挺高兴你终于读了它，"阿米莉娅说，"我求过认识的每个人来读这本书，可没人听我的，除了我妈妈，就算是说服她也不容易。"

　　"有时书本也要到适当的时候才会引起我们共鸣。"

　　"对弗里德曼先生来说，这可没多大安慰啊。"阿米莉娅说。

　　"嗯，我要订一箱封面同样糟糕的平装本。另外，等夏天游客到来时，也许我们可以请弗里德曼先生过来做一次活动。"

　　"如果他能活那么久的话。"阿米莉娅说。

　　"他病了吗？"A.J.问。

　　"没有，不过他好像有九十岁了！"

　　A.J.哈哈大笑。"嗯，阿米莉娅，两周后再见，我想。"

　　"也许下次我跟你说什么是冬季书目上的最佳图书时，你就会听我的了！"阿米莉娅说。

　　"很可能不会。我老了，各方面定型了，秉性难移。"

　　"你还没那么老呢。"她说。

　　"跟弗里德曼先生相比还不老，我想。"A.J.清清喉咙，"你过来时，也许我们可以一起吃个晚饭什么的。"

　　销售代表和书店老板一起吃饭根本没有什么不寻常，但阿米莉娅察觉出A.J.说这话时带着某种语气，她接着澄清道："我们可以过一遍最新的冬季书目。"

　　"对，那当然，"A.J.也回答得太快了，"你来一趟艾丽丝岛真是太远了，你会饿的。我以前从来没有提议过，是我失礼。"

"那我们晚一点吃个午饭吧，"阿米莉娅说，"我需要坐回海恩尼斯的最后一班渡轮。"

A.J.决定带阿米莉娅去裴廓德①餐厅，那是艾丽丝岛上第二好的海鲜餐厅。最好的科拉松②餐厅午市不开，就算开，对于一次不过是生意上的见面，科拉松也会显得太过浪漫。

A.J.先到，那让他有时间后悔自己的选择。在收养玛雅之前，他就不再去裴廓德餐厅了，里面的装修风格让他感到尴尬，还带着观光风味。里面有捕鲸用的鱼叉、鱼网，墙上挂着雨衣，门口有用一根原木雕刻出来的船长，他拿着一桶供人免费品尝的盐水太妃糖，有品位的白色亚麻桌布也没能让人转移多少注意力。一只玻璃纤维做的鲸鱼从天花板上吊下来，眼睛小小的，神情悲哀。A.J.感觉到那只鲸鱼的判断：应该去科拉松餐厅的，伙计。

阿米莉娅晚到了五分钟。"裴廓德，就像《白鲸》里的。"她说。她穿的衣服像是把钩针编织成的桌布重新利用了一下，罩在老式的粉红色衬裙外面。她的金色卷发上插着一朵假雏菊，穿着橡胶套鞋，尽管事实上那天阳光明媚。A.J.觉得橡胶套鞋让她看上去像个童子军，时刻准备应对灾难。

"你喜欢《白鲸》吗？"他问。

---

① 赫尔曼·麦尔维尔代表作品《白鲸》里一艘捕鲸船名。
② 此餐馆的原文为"El Corazon"，西班牙语"心"的意思。

"我讨厌它，"她说，"很多东西我都不会说讨厌。老师布置读这本书时，父母们会高兴，因为他们的孩子在读'有品质的'东西。不过强迫孩子们读那种书，就好像让他们觉得自己讨厌阅读。"

　　"你看到这家餐厅的名字没有取消约会，我倒是感到挺意外。"

　　"哦，我想过，"她声音里透着开心劲儿，"可是我又提醒自己这只是一家餐厅的名字，应该不太会影响食物的品质吧。另外，我在网上查了评论，据说这里的味道挺好。"

　　"你不相信我？"

　　"我只是喜欢在到这里之前，考虑考虑要吃什么。我喜欢——"她拖长了那个词——"有——所——期——待。"她翻开菜单，"我看到他们有几款以《白鲸》里的人物命名的鸡尾酒。"她翻过那页，"话说回来，如果我不想来这里吃饭，我很可能会编造说我对贝壳类食物过敏。"

　　"假装食物过敏，你可真狡猾。"A.J.说。

　　"现在我没法对你使那招了。"

　　侍者穿了件蓬松的白衬衫，那显然跟他的墨镜和鸡冠头格格不入。那种打扮是海盗中的时尚人士。"喂，旱鸭子①，"那位侍者干巴巴地说，"试试主题鸡尾酒？"

　　"我一般点的是老式鸡尾酒，可是怎么能忍得住不点一种主

---

① 水手用语，指新来的水手。

题鸡尾酒呢？"她说。"请来一杯魁魁格①。"她抓住侍者的手，"等等。那酒好喝吗？"

"嗯，"那位侍者说，"游客们好像挺喜欢。"

"嗯，既然游客喜欢……"她说。

"嗯，先让我弄清楚，那意思是你想点还是不想点那种鸡尾酒？"

"我绝对想点，"阿米莉娅说，"不管怎么样，就上吧。"她朝那位侍者微笑。"难喝的话，我不会怪你的。"

A.J.点了一杯这家餐厅的自酿红葡萄酒。

"真可惜，"阿米莉娅说，"我敢说你这一辈子还一次都没有喝过魁魁格鸡尾酒，尽管事实上你住在这里，你卖书，而且你甚至很可能还喜欢《白鲸》。"

"你显然比我进化得更好。"A.J.说。

"对，这我看得出来。我喝了这杯鸡尾酒后，我的整个人生可能就要改变了。"

酒来了。"噢，看，"阿米莉娅说，"叉着一只虾的小捕鲸叉，真是意外惊喜。"她掏出手机拍了张照片，"我喜欢给我喝的酒拍照。"

"它们就像是家人。"A.J.说。

"它们比家人更好。"她举起酒杯跟A.J.的碰了一下。

"怎么样？"A.J.问。

---

① 《白鲸》里的人物，主要的捕鲸手。

"有咸味、水果味、鱼腥味，有点像是虾味鸡尾酒决定向'血腥玛丽'[①]示爱。"

"我喜欢你的说法，'示爱'。对了，这种酒听着挺恶心的。"

她又呷了一口，然后耸耸肩。"我开始喜欢上了。"

"你更喜欢去根据哪本小说而开的餐厅吃饭？"A.J.问她。

"哦，这可不好说。说来没道理，可是我在大学里读《古拉格群岛》[②]的时候，经常会感觉很饿，都是因为对苏联监狱里面包和汤的描述。"阿米莉娅说。

"你真怪。"A.J.说。

"谢谢。你会去哪儿？"阿米莉娅问。

"准确说不是一家餐厅，但是我一直想尝尝《纳尼亚传奇》[③]中提到的土耳其软糖。我小时候读《狮王、女巫与魔衣橱》时，经常想到如果土耳其软糖让爱德蒙背叛了自己的家人，那它肯定难以置信地好吃。"A.J.说，"我想我肯定是跟我妻子说了这件事，因为有一年，妮可送了一盒给我当作节日礼物。结果发现是种表面有粉末的黏黏的糖。我想我这辈子都没有那么失望过。"

"你的童年在那时正式结束了。"

---

① "血腥玛丽"，一种通常用伏特加、蕃茄汁和调味料制成的鸡尾酒。
② 前苏联俄罗斯作家索尔仁尼琴（1918–2008）的长篇小说。
③ 英国二十世纪著名的文学家C.S.刘易斯创作的世界儿童文学经典，这套书一共七本，每本互有关联，亦可独立阅读。下文中《狮王、女巫与魔衣橱》为该系列作品的第二部。

"我再也回不到从前那样了。"A.J.说。

"也许白女巫的不一样，施了魔法的土耳其软糖味道更好。"

"要么也许刘易斯是想说明爱德蒙不需要怎么哄，就会背叛自己的家人。"

"这话说得很尖刻。"阿米莉娅说。

"你吃过土耳其软糖吗，阿米莉娅？"

"没有。"她说。

"我得给你弄点。"他说。

"我要是很喜欢该怎么办？"她问。

"我大概会看低你吧。"

"嗯，我不会为了让你喜欢而撒谎，A.J.。我最突出的优点之一，就是诚实。"

"你刚刚跟我说过你本来会装作对海鲜过敏，好免于在这里吃饭。"A.J.说。

"对，可那只是为了不伤害客户的感情。对于像土耳其软糖这等重要的事，我绝对不会撒谎。"

他们点了食物，然后阿米莉娅从她的大手提袋里取出冬季书目。"好了，奈特利。"她说。

"奈特利。"他也说了一遍。

她轻描淡写地过了一遍冬季书目，对他不会感兴趣的书无情地一带而过，强调出版社寄以厚望的图书，把最奇思妙想的形容词留给她最喜欢的那些。对某些客户，你得提一下这本书上是否有广告语，就是那些印于封底的来自成名作家的常常言过其实的赞誉之词。A.J.不是那种客户。他们第二次或者第三次见面时，他说过那些广告语是"出版业中的噬血钻石"。她现在对他多了点了解，不用说，这个过程就没那么让她感觉辛苦了。他更相信我了，她认为，要么也许只是当爸爸让他平和了。（把诸如此类的想法深藏心间是明智的做法。）A.J.答应读几本试读本。

"我希望，别用四年的时间。"阿米莉娅说。

"我会尽量在三年内把这几本读完。"他顿了一下，"我们点甜点吧，"他说，"他们肯定有'鲸鱼圣代'什么的。"

阿米莉娅叹息了一声说："这种文字游戏真的很差劲。"

"所以，如果你不介意，我想问一下为什么在那份书目上，你最喜欢《迟暮花开》？你是个年轻——"

"我没那么年轻了。我三十五岁了。"

"那还是年轻，"A.J.说，"我的意思是，你很可能没怎么经历过弗里德曼先生所描绘的人生。我看过这本书，现在我看着你，心里纳闷它怎么会让你产生共鸣。"

"天哪，费克里先生，那可是个很私人的问题。"她呷着她第二杯魁魁格鸡尾酒最后剩的一点，"我爱那本书，当然主要是因为它的文笔。"

"那当然，可是那还不够。"

"让我们这么说吧，当《迟暮花开》放到我的办公桌上时，我已经有过很多很多次失败的约会经历。我是个浪漫的人，但有时候那些失败在我眼里算不上浪漫。《迟暮花开》写的是不论在任何年龄，都有可能寻觅到伟大的爱情。这么说听着俗套，我知道。"

A.J.点点头。

"你呢？你为什么喜欢它？"阿米莉娅问。

"文字的水准，等等等等。"

"我还以为我们不可以那样说呢！"阿米莉娅说。

"你不想听我的伤心事，对吧？"

"我当然想听，"她说，"我喜欢听伤心事。"

他简要地跟她讲了妮可的死。"弗里德曼把失去一个人的那种独特感觉写出来了，写出了为什么那并非只是一件事。他写到你怎样失去，失去，再失去。"

"她是什么时候去世的？"阿米莉娅问。

"到现在有一段时间了。当时我只比你现在大一点点。"

"那肯定是很久以前了。"她说。

他没理会她这句玩笑话。"《迟暮花开》确实应该成为一本畅销书的。"

"我知道。我在考虑请人在我的婚礼上读一段。"

A.J.犹豫了一下。"你要结婚了，阿米莉娅，恭喜你。那个幸运的家伙是谁？"

她用那把捕鲸叉在带着西红柿汁颜色的魁魁格鸡尾酒里搅

动，想扎到那只擅离职守的虾。"他叫布雷特·布鲁尔。我正准备放弃时，在网上认识了他。"

A.J.喝着第二杯葡萄酒里味涩的杯底酒。"跟我多讲讲吧。"

"他是军人，在海外部队服役，驻阿富汗。"

"不错哦，你要嫁给一位美国英雄了。"A.J.说。

"我想是这样。"

"我讨厌那些家伙，"他说，"他们让我彻底地自惭形秽。跟我说说他有什么差劲的地方吧，好让我感觉好一点。"

"嗯，他不怎么在家。"

"你肯定很想他。"

"我的确是。不过这样我就有时间大量阅读了。"

"挺好。他也读书吗？"

"事实上，他不读，他不怎么爱读书。可是那有点意思，对吧？我是说，这挺有意思的，嗯，和一个跟我的兴趣很不一样的人在一起。我不知道我干吗老是说'兴趣'。关键是，他是个好人。"

"他对你好吗？"

她点点头。

"那点最重要。不管怎么样，人无完人，"A.J.说，"很可能在中学时有人逼他读过《白鲸》。"

阿米莉娅扎到她的虾。"逮到了，"她说，"你的妻子……

她爱读书吗？"

"还写东西呢。不过我倒不担心那个，大家高看阅读了。看看电视里那么多好东西，比如《真爱如血》[①]。"

"你这是在取笑我。"

"哈！书是给书呆子们看的。"A.J.说。

"像我们这样的书呆子。"

账单拿来时，A.J.付了钱，尽管事实上按照惯例，这种情况下是销售代理埋单。"你确定要付这钱吗？"阿米莉娅问。

A.J.告诉她下次她可以埋单。

到了餐厅外面，阿米莉娅和A.J.握手，互相说了几句通常的职业性的客套话。她转身往渡口走去，重要的一秒钟之后，他也转身朝书店走去。

"嗨，A.J.，"她喊道，"开书店有几分英雄气概，收养一个孩子也有几分英雄气概。"

"我只是做了自己能做的。"他鞠了一躬。鞠到一半时，他意识到自己不太会鞠躬，便立刻又站直身体。"谢谢，阿米莉娅。"

"我的朋友们叫我艾米。"她说。

---

① 《真爱如血》（True Love），根据查琳·哈里斯（Charlaine Harris，1951- ）的畅销系列小说《南方吸血鬼》（The Southern Vampire Mysteries）改编的美国电视剧，共有七季八十集，2008年9月由HBO播出。

玛雅从没见过A.J.这么忙。"爸爸，"她问，"你为什么会有这么多家庭作业？"

　　"有些是课外的。"他说。

　　"'课外的'是什么意思？"

　　"我要是你，就会去查一查。"

　　对于除了有一个爱讲话、上幼儿园的女儿，另外还要打理一份小生意的人来说，读完整整一个季度的书目——即使是像奈特利这样中等规模出版社的——需要花大量时间。他每读完一本奈特利出版社的书，都会给阿米莉娅发一封邮件讲讲他的看法。在邮件中，他没办法让自己用上"艾米"这个昵称，尽管已经得到允许。有时如果他确实感觉对什么很有共鸣，就打电话给她。要是他讨厌哪本书，他会给她发条短信："不适合我。"对阿米莉娅而言，她从来没有被一位客户如此关注过。

　　"你难道没有别的出版社的书要读吗？"阿米莉娅给他发短信。

　　A.J.想了很久该怎样回复。第一稿写的是"我不像喜欢你那样喜欢别的销售代表"，但是他认为在一个有位美国英雄式的未婚夫的女孩眼里，这样说太放肆了。他重写："我想是因为这份奈特利出版社的书目很引人入胜。"

　　A.J.订了太多奈特利出版社的图书，就连阿米莉娅的老板也注意到了。"我从没见过像小岛书店这样的小客户进这么多我们的书，"老板说，"新老板？"

"同一个老板。"阿米莉娅说，"可是他跟我刚认识他的时候不一样了。"

"嗯，你肯定在他身上下了大功夫。那个家伙不会进卖不动的图书，"老板说，"哈维在小岛书店那里从来没有得到过这么多订单。"

终于，A.J.读到了最后一本书。这是本好看的回忆录，关于当母亲、往剪贴簿里添东西和写作生活，作者是A.J.一直喜欢的一位加拿大诗人。那本书只有一百五十页，可是A.J.用了两个星期才读完。他好像没有一章不是读着读着就睡着了，或者是玛雅来打岔。读完后，他发现自己没法告诉阿米莉娅对此书的感想。那本书写得够好，他认为经常光顾书店的那些妇女读了会有共鸣。当然，问题是他一旦回复了阿米莉娅，奈特利出版社冬季书目上的书他就全读完了，在夏季书目出来前，他就没理由联系阿米莉娅了。他喜欢她，而且觉得她有可能也会喜欢他，尽管他们的初次邂逅糟糕透顶。但是……A.J.费克里不是那种认为撬走别人的未婚妻没什么大不了的人。他不相信有什么"命中唯一"，世界上有千千万万的人，没有谁那么特别。另外，他几乎不了解阿米莉娅·洛曼。比如说吧，要是他真的把她撬过来了，却发现他们在床上不和谐又当如何？

阿米莉娅给他发短信："怎么了？你不喜欢吗？"

"不幸的是不适合我，"A.J.回复道，"期待看到奈特利出版社的夏季书目。A.J."

这则回复让阿米莉娅感觉太过公事公办、敷衍了事，她考虑过要打个电话，但却没有。她还是回了短信："趁你期待之际，你绝对应该看看《真爱如血》。"《真爱如血》是阿米莉娅最喜欢的电视节目。这已经成为他们之间的一种玩笑话——只要A.J.肯看《真爱如血》，他就会喜欢吸血鬼。阿米莉娅想象自己是苏琪·斯塔克豪斯①那种人。

　　"我才不看，艾米，"A.J.写道，"三月见。"

　　离三月还有四个半月。A.J.感觉到那时，他这场小小的爱恋肯定将烟消云散，要么至少进入休眠状态，那会让他好受一点。

　　还有四个半月才到三月。

　　玛雅问他怎么了，他跟她说自己不开心，是因为有一阵子见不着他的朋友了。

　　"阿米莉娅？"玛雅问。

　　"你怎么知道是她？"

　　玛雅翻翻眼珠子，A.J.不知道她什么时候从哪里学会了那个动作。

　　那天晚上，兰比亚斯在书店主持了他的"警长精选读书会"（所选书为《洛城机密》②），之后他跟A.J.分享了一瓶葡萄酒，这是他们的老习惯了。

　　"我想我遇到了一个人。"A.J.说，一杯酒下肚后，他心情

---

① 《真爱如血》中的女主角。
② 美国犯罪小说作家詹姆斯·埃尔罗伊（Jame Ellroy，1948- ）的代表作之一。

愉快。

"好消息。"兰比亚斯说。

"问题是,她跟别人订了婚。"

"时机不当啊。"兰比亚斯表示,"我到现在已经当了二十年的警察了,我告诉你,生活中每一桩糟糕事,几乎都是时机不当的结果,每件好事,都是时机恰到好处的结果。"

"这话好像把事情彻底简单化了。"

"好好想想吧。要是《帖木儿》没有被偷,你不会把门留着不锁,玛丽安·华莱士就不会把孩子留在书店里。这就是时机恰到好处。"

"没错。可我是四年前认识阿米莉娅的,"A.J.争辩道,"我只是懒得去注意她,直到几个月前。"

"还是时机不妥。当时你的妻子刚去世,然后你有了玛雅。"

"这话可不怎么安慰人心啊。"A.J.说。

"可是听着,知道你的心还管用,这就挺好,对吧?想让我帮你跟谁撮合一下吗?"

A.J.摇摇头。

"试试吧,"兰比亚斯不肯放弃,"镇上的人我全认识。"

"不幸的是,这个镇很小。"

作为热身,兰比亚斯安排A.J.跟他的表妹约会。那位表妹一头金发,发根是黑色的,眉毛修得太过了,心形脸,说话声音像迈克尔·杰克逊那么尖。她穿着低领口上衣和聚拢型文胸，托起一个不起眼的小平台，她所戴的有她名字的项链就歇在上面。她名叫玛丽亚。在吃莫泽雷勒干酪①条时，他们就无话可谈了。

"你最喜欢哪本书？" A.J.想方设法让她开口。

她嚼着莫泽雷勒干酪条，像抓着一串念珠般抓着有她名字的项链。"这是某种测试，对吧？"

"不，怎样回答都不会错，" A.J.说，"我是好奇。"

她喝了一口葡萄酒。

"要么你可以说哪本书对你的人生影响最大。我是想对你多了解一点。"

她又呷了一口酒。

"或者说说你最近读了什么？"

"我最近读的……"她皱起眉头，"我最近读的是这份菜单。"

"那么我最近读的就是你的项链，"他说，"玛丽亚。"

此后这顿饭吃得融洽无比。他永远不会知晓玛丽亚读了什么。

接下来，书店里的玛吉妮安排他跟她的邻居约会，那是一位活泼的女消防员，名叫罗西。罗西一头黑发，有一道挑染成蓝色，胳膊上的肌肉特别发达，笑起来声音特别洪亮，她把她短短的指甲涂成红色，上面还有橙色的火苗。罗西读大学时曾获得跨栏跑冠军，她喜欢读体育史，特别是运动员的回忆录。

① 一种色白味淡的意大利干酪。

他们第三次约会，当她正在描述何塞·坎塞科①的《棒球如何做大》中的精彩片断时，A.J.打断了她。"你知道那些书全都是有人代笔的吗？"

罗西说她知道，她无所谓。"这些表现突出的人们一直在忙着训练，他们哪有时间去学习写书呢？"

"可这些书……我的看法是，从根本上说来，它们都是谎言。"

罗西的头朝A.J.探过去，用艳红的指甲敲打着桌子。"你是个势利鬼，知道吗？那让你错过很多东西。"

"以前有人这样跟我说过。"

"人这一生就是一部运动员回忆录，"她说，"你努力训练，取得成功，但是到最后你的身体不行了，一切就结束了。"

"听着像是菲利普·罗斯②晚期的一本小说。"他说。

罗西架起胳膊。"你说那种话，就是为了显得聪明，对吧？"她说，"可是说真的，你只是在让别人感觉自己蠢。"

那天夜里在床上做完爱后（做得就像在摔跤），罗西从他身上翻下来说："我不确定还想不想再见你。"

"如果我之前伤害了你的感情，对不起，"他一边说一边穿回裤子，"回忆录那档子事。"

---

① 何塞·坎塞科（Jose Canseco，1964- ），美国职业棒球明星。
② 菲利普·罗斯（Philip Roth，1933- ），美国当今文坛地位最高的作家之一，曾多次被提名诺贝尔文学奖。

她摆摆手，"别担心，你就是那种人。"

他怀疑她说得对，他的确是个势利鬼，不适合跟人谈恋爱。他会抚养自己的女儿，管好自己的书店，读自己的书，他想好了，那样的生活就已经足够了。

在伊斯梅的坚持下，确定了玛雅要去学舞蹈。"你不想对她有什么亏欠，对吧？"伊斯梅说。

"当然不想。"A.J.说。

"那好，"伊斯梅说，"跳舞很重要，不仅是对身形，在社会交往中也很重要。你总不想让她最后发育迟缓吧。"

"我不知道。让一个小女孩报名去学跳舞这种事，那种观念是不是有点老式，还有点性别歧视的倾向？"

A.J.拿不准玛雅是否适合跳舞。即使才六岁，她更喜欢用脑——书不离手，在家里或者在书店她都惬意。"她没有发育迟缓，"他说，"她现在读有章节的书了。"

"智力上显然没有，"伊斯梅坚持说，"可是她似乎只要你的陪伴，别的人都不要，甚至同龄的小伙伴也不要。这或许不太健康。"

"为什么不健康？"这时，A.J.的脊骨有种不舒服的刺痛感。

"她到头来会跟你一模一样。"伊斯梅说。

"那又有什么问题？"

伊斯梅摆出一副这个问题的答案显而易见的表情。"你看，A.J.，你们自己的小小世界里只有你们两个人。你从来不跟人约会——"

"我约会的。"

"你从来不去旅行——"

A.J.打断她的话。"我们不是在谈论我。"

"别这么爱争辩了。你请我当教母，我现在跟你说，给你的女儿报名学跳舞。我出钱，所以别再跟我吵了。"

艾丽丝岛上只有一间舞蹈工作室，只有一个班收五六岁的女孩。奥伦斯卡夫人既是老板，又是老师。她六十多岁，尽管并不肥胖，却皮肤松弛，说明她的骨头过了这么多年收缩了。她总是戴着珠宝的手指似乎多了个关节。那些小孩对她既着迷，又害怕。A.J.亦有同感。他第一次把玛雅送去时，奥伦斯卡夫人说："费克里先生，你是二十年来第一次踏足这间舞蹈房的男人。我们一定要劳你大驾一下。"

她说这话时带着俄罗斯口音，听着像某种性方面的邀请，但她需要的主要是体力劳动。为了节日表演，他做了一个样子像是一块儿童积木的巨大板条箱并上了油漆，用热熔胶枪做了鼓凸凸的眼睛、铃铛和花朵，把闪着光的烟斗通条做成胡须和触角。（他怀疑自己再也弄不干净指甲里掺进的亮粉。）

那年冬天，他的空闲时间大多是跟奥伦斯卡夫人一起度过的，他知道了她的很多事情。例如，奥伦斯卡夫人的明星学生是她的女儿，她当时在百老汇的一场演出中跳舞，而奥伦斯卡夫人有太久没有跟她说过话了。她朝他晃动她多了一段关节的手指。"你可别遇到这种事。"她表情夸张地望向窗外，然后又转向A.J.，"你会在节目单上购买广告位，对。"这不是提问。小岛书店成了《胡桃夹子》《鲁道夫和朋友们》的唯一赞助商，节目单背面有一份小岛书店的假日优惠券。A.J.甚至好人做到底，提供了一个里面放着以跳舞为主题的图书礼品篮供抽奖，收益将会捐给波士顿芭蕾舞团。

A.J.站在抽奖桌那里观看演出，他精疲力竭，还有轻微的流感症状。因为演出是根据舞蹈技巧安排的，玛雅那组率先出场。她就算不是一只特别优雅的老鼠，也算是一只特别热情的。她放开了跑，鼻子皱得一看就像老鼠。她晃动用烟斗通条做的尾巴，那是他辛辛苦苦盘出来的。他知道她吃不了跳舞这碗饭。

在抽奖桌旁边帮忙的伊斯梅递给他一张舒洁纸巾。

"冷。"他说。

"当然冷。"伊斯梅说。

那天晚上结束时，奥伦斯卡夫人说："谢谢，费克里先生，你是个好人。"

"也许是我有个好孩子。"他还需要把他的老鼠从化妆间里领走。

"对，"她说，"可是这还不够，你必须给自己找个好女人。"

"我喜欢我的生活。"A.J.说。

"你觉得有孩子就够了，可孩子会长大。你觉得有工作就够了，可工作并不像温暖的身体。"他怀疑奥伦斯卡夫人已经猛灌了几杯苏红伏特加。

"节日愉快，奥伦斯卡夫人。"

跟玛雅一起走回家时，他思忖着那位老师的话。他已经独身过了近六年。悲伤让他不堪承受，但是独自生活呢，他倒是从不特别在意。另外，他不想要一个温暖却朽老的身体，他想要阿米莉娅·洛曼，还有她那宽阔的胸怀和糟糕的着装。至少是某个像她那样的人。

开始下雪了，雪花沾在玛雅的胡须上。他想拍张照片，但是他不想专门去做停下来拍一张照片这种事。"胡须跟你挺称。"A.J.告诉她。

这句对她胡须的赞美引出一连串对于那场表演的评论，可A.J.心不在焉的。"玛雅，"他说，"你知道我有多少岁吗？"

"知道，"她说，"二十二。"

"我比那要大得多。"

"八十九岁？"

"我……"他把两只手掌举了四次，然后伸出三根手指。

"四十三岁？"

"算得好。我四十三岁了，这些年，我学到的是爱过然后失去只有更好，等等等等，和跟某个你并不是很喜欢的人在一起相比，更好的是一个人过。你同意吗？"

她严肃地点点头，她的老鼠耳朵几乎要掉了。

"不过有时候，我会厌倦吸取教训。"他低头看着女儿困惑的脸，"你的脚快湿了吧？"

她点点头，他蹲下来，好让她趴到他的背上。"搂住我的脖子。"她爬上去后，他站立起来，呻吟了一两声，"你比以前重了。"

她抓住了他的耳垂。"这是什么？"她问。

"我以前戴耳环。"他说。

"为什么？"她问，"你当过海盗吗[①]？"

"我当时年轻。"他说。

"跟我这么大？"

"比你要大。有那么一个女孩。"

"一个姑娘？"

"一个女人。她喜欢一支名叫'治疗'的乐队，她觉得把我的耳朵扎个眼挺酷。"

玛雅想了想。"你养过鹦鹉吗？"

"没有，我有过女朋友。"

"那只鹦鹉会说话吗？"

"不会，因为没养过鹦鹉。"

她想捉弄一下他："那只鹦鹉叫什么？"

---

① 据说为了给可能为其收尸的人一点酬劳，海盗通常都戴耳环。

"没养过鹦鹉。"

"但是如果你养过的话，你会叫那只雄鹦鹉什么？"

"你怎么知道是只雄鹦鹉？"他问道。

"哈！"她把手放到嘴边，身子开始往后倾。

"搂住我的脖子，要不然你会掉下去的。也许是只雌的，叫艾米？"

"鹦鹉艾米。我就知道。你有一艘船吗？"玛雅问。

"有的。船上有书，事实上那是一艘考察船。我们做很多研究。"

"你把这个故事讲坏了。"

"这是事实，玛雅。有杀人的海盗，也有做研究的海盗，你的爸爸是后一种。"

冬天时，小岛书店从来不是很多人都想去的地方，但是那一年，艾丽丝岛上出奇的寒冷。马路成了溜冰场，渡轮一取消就是好几天。就连丹尼尔·帕里什也不得不待在家里。他写得不多，躲开他的妻子，其他时间都跟A.J.和玛雅待在一起。

跟大多数女人一样，玛雅喜欢丹尼尔。他来书店时，不会因为她是个孩子，就在跟她说话时把她当成什么都不懂。尽管才六岁，玛雅就不待见那些居高临下跟她说话的人。丹尼尔总是问她在读什么书，她在想什么。另外，他有着浓密的金色眉毛，说话的声音让她想到绵缎。

就在进入新年大约一周后的一天下午，丹尼尔和玛雅坐在书店的地板上读书，这时她扭头跟他说："丹尼尔叔叔，我有个问题。你难道从来不用工作吗？"

"我现在就在工作，玛雅。"丹尼尔说。

她摘下眼镜，在衬衫上面擦了擦。"你看样子不像在工作啊，你看样子在读书。你难道没有一个可以去上班的地方吗？"她又进一步阐述道，"兰比亚斯是个警官。爸爸是个卖书的。你是干吗的？"

丹尼尔把玛雅抱起来，把她抱到小岛书店的本地作家专架那里。出于对其连襟的礼貌，丹尼尔的书在A.J.的书店里全有存货，但只有一本卖得动，即他的处女作《苹果树上的孩子们》。丹尼尔指着书脊上自己的名字。"这就是我，"他说，"这就是我的工作。"

玛雅瞪圆了眼睛。"丹尼尔·帕里什。你写书，"她说，"你是个——"她说这个词时带着敬意——"作家。这本书是写什么的？"

"是关于人类的愚蠢。这是个爱情故事，还是个悲剧。"

"那样说得很笼统啊。"玛雅告诉他。

"说的是一位一辈子都在照顾别人的护士。她出了车祸，在她这一辈子里，第一次别人得照顾她。"

"听着好像不是我会去读的。"玛雅说。

"有点老套，呃？"

"不——"她不想伤害丹尼尔的感情，"只是我喜欢情节更丰富的书。"

"情节更丰富，啊？我也是。好消息呢，费克里小姐，我一直都在读书，我在学习怎样写得更好。"丹尼尔解释道。

玛雅想了想。"我想做这种工作。"

"很多人都想，小姑娘。"

"我怎样才能做上呢？"玛雅问。

"读书，就像我说过的。"

玛雅点点头。"我读的。"

"一张好椅子。"

"我有一张。"

"那你就完全上路了，"丹尼尔告诉她，然后把她放下来，"以后我会教你其他的。有你做伴真好，你知道吗？"

"爸爸也是这么说的。"

"他是个聪明人，幸运儿，好人。你也是个聪明的孩子。"

A.J.叫玛雅上楼吃饭。"你想跟我们一起吃吗？"A.J.问他。

"我觉得有点早，"丹尼尔说，"况且我还有工作要做。"他朝玛雅挤了一下眼睛。

终于，三月到了。道路解冻了，一切都变得污秽不堪。渡轮服务恢复了，丹尼尔·帕里什又开始了漫游。销售代表们带着夏季的书目来到这里，A.J.不辞辛劳地对他们热情相待。他开始以打领带来向玛雅表明他"在工作"，与"在家"相区别。

或许因为这是他最期待的会面，他把阿米莉娅的上门推销安排到了最后。在他们约定日期的前两周，他给她发了条短信："你觉得裴廓德餐厅可以吗？还是你更想试试新地方？"

"这次去裴廓德我请客。"她回复道，"你看《真爱如血》了吗？"

那年冬天的天气特别不方便人们社交，所以晚上玛雅入睡后，A.J.看完了四季《真爱如血》。他挺快就看完了，因为他比预期的更喜欢——它把几种元素杂糅在一起：弗兰纳里·奥康纳式的南方哥特风格、《厄舍古屋的倒塌》加上《罗马帝国艳情史》。他一直计划着阿米莉娅来到这里后，随意引用他所掌握的《真爱如血》的知识，让她叹服。

"来了你就知道。"他写道，但是没有按发送键，因为他觉得这则短信听着调情意味太浓。他不知道阿米莉娅的婚礼定的是什么时候，所以现在她有可能是位已婚女士。"下星期四见。"他写道。

星期三，他接到一个电话，是陌生号码。打来电话的是布雷特·布鲁尔，那位美国英雄，他的声音听起来就像《真爱如血》

中的比尔①。A.J.认为布雷特·布鲁尔的口音是装出来的，但是显然，一位美国英雄不需要伪装出南方口音。"费克里先生，我是布雷特·布鲁尔，打电话是为阿米莉娅的事。她出了点意外，所以让我告诉您她得改一下你们见面的时间。"

A.J.扯松领带。"但愿不严重。"

"我一直想让她别穿那种橡胶套鞋。下雨时穿不错，可是在冰上就有点危险了，你知道吗？嗯，她在普罗维登斯这里结了冰的几级台阶上滑了一下——我跟她说过会出那种事的——她的脚踝骨折了。她目前正在手术中，所以没什么严重的，不过她要卧床一段时间。"

"请代我向您的未婚妻问好，行吗？"A.J.说。

对方有一阵子没说话，A.J.不知道是不是电话掉线了。"会的。"布雷特·布鲁尔说完就挂断了电话。

阿米莉娅的伤势不是很严重，这让A.J.松了口气，但还是对她来不了感到有点失望（还因为那位美国英雄的的确确还存在于她的生活中这个消息）。

他考虑要送阿米莉娅一束花或者一本书，但最终决定发条短信。他想引用《真爱如血》中的台词，能让她笑起来的什么话。他就此搜索谷歌时，那些引语似乎全都颇具调情意味。他写道："很遗憾你受伤了。一直盼望听听奈特利出版社夏季书单上都有什么。希望我们可以很快重新安排时间。另外，我这话说得可是

---

① 《真爱如血》中的男主角。

不容易——'给贾森·斯塔克豪斯①喂吸血鬼的血，就好像给糖尿病患者奶油巧克力蛋糕'。"

六个小时后，阿米莉娅回复道："你看了！！！"

A.J.："我看了。"

阿米莉娅："我们可以通过电话或者Skype把书单过一下吗？"

A.J.："什么是'Skype'？"

阿米莉娅："我什么都得教你吗？！"

阿米莉娅解释了什么是Skype之后，他们决定那样见面。

A.J.很高兴见到她，哪怕只能在显示器上。在她梳理书单时，他发现自己几乎无法集中注意力。画面里她身后那些具备阿米莉娅特性的东西让他入了迷：一个玻璃食品罐，里面插满即将枯萎的向日葵，一份瓦萨学院②的文凭（他如是认为），一个赫敏·格兰杰③模样的摇头娃娃，一张放在镜框里的照片，他想照片上是年轻的阿米莉娅和她的父母，一盏上面搭着小圆点围巾的台灯，一个样子像是基思·哈林④画作中的订书机，一本A.J.看不出书名是什么的旧书，一瓶亮闪闪的指甲油，一只发条龙虾，一对吸血鬼的塑料尖牙，一瓶未开的好香槟，一个——

"A.J.，"阿米莉娅打断了他，"你在听吗？"

---

① 《真爱如血》中女主角苏琪的哥哥。
② 位于美国纽约州的一所文理学院，成立于1861年，建校之初是一所女校。2013USNews美国大学排名在文理学院中名列第十位。
③ 英国作家J.K.罗琳（J.K. Rowling, 1965- ）著名魔幻小说《哈利·波特》系列中的主要人物之一。
④ 基思·哈林（Keith Haring, 1958-1990），美国街头绘画艺术家和社会运动者。

"在听，当然，我在……"盯着你的东西看？"我不习惯Skype。我可以把'Skype'当动词用吗？"

"我觉得《牛津英语词典》还没有考虑这件事，不过我认为你用着没事。"她说，"我刚才只是在说奈特利的夏季书单上不是有一本，而是有两本短篇小说集。"

阿米莉娅接着说那两本短篇小说集，A.J.继续偷看。那是本什么书？太薄了，不会是《圣经》或者词典。他往前凑，试图看得更清楚些，但是磨损了的烫金字在视频会议中还是颜色淡得认不出来。真是讨厌，他没法放大或改变角度去看。她没在说话了。显然，她需要A.J.的回应。

"对，我盼望读到。"他说。

"太棒了。我今天或明天就给你寄去。那么等秋季书目出来了再说吧。"

"但愿到那时你能亲自过来。"

"能的，绝对能。"

"那是什么书？"A.J.问。

"什么什么书？"

"那本靠着台灯的旧书，在你后面的桌子上。"

"你想知道，是吗？"她说，"那是我的最爱。是我父亲送给我的大学毕业礼物。"

"那么，是什么书呢？"

"如果你哪天能来一趟普罗维登斯，我会让你看看的。"

她说。

A.J.看着她。这听上去也许语带调情，只不过她说这话时低头看着所做的笔记，根本没抬头。然而……

"布雷特·布鲁尔好像人挺不错的。"A.J.说。

"什么？"

"他打电话给我说你受了伤，没法来的时候。"A.J.解释道。

"对。"

"我觉得他说起话来就像《真爱如血》中的比尔。"

阿米莉娅大笑起来。"你瞧你，随随便便就掉一下《真爱如血》的书袋。下次我见到布雷特时，得跟他说说。"

"对了，婚礼是什么时候？还是已经举办过了？"

她抬头看着他。"事实上，婚礼取消了。"

"对不起。"A.J.说。

"有段时间了，圣诞节的时候。"

"因为是他打的电话，我才想着……"

"他当时正好闯上门来。我跟我的前男友们努力做朋友，"阿米莉娅说，"我就是那种人。"

A.J.知道自己冒昧了，但还是忍不住问："出了什么事呢？"

"布雷特人很不错，但悲哀的事实是，我们真的没有多少共同点。"

"情趣相投的确挺重要。"A.J.说。

阿米莉娅的手机响了。"是我妈妈，我得接这个电话，"她说，"几个月后见，好吗？"

A.J.点头。Skype断掉了，阿米莉娅的状态变成了"离开"。

他打开浏览器，搜索下面的短语："教育性家庭景点，普罗维登斯，罗得岛。"没搜到什么很特别的：一家儿童博物馆、一家玩具娃娃博物馆、一座灯塔和一些他在波士顿更容易去到的地方。他选定了朴茨茅斯的一座格林动物造型园艺公园。不久前，他和玛雅看过一本绘本，里面有园艺造型的动物，她似乎对这个主题有点兴趣。另外，他们出一下小岛也挺好，对吧？他会带玛雅去看那些动物，然后往普罗维登斯拐一下，去看望一位生病的朋友。

"玛雅，"当天晚饭时他说，"你觉得去看一头巨大的园艺造型而成的大象怎么样？"

她看了他一眼。"你的声音听着怪怪的。"

"那挺酷的，玛雅。你记得我们看过的里面有园艺造型动物的那本书吗？"

"你是说，在我小的时候。"

"对，我发现这个地方有座动物造型园艺公园。反正我得去普罗维登斯看望一位生病的朋友，所以我觉得我们在那里的时候去看看这座动物造型园艺公园也挺酷。"他打开电脑，让她看那个动物造型园艺公园的网页。

"好吧，"她认真地说，"我想看那个。"她指出那个网页上说这个公园在朴茨茅斯，而非普罗维登斯。

"朴茨茅斯和普罗维登斯靠得很近，"A.J.说，"罗得岛是我国最小的州。"

然而，结果证明朴茨茅斯跟普罗维登斯并不是那么近。尽管有大巴，最方便的还是开车过去，而A.J.没有驾驶执照。他打电话给兰比亚斯，要他跟他们一起去。

"小孩子们真的很喜欢园艺造型动物，嗯？"兰比亚斯问。

"她迷得要命。"A.J.说。

"小孩子会喜欢那个，挺古怪的，我只能这么说。"

"她是个古怪的小孩。"

"可这大冬天的，真的是去公园的最佳时间吗？"

"现在几乎是春天了。另外，现在玛雅真的很喜欢园艺造型动物。谁知道等到夏天来后，她还喜不喜欢了？"

"小孩子变化快，这倒是真的。"兰比亚斯说。

"听着，你不是非得去。"

"哦，我会去的。谁不想看一头巨大的绿色大象？但问题是，有时候别人跟你说你踏上一种旅程，结果却成了另外一种旅程。你懂我的意思吗？我只是想知道我要踏上的是什么样的旅程。我们是要去看园艺造型动物呢，还是要去看别的什么？比如说也许去看你的那位女性朋友？"

A.J.吸了口气，"我是想我或许可以顺路去看看阿米莉娅，是的。"

第二天，A.J.给阿米莉娅发短信："忘了说，下个周末我和玛雅要去罗得岛。你不用把样书寄来了，我可以去拿。"

阿米莉娅："样书不在这里。已经让人从纽约寄出了。"

计划太不周全了，A.J.暗道。

几分钟后，阿米莉娅又发了条短信："不过你们来罗得岛做什么？"

A.J.："去朴茨茅斯的动物造型园艺公园。玛雅很喜欢园艺造型动物！"（夸张地用上感叹号，他也只感到一点点不好意思。）

阿米莉娅："不知道有这么一座公园。真希望我能跟你们一起去，但我只能勉强走动。"

A.J.等了两分钟，然后又发短信："你需要有人去看你吗？也许我们可以顺路过去看看。"

她没有马上回答。A.J.把她的沉默理解为去看望她的人够多的了。

第二天，阿米莉娅的确回了短信："当然，我很乐意。别吃东西，我会给你和玛雅做饭吃。"

"你差不多能看得到，要是你踮起脚尖隔着墙头往里看的话，"A.J.说，"在远处那儿。"他们那天早上七点钟离开艾丽丝岛，搭渡轮到海恩尼斯，然后开车两个小时到了朴茨茅斯，却发现格林动物造型园艺公园从十一月到五月不开放。

A.J.发现自己无法跟女儿或者兰比亚斯有任何视线接触。气温只有零下一二摄氏度，但是因为惭愧，他感到通体发热。

玛雅踮脚站着，但那不管用，她又试着跳起来。"我什么都看不到。"她说。

"来，我把你弄得更高一点。"兰比亚斯说，把玛雅举到了自己的肩膀上。

"也许，我能看到点什么了，"玛雅犹豫不决地说，"不，我还是什么都看不到。全都盖着呢。"她的下嘴唇开始颤抖。她眼神痛苦地看着A.J.。他感觉自己再也受不了了。

突然，她朝A.J.露出灿烂的笑容。"可是你知道吗，爸爸？我可以想象毯子下面的大象是什么样。还有老虎！还有独角兽！"她朝父亲点点头，似乎是说，大冬天的你带我来这里，显然就是为了训练想象力。

"很好，玛雅。"他觉得自己是世界上最糟糕的父亲，但玛雅对他的信心似乎恢复了。

"看，兰比亚斯！那头独角兽在颤抖，它披着毛毯挺高兴的。你能看到吗，兰比亚斯？"

A.J.走到保安亭那边，保安送上一副同情的表情。"一天到晚都有这种事。"她说。

"那么你不认为我给我的女儿留下了终身的伤痕？"A.J.问道。

"当然，"保安说，"你很可能已经留下了，但我想不是因为你今天所做的任何事。没有哪个孩子会因为没看到园艺造型动物而变坏。"

"即使她爸爸真正的目的，是为了去见普罗维登斯的一个性感女孩？"

那位保安似乎没听到那句话。"我的建议是，你们可以去参观那座维多利亚时代的老宅子。孩子们喜欢那些。"

"他们会喜欢吗？"

"有些喜欢。当然啦。为什么不呢？也许你的孩子就会喜欢。"

在那座豪宅里，玛雅想起了《天使雕像》，兰比亚斯没有看过那本书。

"哦，你一定要看，兰比亚斯，"玛雅说，"你会爱上它的。里面有个女孩还有她的弟弟，他们离家出走了……"

"离家出走不是件可以一笑置之的事。"兰比亚斯皱起眉头，"作为警察，我可告诉你在街头的小孩不会学好。"

玛雅接着说："他们去了纽约的一家大博物馆，藏在那里。那……"

"那是犯法的，就是这样，"兰比亚斯说，"那绝对是非法闯入。很可能还是打破什么东西闯进去的。"

"兰比亚斯，"玛雅说，"你没有抓住重点。"

在豪宅里吃过一顿不菲的午餐后，他们开车前往普罗维登斯，登记入住宾馆。

"你去看阿米莉娅吧，"兰比亚斯对A.J.说，"我在考虑和孩子去市里的儿童博物馆。我想让她看看藏身一家博物馆里不可行的诸多原因。至少在'九一一'之后的世界是这样。"

"你不必那么做。"A.J.本计划带着玛雅一起去，好让去看望阿米莉娅这件事显得没那么刻意。（是的，他就是这么不争气，还想用自己的宝贝女儿打掩护。）

"别满脸愧疚的，"兰比亚斯说，"教父就是干这个的。后援。"

刚好快五点时，A.J.到了阿米莉娅的家。他给她带了个小岛书店的手提袋，里面装的是查琳·哈里斯的长篇小说、一瓶上好的马尔贝克红葡萄酒和一束向日葵。按了门铃后，他又认为带花太招摇了，就把花放在前廊秋千垫子的下面。

她来应门时，膝盖架在那种轮滑车上。她打的石膏是粉红色的，上面的签名有在学校里最受欢迎学生的纪念册上的签名那么多[1]。她穿着一条海军蓝超短连衣裙，脖子上还时髦地围了块有图案的红色围巾。她看上去就像是位空中小姐。

"玛雅呢？"阿米莉娅问。

"我的朋友兰比亚斯带她去普罗维登斯儿童博物馆了。"

阿米莉娅歪着脑袋。"这不是约会，对吧？"

---

[1] 一种习俗，朋友、同事等在伤者所打的石膏上签名及写祝愿康复的话。

A.J.试图解释那个动物造型园艺公园不开放的事。这故事听上去让人难以信服——讲到一半，他差点要扔下手提袋转身逃跑。

　　"我在逗你玩呢，"她说，"进来吧。"

　　阿米莉娅的家里虽然乱，但是干净。她有一张紫色天鹅绒沙发、一架小型三角钢琴、一张能坐十二个人的餐桌、很多她朋友和家人的相框、长势不一的室内盆栽、一只名叫"忧郁坑"的独眼虎斑猫，当然还有无处不在的书。她家里发散着她在做什么饭的气味，后来发现她做的是意大利千层面和大蒜面包。他脱了皮靴，免得把泥巴带进她家。"家如其人。"他说。

　　"凌乱，不协调。"她说。

　　"兼容并蓄，富于魅力。"他清清喉咙，尽量不要说得听起来俗不可耐。

　　等他们吃过晚饭，开了第二瓶葡萄酒时，A.J.才终于鼓起勇气问她跟布雷特·布鲁尔怎么了。

　　阿米莉娅微微一笑。"如果我跟你说实话，我不想让你产生误解。"

　　"我不会的，我保证。"

　　她喝完杯里的最后一点酒。"去年秋天，当时我们还一天到晚联系……听着，我不想让你以为我跟他分手是因为你，因为不是。我跟他分手，是因为跟你的谈话，让我想起跟一个人心意相通、分享激情有多么重要。我这话很可能听起来傻傻的。"

　　"不会。"A.J.说。

她眯起她漂亮的褐色眼睛。"我们第一次见面的时候，你对我很差劲。到现在我都还没有原谅你，你要知道。"

"我希望你能忘了那桩事儿。"

"我没有。我记性很好，A.J.。"

"我是挺糟糕的，"A.J.说，"为自己辩解一下吧，我当时正在经历一段艰难时期。"他从桌子对面探身，拨开她脸上的一绺金色卷发，"我第一次看到你时，觉得你就像是一团蒲公英。"

她难为情地拍拍自己的头发。"我的头发很烦人。"

"那是我最喜欢的花。"

"我觉得那实际上是种野草。"她说。

"你真的能让人印象深刻，你知道的。"

"上学时他们叫我'大鸟'。"

"抱歉。"

"还有更糟的外号呢，"她说，"我跟我妈妈讲了你的事。她说你听着不像是个好男朋友的料，A.J.。"

"我知道。对此我很难过，因为我真的非常喜欢你。"

阿米莉娅叹了口气，起身准备清理桌子。

A.J.站了起来。"不，别动。让我来吧，你应该坐着。"他把盘子摞起来端到洗碗机旁边。

"你想看看那是本什么书吗？"她说。

"什么书？"A.J.一边问，一边把盛烤宽面条的盘子放进水里。

"我办公室里的那本，你问起过的。你来不就是要看那个的吗？"她站了起来，没用滚动的设备，而是用拐杖，"对了，穿过我的卧室就是办公室。"

A.J.点点头。他快步走过卧室，以免显得不把自己当外人。他就要走到办公室的门口时，阿米莉娅坐到床上说："等一下，我明天再给你看那本书吧。"她拍拍床上她旁边的地方，"我的脚踝受了伤，所以如果我的引诱不像通常可能的那样巧妙，请原谅。"

A.J.退回来，走过房间往阿米莉娅的床边去时，想尽量表现得酷一点，但他从来都酷不起来。

阿米莉娅睡着后，A.J.轻手轻脚地进了办公室。

那本书靠在台灯上，跟他们那天通过电脑交谈时一模一样。即使拿到眼前，那本书的封面还是褪色得看不出是什么书。他打开扉页：弗兰纳里·奥康纳的短篇小说集《好人难寻》。

"亲爱的艾米，"那本书上有这样的题词，"妈妈说这是你最喜欢的作家。我希望你不介意我读了同名的那篇。我感觉有点黑暗，可是我的确喜欢。祝你毕业日快乐！我为你感到很自豪。永远爱你的，爸爸。"

A.J.合上那本书，把它靠着台灯放回去。

他写了张纸条："亲爱的阿米莉娅，如果你要一直等到奈特利的秋季书目出来才会再来艾丽丝岛，我真觉得我会无法忍受。——A.J.F."

《卡拉维拉县驰名的跳蛙》

1865/马克·吐温

    一个初具后现代主义风貌的故事，讲的是一个嗜赌之人和他被打败的青蛙的故事。情节没什么，但是值得一读，因为吐温信笔书写的叙述富有乐趣。（读吐温的作品时，我经常怀疑他比我更开心。）

    《跳蛙》总是让我想到利昂·弗里德曼来这里的时候。你还记得吗，玛雅？如果不记得，哪天让艾米跟你说说吧。

    隔着门，我能看到你们俩都坐在艾米的那张紫色旧沙发上。你在读托妮·莫里森[1]的《所罗门之歌》，她在读伊丽莎白·斯特鲁特[2]的《奥丽芙·基特里

---

[1] 托妮·莫里森（Toni Morrison，1931- ），美国黑人女作家，1993年获诺贝尔文学奖。《所罗门之歌》为其代表作品之一。

[2] 伊丽莎白·斯特鲁特（Elizabeth Strout，1956- ），美国著名女作家。《奥丽芙·基特里奇》获得2009年普利策小说奖。

奇》。那只虎斑猫"忧郁坑"在你们俩中间，我比记忆中的任何时候都快乐。

——A.J.F.

那年春天，阿米莉娅开始穿平底鞋，而且发现自己去小岛书店上门推销的次数，严格说来比客户需要的还要多。如果她的老板注意到了，他倒是没有说什么。出版依旧是个文雅人从事的职业，另外，A.J.费克里进的奈特利出版社的书特别多，几乎比东北走廊上其他任何一家书店都进得多。那么大的数量，是因为爱情还是商业考虑或是两者皆有，阿米莉娅的老板并不关心。"也许，"老板对阿米莉娅说，"你可以向费克里先生提个建议，给店面前放奈特利出版社图书的桌子上打个聚光灯？"

　　那年春天，就在阿米莉娅踏上回海恩尼斯的渡轮之前，A.J.吻了她，然后说："你不能以一座岛为根据地。为了工作，你不得不经常出差。"

　　她伸手搭在他身上，跟他保持一臂之遥，笑他。"这话我同意，可是你就这样劝我搬到艾丽丝岛？"

"不，我在……嗯，我在替你着想，"A.J.说，"你搬来艾丽丝岛不实际，这是我的看法。"

"对，不实际。"她说。她用她粉红荧光色的指甲在他的胸口画了个心形。

"那是什么颜色？"A.J.问。

"'玫瑰色酒杯'。"汽笛响了，阿米莉娅上船。

那年春天，在等灰狗巴士时，A.J.跟阿米莉娅说："甚至让你每年在艾丽丝岛待三个月都不行。"

"我就算去阿富汗上下班，交通也会更便当一些，"她说，"对了，我喜欢你这样在大巴站提起这件事。"

"我尽量不去想这件事，直到最后一刻。"

"那也是种办法。"

"我认为，你的意思是说这不是种好办法。"他抓过她的手。她的手大，但是匀称美观。是钢琴家的手，雕塑家的手。"你有双艺术家的手。"

阿米莉娅翻翻眼睛。"却有着图书销售代表的心智。"

她把指甲涂成了深紫色。"这次是什么颜色？"他问。

"'布鲁斯旅行者'。我在考虑这件事呢，下次我来艾丽丝岛，给玛雅涂指甲好不好？她一直缠着我。"

那年春天，阿米莉娅领着玛雅来到药店，让她挑选自己喜欢的指甲油颜色。"你是怎么选的？"玛雅问。

"有时候我问自己是何感觉，"阿米莉娅说，"有时候我问自己想要什么感觉。"

玛雅仔细研究那一排排玻璃瓶。她拿起一瓶红色的，然后又放回去。她从架子上取下彩虹银色。

"哦，漂亮。这是最好的一点，每种颜色都有个名字，"阿米莉娅告诉她，"你把瓶子倒过来。"

玛雅把瓶子倒过来。"它的名字就像书名！'叛逆珍珠'。"她读道，"你那种叫什么？"

艾米选了种浅蓝色。"'保持轻松'。"

那个周末，玛雅陪着A.J.去到码头。她一下子搂住阿米莉娅，让她不要走。"我也不想走。"阿米莉娅说。

"那你干吗非得走？"玛雅问。

"因为我不在这里住。"

"你为什么不在这里住？"

"因为我的工作在别的地方。"

"你可以来书店工作啊。"

"我不能。你爸爸很可能会杀了我。再说，我喜欢我的工作。"她看着A.J.，他正煞有介事地查看手机。汽笛响了。

"跟艾米说再见。"A.J.说。

阿米莉娅在渡轮上打电话给A.J.："我不能搬离普罗维登斯，你不能搬离艾丽丝岛。这种状况挺难解决的。"

"的确。"他也同意，"你今天涂的是什么颜色？"

"'保持轻松'。"

"有那么重要吗？"

"没有。"她说。

那年春天，阿米莉娅的妈妈说："这对你不公平。你三十六岁了，早已不年轻了。如果你真的想生个孩子，你就不能再在一段不可能成功的关系上浪费时间了，艾米。"

伊斯梅对A.J.说："这个叫阿米莉娅的人在你的生活中占了这么大的一部分，如果你对她不是真心的，可就对玛雅不公平。"

而丹尼尔对A.J.说："你不应该为任何一个女人改变自己的生活。"

那年六月，好天气让A.J.和阿米莉娅忘了这些以及别的反对意见。阿米莉娅来介绍秋季书目时，逗留了两个星期。她穿着泡泡纱短裤和饰有雏菊的人字拖鞋。"今年夏天我恐怕没法多见你，"她说，"我一直要出差，然后我妈妈八月要来普罗维登斯。"

"我可以去看你。"A.J.提议道。

"我真的没时间，"阿米莉娅说，"除了八月，而我妈妈的看法已定型。"

A.J.把防晒霜抹到她强壮而柔软的背部，想着他真的不能没有她，想着要创造一个让她来艾丽丝岛的理由。

她一回到普罗维登斯，A.J.就在Skype上联系她。"我一直在想，我们应该请利昂·弗里德曼八月份来书店签售，那时夏季来度假的人还在。"

"你讨厌夏天时的那些人。"阿米莉娅说。她已经不止一次听到A.J.大声抱怨艾丽丝岛上那些季节性的居民：一家一家的人在"布默船长[1]"商店买好冰淇淋后马上拐进书店，让他们还在学走路的小孩子在书店里到处跑，什么东西都碰；参加戏剧节的人，他们笑的声音总是太大；那些从寒冷地带过来的人们以为一周去一次海滩洗个澡就解决个人卫生问题了。

"事实并非如此，"A.J.说，"我喜欢抱怨他们，但是我卖给他们很多书。另外，妮可曾说过，跟通行的观念相反，为作家举办活动最好的时间是八月。那时人们都会感到很无聊，为了解闷干什么都行，甚至去听作家朗诵。"

"作家朗诵会，"阿米莉娅说，"天哪，那可算不上是种娱乐。"

"跟《真爱如血》比起来吧，我想就算不上了。"

她充耳不闻。"事实上，我喜欢朗诵会。"她刚入出版这一行时，有位男朋友拉她去参加了在九十二街Y[2]举办的一次凭票入内的艾丽丝·麦克德莫特[3]的朗诵会。阿米莉娅本以为她不喜欢《迷人的比利》，但是当她听到麦克德莫特朗读时——她挥动胳膊的样子、她对某些词的强调——她意识到之前自己根本没有看懂那本小说。他们参加完朗诵会离开时，那位男朋友在地铁上

---

① 《白鲸》当中一艘捕鲸船的船长。
② 位于纽约曼哈顿上东区，世界级非营利社团和文化中心。
③ 艾丽丝·麦克德莫特（Alice McDermott，1953— ），美国作家，凭借《迷人的比利》荣获1998年美国国家图书奖。

向她道歉："如果这次安排得有点糟糕，对不起。"一周后，阿米莉娅结束了他们的关系。她现在禁不住想当时自己是多么年轻气盛，标准是高得多么离谱。

"好吧，"阿米莉娅对A.J.说，"我会安排你跟宣传人员联系。"

"你也会来的，对吧？"

"我尽量。我妈妈八月份来看我，所以……"

"带她来！"A.J.说，"我想见见你妈妈。"

"你这样说，只是因为你还没有见过她。"阿米莉娅说。

"阿米莉娅，我亲爱的，你得来。我是为了你才请利昂·弗里德曼来的。"

"我不记得我说过想见利昂·弗里德曼。"阿米莉娅说。但视频通话的妙处就在这里，A.J.想——他能看到她在微笑。

A.J.星期一上午做的第一件事，就是打电话给奈特利出版社负责宣传利昂·弗里德曼的人员。她二十六岁，是个新人，出版社从来都是新人。她得去谷歌上搜索"利昂·弗里德曼"，才知道是哪本书。"噢，关于《迟暮花开》这本书，您请作者公开露面，我第一次收到这样的要求。"

"这本书在我们这家书店的确受欢迎。我们已经卖了好多本。"A.J.说。

"您可能是第一个组织利昂·弗里德曼相关活动的人。说真的，以前没有过。我想大概是的。"那位宣传人员顿了一下，"让我跟他的编辑谈谈，看他能不能出席活动。我从来没有见过他，不过我现在正看着他的照片，他挺……成熟的。我可以给您回电话吗？"

"假如他还没有成熟得出不了门，我想把活动安排在八月底，在夏季度假人群离开之前。那样他就能多卖一点书。"

一周后，那位宣传人员回了话，称利昂·弗里德曼尚在人世，八月份能来小岛书店。

A.J.有好多年没有组织过作家活动了，原因在于他根本没有安排此类事件的才能。艾丽丝岛上一次为作家举办活动还是妮可在世时，总是她安排一切。他努力回忆她都做了一些什么。

他订购书，在店里挂上有利昂·弗里德曼苍老面容的海报，发送相关的社交媒体消息，并要求他的朋友和雇员也这样做。然而，他做了这些还感觉不够。妮可的图书派对总是有什么噱头，所以A.J.试图构想出一个来。利昂·弗里德曼年纪大，那本书也失败了。这两项事实，似乎都不足以撑起一次图书派对。这是本浪漫的书，但又出奇地令人沮丧。A.J.决定打电话给兰比亚斯，后者建议用从好市多买来的冻虾，A.J.现在意识到这是兰比亚斯必定会给出的派对建议。"嗨，"兰比亚斯说，"既然你现在开始做活动了，我的确很想见到杰弗里·迪弗。我们艾丽丝岛警察局的人都是他的铁杆粉丝。"

A.J.接着给丹尼尔打电话，后者告诉他："一场好的图书派对唯一需要的，就是有充足的酒水供应。"

"让伊斯梅来听电话。"A.J.说。

"这本书的文学性不是特别高或者特别精彩，可是举办一场花园派对怎么样？"伊斯梅说，"《迟暮花开》。开花，明白吗？"

"我明白。"他说。

"每个人都戴上用花装饰的帽子。你让作者来为帽子比赛当评委什么的。这样能活跃气氛，你的那些妈妈朋友们很可能都会参加，就算只是为了互相拍下戴着可笑帽子时的照片也会。"

A.J.考虑了一下。"那听着挺可怕。"

"只是个建议。"

"可是我想了想，它很可能是好的那种可怕。"

"我接受这样的恭维。阿米莉娅来吗？"

"我当然希望她会来，"A.J.说，"我就是为了她才举办这场破派对的。"

那年七月，A.J.和玛雅去了艾丽丝岛上唯一的一家珠宝首饰店。A.J.指着一个老式戒指，简单的底座上有一块方方的宝石。

"太普通了。"玛雅说。她选了一个有着像里兹饭店那么大的黄色钻石的，结果发现它差不多是一本品相绝佳的初版《帖木儿》的价钱。

他们选定一枚二十世纪六十年代风格的戒指，中间有一颗钻石，底座是珐琅质的花瓣。"就像一朵雏菊，"玛雅说，"艾米喜欢花和让人开心的东西。"

A.J.觉得这个戒指有点华而不实，但他知道玛雅说得对——阿米莉娅会选择这样的一枚戒指，它会让她开心。最起码，这枚戒指会跟她的人字拖鞋相配。

走回书店的路上，A.J.提醒玛雅说阿米莉娅有可能拒绝。"她跟我们还会是朋友，"A.J.说，"即使她拒绝我们。"

玛雅点点头，接着又点了几下。"她为什么会拒绝？"

"嗯……事实上有很多原因。准确说来，你的爸爸并不抢手。"

玛雅笑了起来。"你真傻。"

"而且我们住的这个地方交通不便，艾米因为工作得出很多差。"

"你打算在这次图书派对上向她求婚吗？"玛雅问。

A.J.摇摇头。"不，我不想让她难堪。"

"为什么会让她难堪呢？"

"嗯，我不想让她感觉被逼到了墙角，不得不答应，因为周围有好多人，你懂吧？"他九岁时，他爸爸带他去看了一场巨人队的比赛。结果他们坐到了一个女人旁边，中场休息时，有人在超大屏幕上向这个女人求婚。摄像机对准那个女人时，她说"我愿意"。但是第三节刚一开始，那个女人就无法控制地哭了起来。从那以后，A.J.就不再喜欢橄榄球了。"或许我也不想让自己感到难堪。"

"在派对之后？"玛雅说。

"对，如果我能鼓起勇气的话。"他看着玛雅，"对了，你赞同的吧？"

她点头，然后在T恤衫上擦了擦她的眼镜片。"爸爸，我跟她说了动物造型园艺公园的事。"

"你到底说了什么？"

"我告诉她我根本不喜欢，而且我相当肯定我们那次去罗得岛就是为了看她。"

"你为什么要跟她说这个？"

"她几个月前说过，你这个人有时候让人难以猜到心思。"

"恐怕那大概是真的。"

作家跟他们书上的照片从来不是很像，但A.J.见到利昂·弗里德曼时首先想到的，是他跟照片完全不像。照片上的利昂·弗里德曼要瘦一点，鼻子显得长一点，脸上刮得干干净净的。现实中的利昂·弗里德曼长得介于老年海明威和百货商场里的圣诞老人之间：红红的大鼻子，大肚子，茂密的白色大胡子，闪烁的眼神，显得比作家像上的他年轻约十岁。A.J.想，那也许只是体重超重和大胡子的原因。"利昂·弗里德曼，杰出的小说家。"弗里德曼这样介绍自己。他把A.J.拉过去熊抱了一下，"很高兴见到你。你肯定是A.J.，奈特利的那个姑娘说你很喜欢我的书。你的品位不错，如果非要我说的话。"

"您称这本书为小说，挺有趣的，"A.J.说，"您会说它是一部小说还是回忆录？"

"那个嘛，我们可以无止境地一直讨论下去，不是吗？你不会刚好有杯酒可以给我喝吧。对我来说，一点老酒能让这种活动办得更好。"

伊斯梅为这次活动准备了茶和手指三明治，但是没有酒。这次活动定在星期天下午两点钟，伊斯梅没有想到会需要酒，想着酒跟这次派对的氛围不合。A.J.上楼去找了瓶葡萄酒。

等他回到楼下时，玛雅坐在利昂·弗里德曼的膝头。

"我喜欢《迟暮花开》，"玛雅在说，"可我不是很肯定我是这本书的目标读者。"

"噢嘀嘀，你这句话说得很有意思，小姑娘。"利昂·弗里德曼回答道。

"我说过很多这样的话。别的作家我只认识丹尼尔·帕里什。你认识他吗？"

"我说不准。"

玛雅叹了口气。"跟你说话比跟丹尼尔·帕里什讲话费劲。你最喜欢什么书？"

"我不知道有什么书是我最喜欢的。不说这个了，你干吗不告诉我你想要什么圣诞礼物呢？"

"圣诞礼物？"玛雅说："还有四个月才到圣诞节呢。"

A.J.从弗里德曼的膝上领走自己的女儿，作为交换，给了他一杯葡萄酒。"衷心感谢你。"弗里德曼说。

　　"在朗诵之前，您会不会很介意为书店的书签几本？"A.J.把弗里德曼领到后边，给他搬来一箱平装书，送上一杆笔。弗里德曼正要把自己的名字签到封面上，A.J.拦住了他，"我们一般是让作者签在扉页，如果您没意见的话。"

　　"不好意思，"弗里德曼回答，"我是个新手。"

　　"没关系。"A.J.说。

　　"你不介意跟我说一下你想让我在那边怎样表演吧？"

　　"对，"A.J.说，"我会用几句话来介绍您，然后我想您可以介绍这本书，说说是什么给你灵感写了这本书，接着你也许可以读两页，之后如果有时间的话，可以接受现场观众的提问。另外，为了向这本书致敬，我们还要举办一场帽子比赛，如果您能挑选出一名获胜者，我们会很荣幸的。"

　　"听着很奇幻，"弗里德曼说，"弗里德曼，F－R－I－E－D－M－A－N，"他边说边签，"很容易忘记那个'I'。"

　　"是吗？"A.J.说。

　　"是不是应该还有个'e'，对吧？"

　　作家都是些古怪人，A.J.决定听之任之。"您好像跟小孩子相处得很好。"A.J.说。

　　"是啊……圣诞节的时候，我经常在当地的梅西百货里扮演圣诞老人。"

"真的吗？那可不简单。"

"我有窍门，我想。"

"我是想说——"A.J.犹豫一下，想确定一下他要说的话会不会冒犯弗里德曼——"我只是想说，因为您是犹太人^①。"

"没——错。"

"您在您的书中特别强调过这点。迷失的犹太人。这样说得正确吗？"

"你想怎么说就可以怎么说，"弗里德曼说，"哎，你有没有什么比葡萄酒更有劲儿的？"

等到朗诵开始时，弗里德曼已经喝了好几杯，这位作家把几个长一点的名词和外来短语——Chappaqua^②，Après moi le déluge^③，Hadassah^④，L'chaim^⑤，challah^⑥，等等——念得含糊不清时，A.J.认为肯定是这个原因。有些作家不习惯大声朗诵。在问答环节，弗里德曼尽量回答得简短。

问：您妻子去世时你感觉如何？

① 犹太人不过圣诞节。
② 查帕瓜，美国纽约一地名。
③ 法国皇帝路易十五的名言，意为"我死后哪管洪水滔天"。一说为蓬皮杜夫人的名言。
④ 哈达萨，应为位于以色列耶路撒冷的希伯莱大学医疗中心。
⑤ 希伯来语，意为"为了生命"，常用于祝酒辞。
⑥ 白面包卷，是犹太人传统的节日面包。犹太人在安息日前，把剩下的鸡蛋全部用掉，做成challah。这款面包不切开，得撕着吃，如同分享节日里的大花环。

答：悲伤，特别悲伤。

问：您最喜欢哪本书？

答：《圣经》，要么是《相约星期二》①，不过很可能是《圣经》。

问：您比照片上年轻。

答：哎，谢谢您！

问：在报社上班怎么样？

答：我的手总是脏脏的。

在挑选最漂亮的帽子和签售时，他表现得更为自如。A.J.成功地让挺多人来参加活动，排队排到了书店的门外。"你应该像我们在梅西百货一样立起围栏。"弗里德曼建议道。

"在我这一行，极少需要围栏。"A.J.说。

最后轮到阿米莉娅和她妈妈请作家在她们的书上签字。

"能见到您真是太好了，"阿米莉娅说，"要不是因为您的书，我和我的男朋友很可能不会在一起呢。"

A.J.摸了摸他口袋里的订婚戒指。现在时机恰当吗？不，太引人注目了。

"拥抱我一下。"弗里德曼告诉阿米莉娅。她身子探过桌子，A.J.觉得自己看到那位老先生低头往阿米莉娅的上衣里面看。

"那就是小说在你们身上产生的力量。"弗里德曼说。

---

① 美国著名作家、广播电视主持人米奇·阿尔博姆（Mitch Albom，1958— ）的代表作品。

阿米莉娅端详他。"我想是这样。"她顿了一下，"只不过这不是小说，对吗？是真人真事。"

"是的，亲爱的，那当然。"弗里德曼说。

A.J.插话道："也许，弗里德曼先生是想说这就是叙事的力量。"

阿米莉娅的妈妈——她的个头像蚂蚱，性格像螳螂——说："也许，弗里德曼是想说以喜欢一本书为基础建立起来的一段关系算不上什么关系。"阿米莉娅的妈妈这时把手伸向弗里德曼先生。"玛格丽特·洛曼。我的丈夫也是几年前去世的。我的女儿阿米莉娅非要我在查尔斯顿丧偶者读书会读您的这本书。大家都觉得这书很精彩。"

"哦，真好，真……"弗里德曼对着洛曼太太露出灿烂的笑容。"真……"

"怎么？"洛曼太太又说了一遍。

弗里德曼清清喉咙，擦了一下眉毛和鼻子上的汗。红着脸的他比之前更像圣诞老人。他张开嘴巴，像是要说话，却把那摞刚刚签过名的书和阿米莉娅的妈妈的菲格拉慕米色帆布鞋上呕吐得到处都是。"我好像喝得太多了。"弗里德曼说。他打了个嗝。

"显然是。"洛曼太太说。

"妈妈，A.J.住的地方就在这楼上。"阿米莉娅指着楼梯让她妈妈上去。

"他住在书店上面？"洛曼太太问，"你从来没有提到过这则让人振奋的……"这时，洛曼太太在迅速漫开的那摊呕吐物上滑了一下。她站直身子，但是她那顶获得鼓励奖的帽子却完蛋了。

弗里德曼转身对着A.J.说："对不起，先生。我好像喝得太多了。抽一根烟，再呼吸点新鲜空气，有时候能让我不再反胃。要是谁能指一下怎么出去……"A.J.把弗里德曼领出后门。

"怎么了？"玛雅问。她对弗里德曼说的话不感兴趣，就把注意力放回到《波西·杰克逊与神火之盗》[①]上。她走过来，来到签售桌旁，看到那堆呕吐物时，她自己也吐了。

阿米莉娅赶紧到玛雅身边。"你没事吧？"

"我没想到会看到那个。"玛雅说。

同时，在书店旁边的小巷里，利昂·弗里德曼又在呕吐。

"您觉得可能是食物中毒吗？"A.J.问。

弗里德曼没有回答。

"也许是因为坐渡轮的关系？或者是很兴奋的原因？气温高？"A.J.不知道为什么感觉自己需要说这么多话，"弗里德曼先生，也许我能给您弄点东西吃？"

"你有打火机吗？"弗里德曼声音沙哑地说，"我把我的打火机忘在里面我的袋子里了。"

A.J.又跑进书店。他找不到弗里德曼的袋子。"我需要一个打火机！"他大叫。他很少大声说话。"拜托，在这儿工作的有

---

① 美国畅销童书作家雷克·莱尔顿（Rick Riordan, 1964- ）的代表作品"波西·杰克逊奥林匹斯英雄系列"的第一部。

谁能给我找个打火机？"

但是人们都走了，除了一位店员，他在收款台那边忙着，另外还有参加弗里德曼签售活动后留下的一些零散顾客。一个穿着很漂亮、跟阿米莉娅岁数差不多的女人打开她能装很多东西的皮手袋。"我也许有一个。"

A.J.站在那里，心里翻江倒海，那个女人把她的手袋翻了个遍，那事实上更像是个行李包。他想这就是之所以不能让作家来书店的原因。结果那个女人什么也没找到。"对不起，"她说，"我父亲死于肺气肿之后，我就戒烟了，可是我原以为我还留着打火机。"

"不，没关系。我楼上有一个。"

"那位作家出什么问题了吗？"那个女人问。

"跟通常一样。"A.J.说着朝楼梯走去。

在他的住处，他发现玛雅独自待着，她的眼睛看上去湿湿的。"我吐了，爸爸。"

"我很难过。"A.J.在抽屉里找到那个打火机。他"啪"的一声关上那个抽屉。"阿米莉娅呢？"

"你要求婚吗？"玛雅问。

"不，亲爱的，不是在这个时候。我得给一个酒鬼送打火机。"

她听后考虑了一下。"我能跟你一起去吗？"她问。

A.J.把打火机放进口袋，为了赶时间，一下子抱起玛雅，而其实她已经个子高得不好抱了。

他们下了楼，穿过书店到了A.J.让弗里德曼待着的外面。弗里德曼的脑袋笼罩在一团烟雾中，他手指间无力垂着的烟斗发出冒泡的奇怪声音。

"我找不到你的包。"A.J.说。

"我一直带着呢。"弗里德曼说。

"那是什么烟斗？"玛雅问，"我以前从来没见过那样的烟斗。"

A.J.的第一反应，是想捂住玛雅的眼睛，但是他又哈哈大笑起来。弗里德曼居然带着吸毒工具坐飞机？他转而对着女儿说："玛雅，你还记得我们去年读的《艾丽丝漫游奇境》吗？"

"弗里德曼呢？"阿米莉娅问。

"在伊斯梅的多功能越野车后座上不省人事。"A.J.回答道。

"可怜的伊斯梅。"

"她习惯了。她已经当了好多年丹尼尔·帕里什的媒体陪同。"A.J.做了个鬼脸，"我想我跟他们一起去才像话。"计划本来是伊斯梅开车送弗里德曼去坐渡轮，然后送去机场，可A.J.不能就这样都扔给他的妻姐。

阿米莉娅吻了他一下。"好人啊。我会照顾玛雅，并把这里清理一下。"她说。

"谢谢你。不过一切都糟糕透顶，"A.J.说，"这是你在这里的最后一夜。"

"嗯，"她说，"至少这令人难忘。谢谢你把利昂·弗里德曼请到这里，尽管他跟我想象中的有点不一样。"

"只是有一点。"他吻了阿米莉娅一下，随后又皱起眉头，"我本来想着会挺浪漫，没想到结果是这样。"

"这很浪漫啊。有什么比一个好色的老酒鬼往我的上衣里面看更浪漫呢？"

"他还不仅仅是个酒鬼……"A.J.模仿了一下那个吸毒的惯常动作。

"也许他患了癌症什么的？"阿米莉娅说。

"也许吧……"

"至少他一直坚持到了活动结束。"她说。

"我倒是觉得这让活动更糟糕了。"A.J.说。

伊斯梅在按喇叭。

"叫我的，"A.J.说，"你晚上真的得在旅馆里陪你妈妈？"

"我不是非得要。我是个成年人了，A.J.，"阿米莉娅说，"只不过我们明天要起早回普罗维登斯。"

"我觉得我没有给她留下很好的印象。"A.J.说。

"没人能够，"她说，"我不会为此担心的。"

"嗯，等我回来，如果你可以的话。"伊斯梅又按响了喇叭，A.J.朝车跑去。

阿米莉娅开始清理书店，从那摊呕吐物开始，让玛雅收拾一些没那么让人反胃的杂物，比如花瓣和塑料杯。没从包里找出打火机的那个女人坐在最后一排。她戴了一顶松松的灰色软呢帽，穿着一条丝绸长裙。她的衣服就像是从旧货店里淘来的，不过阿米莉娅这位真的在旧货店淘衣服的人，看得出那身行头价格不菲。"您是来参加朗诵会的吗？"阿米莉娅问。

　　"对。"那个女人说。

　　"您觉得怎么样？"阿米莉娅问。

　　"他很活跃啊。"那个女人说。

　　"对，确实是。"阿米莉娅把海绵里的水挤到一个桶里，"我不能说他完全就是我所期望看到的那样儿。"

　　"您期望什么？"那个女人问。

　　"更知性的一个人，我想。那听着势利。也许这个词用得不对。也许是一个更睿智的人吧。"

　　那个女人点点头。"是，我看得出来。"

　　"我大概期望太高了。我为他的出版商工作。事实上，这是我卖过的书中最喜欢的一本。"

　　"为什么是您最喜欢的？"那个女人问。

　　"我……"阿米莉娅看着那个人。她眼神和蔼，阿米莉娅经常被和蔼的眼睛所愚弄。"在那之前不久，我失去了父亲，我想那种腔调里有什么东西让我想到了他。另外，书中还有很多真情实感。"阿米莉娅继续扫地。

"我碍您事了吗？"那个女人问。

"没有，您在那里就挺好。"

"只是袖手旁观让我感觉不好。"那个女人说。

"我喜欢扫地，而且您穿得那么好，不方便帮忙。"阿米莉娅有节奏地扫地，每一下都挺久。

"他们让出版商在朗诵会后清理现场？"那个女人问。

阿米莉娅哈哈笑了。"不，我还是这家书店老板的女朋友。我今天过来帮忙的。"

那个女人点头。"他肯定是特别喜欢这本书，才会在这么多年后，把利昂·弗里德曼请过来。"

"是啊。"阿米莉娅把声音压低得像是说悄悄话，"事实上，他是为了我而这么做的。这是我们都喜欢的第一本书。"

"真贴心啊。类似于你们一起去的第一家餐厅或你们共舞的第一支曲子什么的。"

"一点儿没错。"

"也许他在计划向你求婚？"那个女人说。

"我曾这样想过。"

阿米莉娅把簸箕里的东西倒进垃圾桶。

"您为什么觉得这本书不会畅销？"过了一会儿，那个女人问道。

"《迟暮花开》？嗯……因为竞争挺厉害。哪怕一本书很好，有时也会不畅销。"

"那肯定很残酷。"那个女人说。

"您在写书什么的吗？"

"我试过，对。"

阿米莉娅停下手里的活去看那个女人。她一头褐色长发，精心修剪过，而且头发特别直。她的手袋很可能跟阿米莉娅的汽车一样贵。阿米莉娅伸出手跟那个女人作自我介绍："阿米莉娅·洛曼。"

"利昂诺拉·费里斯。"

"利昂诺拉，就像利昂。"玛雅大声说。她喝了杯奶昔，这时已经恢复过来。"我是玛雅·费克里。"

"您是艾丽丝岛上的人吗？"阿米莉娅问利昂诺拉。

"不，我只是今天过来。为了这次朗诵会。"

利昂诺拉站了起来，阿米莉娅把她坐的那把椅子折起来靠墙放着。

"您肯定也很喜欢这本书，"阿米莉娅说，"就像我刚才说的，我的男朋友在这里生活，我的经验之谈是，艾丽丝岛并不是世界上最容易到达的地方。"

"对，不是。"利昂诺拉说着拿起她的手袋。

突然，阿米莉娅想到了什么。她转过身大声说："没有人会漫无目的地旅行，那些迷路者是希望迷路。"

"您是在引用《迟暮花开》中的话，"利昂诺拉顿了很久说，"这确实是您最喜欢的书啊。"

"的确是，"阿米莉娅说，"'我年轻时，我从来没有感觉年轻过'诸如此类的话。您还记得这一句的后半句吗？"

"不记得。"利昂诺拉说。

"作家对自己写的东西不会全都记得，"阿米莉娅说，"他们怎么可能全记得呢？"

"跟您聊得挺愉快。"利昂诺拉开始往门口走去。

阿米莉娅把手搭在利昂诺拉的肩膀上。

"您就是他，难道不是吗？"阿米莉娅说，"您就是利昂·弗里德曼。"

利昂诺拉摇摇头。"也不全是。"

"此话怎讲？"

"很久以前，有个女孩写了部长篇小说，她试图把它卖出去，但是没人想要。这部小说是关于一个失去了妻子的老人，里面没有超自然的生物，也没有什么可以一提的高深概念。所以她想如果她给这本书换个书名，称它为回忆录，也许会更容易出手一些。"

"那……那……是不对的。"阿米莉娅结结巴巴地说。

"不，这没有不对。里面的所有东西虽然不一定有这么回事，但感情上说来仍是真实的。"

"这么说，那个人是谁？"

"我打电话给选角中介找来的。他通常扮演圣诞老人。"

阿米莉娅摇摇头。"我不明白。为什么要办这场朗诵会呢？

为什么要花那么多钱、费那么多事呢？为什么要冒这个险呢？"

"那本书已经失败了。有时候你只是想知道……亲眼看看你的作品对某个人有某种意义。"

阿米莉娅看着利昂诺拉。"我有点感觉被愚弄了，"她最后说，"您是位很好的作家，你知道吗？"

"我确实知道。"利昂诺拉说。

利昂诺拉·费里斯消失在那条街道的尽头，阿米莉娅又走回书店。

玛雅跟她说："这是很古怪的一天啊。"

"这话我同意。"

"那个女人是谁，艾米？"玛雅问。

"说来话长。"阿米莉娅告诉她。

玛雅做了个鬼脸。

"她是弗里德曼先生的远亲。"阿米莉娅说。

阿米莉娅让玛雅上床睡觉，然后给自己倒了一杯酒，心里斗争了一番要不要告诉A.J.利昂诺拉·费里斯的事。她不想打击他为作家举办活动的想法，也不想让自己在他眼里显得愚蠢或者让自己显得不够专业：她卖给他一本书，现在却揭露这本书是一部伪作。也许利昂诺拉·费里斯说得对，也许这本书在严格意义上是否真实并不重要。她回想起她大二时文学理论课上的一次讨论会。"什么是真实的？"那位教课的会问他们。"难道回忆录不管怎么样还是构建起来的吗？"上这门课时，她总是会睡着，那让人尴尬，因为只有九个人上这门课。这么多年之后，阿米莉娅发现自己仍然会不由自主想起那件事。

十点过后不久，A.J.回到住处。"送得怎么样？"阿米莉娅问。

"我只能说，最好的一点是弗里德曼大部分时间都不省人事。我花了二十分钟时间清洁伊斯梅的后座。"A.J.汇报道。

"嗯，我可真的是盼望你的下次作家活动啊，费克里先生。"阿米莉娅说。

"有那么一败涂地吗？"

"没有，我想事实上每个人都过得很开心。而且书店的确卖了不少书。"阿米莉娅站起身要走。她这时不走的话，就会忍不住要告诉A.J.关于利昂诺拉·费里斯的事。"我该回旅馆了。因为我们明天走得很早。"

"不，等一下。再待一会儿吧。"A.J.摸索口袋里的首饰盒。他不想夏天过完都没有向她求婚，管它结果如何。他就要错过时机了。他突然从口袋里掏出那个盒子扔给她。"快点考虑。"他说。

"什么？"她说着转过身。那个首饰盒"啪"的一声打在她额头中央。"噢，见鬼，A.J.？"

"我是想让你别走。我以为你能接住。对不起。"他走到她跟前，吻她的额头。

"你扔得有点高了。"

"你比我高。我有时候对高多少估多了。"

她从地板上捡起那个盒子，打开。

"是给你的，"A.J.说，"是……"他单膝跪下，两只手攥着她的手，想避免感觉假惺惺的，不要像一出戏里的演员。"我们结婚吧。"他说，带着几乎是痛苦的表情，"我知道我被困在这个岛上，我穷，是个单身父亲，做生意的收入越来越少。我知道你妈妈讨厌我，在主持作家活动这方面显然我表现糟糕。"

"这样求婚挺怪的，"她说，"先说你的强项嘛，A.J.。"

"我只能说……我只能说我们会找到解决办法的，我发誓。当我读一本书时，我想让你也同时读。我想知道阿米莉娅对这本书有什么看法。我想让你成为我的。我可以向你保证有书、有交流，还有我的全心全意，艾米。"

她知道他说的是真心话。因为他说的那些原因，他跟她（说起来是跟任何人）特别不相称。出差会累死人的。这个男人，这位A.J.，容易发火，爱争论。他自以为从来不会错。也许他的确从来没有错过。

但是他出过错。一贯正确的A.J.没有发觉利昂·弗里德曼是个冒牌货。她拿不准为什么这一点此时是重要的，但的确是。也许证明了他身上有男孩子气和妄想的一面。她仰起头。我会保守这个秘密，因为我爱你。就像利昂·弗里德曼（利昂诺拉·费里斯？）曾写过的："好的婚姻，至少有一部分是阴谋。"

她皱起眉头，A.J.以为她要拒绝。"好人难寻。"她终于说。

"你指的是弗兰纳里·奥康纳的短篇？你书桌上的那本？在这种时候提到它，是件特别黑暗的事。"

"不，我是指你。我始终都在寻找。不过是两趟火车、一趟船的距离。"

"你开车的话，可以少坐点火车。"A.J.告诉她。

"你又懂什么开车的事？"阿米莉娅问。

第二年秋天，就在树叶变黄后不久，阿米莉娅和A.J.结婚了。

兰比亚斯的妈妈——作为他的女伴，和他一起参加婚礼——对她的儿子说："凡是婚礼我都喜欢，但是当两个真正长大的人决定结婚时，这不是尤其让人高兴吗？"兰比亚斯的妈妈乐见自己的儿子哪天再婚。

"我懂你的意思，妈。他们看来不像是闭着眼睛结婚的，"兰比亚斯说，"A.J.知道阿米莉娅不是十全十美，阿米莉娅也知道A.J.绝对不是十全十美，他们知道世界上没有十全十美这种事。"

玛雅选择了保管戒指，因为这项工作比当花童的责任更大。"要是你把花丢了，你可以再拿另一束，"玛雅如是陈述理由，"要是你把戒指丢了，所有人都会永远悲伤。保管戒指的人责任要大得多。"

"说得好像你是咕噜。"A.J.说。

"谁是咕噜？"玛雅想知道。

"你爸爸喜欢的一个呆头呆脑的人。"阿米莉娅说。

婚礼前夕，阿米莉娅送了玛雅一件礼物：一小盒上面有"玛雅·帖木儿·费克里藏书"字样的藏书票。在她人生的这个阶段，玛雅喜欢上面有她名字的东西。

"我挺高兴我们要成一家人了，"阿米莉娅说，"我很喜欢你，玛雅。"

玛雅在忙着把她的第一张藏书票贴到她正在读的一本书上：《令人惊讶的屋大维》[①]。"是啊，"她说，"哦，等一下。"她从口袋里掏出一瓶橘黄色指甲油，"送给你的。"

"我没有橘黄色的呢，"艾米说。"谢谢你。"

"我知道，所以我选了这瓶。"

艾米把瓶子翻过来看瓶底的字。"好橘难寻"。

A.J.提议过邀请利昂·弗里德曼来参加婚礼，阿米莉娅拒绝了。但他们的确商量好让阿米莉娅大学时的一位朋友在婚礼上读《迟暮花开》中的一段。

"因为从心底害怕自己不值得被爱，我们独来独往，"那一段是这样的，"然而就是因为独来独往，才让我们以为自己不值得被爱。有一天，你不知道是什么时候，你会驱车上路。有一天，你不知道是什么时候，你会遇到他（她）。你会被爱，因为你今生第一次真正不再孤单。你会选择不再孤单下去。"

---

① 美国著名童书作家M.T.安德森（M.T.Anderson，1968- ）的作品。

阿米莉娅其他的大学朋友都不认识读这一段的那个女人，但她们谁都没有感到特别古怪。瓦萨学院虽小，但当然也不是那种小到谁都认识谁的地方，而且在跟各种社交圈子里的人交朋友这方面，阿米莉娅自有一套。

《穿夏裙的女孩》

1939/欧文·肖[①]

男人看着妻子旁边的女人们。妻子不高兴了。最后有个可爱的转折，更像是个逆转。你是个出色的读者，你大概能看出会有逆转。（如果能看出来，逆转是否就没那么令人满意呢？无法预见的逆转是否表明架构有缺陷呢？这些是写作时要考虑的方方面面。）

不是专门说写作，不过……有一天，你也许会想到婚姻。要是有谁觉得你在一屋子人中是独一无二的，就选那个人吧。

——A.J.F.

---

① 欧文·肖（Irwin Shaw，1913–1984），当代美国作家，短长篇创作俱佳。

伊斯梅在自家门厅里等着。她双腿交叉，一只脚兜着另一条腿的腿肚子。她曾见过一位新闻节目女主持人那样坐，给她留下了深刻印象。对一个女人来说，需要腿瘦、膝盖灵活才能做到。她在想她为这天挑的裙子是否颜色太浅。料子是绸子的，而夏天已经结束了。

　　她看看手机。上午十一点了，那意味着婚礼已经开始。也许她应该自个儿去，不跟他一起？

　　因为已经迟了，她觉得一个人去也没什么意义。如果她等的话，他回来后她还可以吼一吼他。她要及时行乐。

　　丹尼尔十一点二十六分进了门。"对不起，"他说，"我那个班上的几个孩子想去喝一杯。一来二去的，你知道怎么回事。"

　　"对。"她说。她觉得不想吼了，沉默更好。

"我在办公室摔了一跤，我的背疼死了。"他在她的脸上吻了一下，"你看着真迷人，"他悄声说，"你的腿还是很棒，伊西[1]。"

"换衣服吧，"她说，"你身上的味道像是酒铺里的。你是自己开车回来的吗？"

"我没醉，我只是有点宿醉。那不一样，伊斯梅。"

"你还活着，这真是让人吃惊。"她说。

"很可能是这样。"他一边上楼一边说。

"你下来时，把我的披肩拿下来好吗？"她说。但是她拿不准他是否听到。

这场婚礼，就像婚礼本该的那样，就像婚礼永远的那样，伊斯梅想。A.J.穿着他的蓝色薄布西装，显得邋里邋遢的。他难道不能去租套燕尾服吗？这是艾丽丝岛，而不是泽西海岸[2]。阿米莉娅又是从哪儿弄来的那件难看的文艺复兴风格的裙子？它颜色偏黄而不是白，她穿上显得有点嬉皮。她总是穿样式古老的衣服，但事实上她又没有正好适合穿那种衣服的体型。她的头发上插着大朵非洲菊，她跟谁开玩笑呢——看在上帝的份上，她又不是二十岁。她微笑时，牙龈全都露了出来。

---

[1] 伊斯梅的昵称。
[2] 《泽西海岸》是美国一档以新泽西海岸几位意大利裔年轻人为主角的真人秀节目，这群年轻人疯狂玩乐，彼此间嬉笑怒骂，甚至连冲突斗殴的言行举止都被记录下来，从2009年开播后引发极大争议。

我什么时候这么事事看不顺眼？伊斯梅心想。他们的幸福并非她的不幸；除非是，那才说得过去。如果在任何一个时间点，世界上总是有相同比例的幸与不幸又当如何？她应该友善一点。众所周知，一旦年过四十，憎恶就会流露在脸上。另外，阿米莉娅长得漂亮，即使她不像妮可那样美丽。看看玛雅的笑容多么灿烂，她又掉了颗牙。A.J.也那么开心。看看那个幸运的家伙吧，他在忍着不哭出来。

伊斯梅为A.J.感到高兴，不管那意味着什么，然而婚礼本身让她感到难熬。婚礼让她的妹妹似乎死得更彻底了，也让她不想却偏要想起自己的种种失意。她四十四岁了，嫁给了一个长得太帅的男人，她已经不再爱他。在过去的十二年里，她流产七次。根据她的妇科医生所言，她已经出现了停经期前症候，到此为止吧。

她望向婚礼现场那边的玛雅，她长得可真是漂亮啊，还很聪明。伊斯梅朝她挥手，但是玛雅在埋头看一本书，好像没有注意到。这小姑娘跟伊斯梅从来不是特别亲，大家都觉得挺怪。通常，玛雅更喜欢跟大人在一起，而伊斯梅擅长跟孩子相处，她已经教书教了二十年。二十年啊，老天。不知不觉地，她就从一位聪明的新老师（所有男生都盯着她的腿看）变成了负责学校里戏剧排演的帕里什老太太。他们觉得她那样关心上演的戏剧挺傻的。当然，他们高估了她的投入。一场接着一场平庸的戏剧，又能指望她坚持多少年呢？不同的面孔，但是这些小孩子中没有一个会成为梅丽尔·斯特里普[1]。

伊斯梅裹紧披肩，决定去走一走。她朝码头走去，然后脱下中跟鞋，走过空无一人的海滩。时值九月底，感觉像是秋天已临。她想回忆起一本书的名字，书里有个女人朝大海远处游去，最后淹死在海里。

会很容易的，伊斯梅想。你走出去，游一阵子，游得太远了，不去努力游回来，你的肺里全是水，会难受一会儿，可是随后一切都结束了，哪里都不会再疼，意识一片空白。你不会留下一个烂摊子。也许有一天你的尸体会被冲上来，也许不会。丹尼尔根本不会去找她。也许他会找，但是他肯定不会很尽力地去找。

当然！那本书是凯特·肖邦[2]的《觉醒》。她十七岁时，可真是爱那部长篇小说（中篇小说？）啊。

玛雅的妈妈也是这样结束了自己的生命。伊斯梅想知道玛丽安·华莱士是否读过《觉醒》，这个念头可不是第一回出现。这几年她想到过玛丽安·华莱士很多次。

伊斯梅走进水里，水比她原以为的还要冷。我做得到的，她想。只要继续走。

我也许就是要这样做。

"伊斯梅！"

---

① 梅丽尔·斯特里普（Meryl Streep，1949- ），美国著名演员，曾两次获得奥斯卡金像奖最佳女主角，一次最佳女配角。
② 凯特·肖邦（Kate Chpin，1850-1904），美国女权主义文学创作的先驱之一。《觉醒》为其最为知名的作品。

伊斯梅不由自主转过身。是兰比亚斯，A.J.那位讨厌的警察朋友。他拿着她的鞋子。

"游泳有点冷吧？"

"有点儿，"她回答，"我只是想让自己的脑子清醒一下。"

兰比亚斯走到她身边，"当然可以。"

伊斯梅的牙齿在打架，兰比亚斯把自己的西装外套脱下来披在她的肩膀上。"肯定不好受，"兰比亚斯说，"看到A.J.跟不是你妹妹的人结婚。"

"是啊。不过阿米莉娅看着挺好的。"伊斯梅哭了起来，可是太阳基本下山了，她拿不准兰比亚斯是否能看到她哭。

"婚礼就是这样，"他说，"会让人感觉孤独得要命。"

"对。"

"我希望这话说得不过分，我也知道我们彼此并没有那么熟。可是呢，嗯，你的丈夫是个白痴。如果我有像你这样一个有职业的漂亮妻子……"

"你说得过分了。"

"对不起，"兰比亚斯说，"我失礼了。"

伊斯梅点点头。"我不会说你失礼的，"她说，"你的确把你的外套借给了我。谢谢。"

"艾丽丝岛上的秋天来得急，"兰比亚斯说，"我们最好回屋里去。"

丹尼尔在吧台那边跟阿米莉娅的伴娘大声地讲话，头顶上是裴廓德餐厅的那条鲸鱼，这次鲸鱼身上应景地缠了圣诞灯饰。雅尼纳是位希区柯克电影中的那种金发女郎，戴着眼镜，跟阿米莉娅一样在出版业一路干过来。丹尼尔不知情的是，雅尼纳已经领了任务，确保这位大作家不要失了分寸。

为了这次婚礼，雅尼纳穿了一件黄色的条格平布裙子，阿米莉娅帮她挑的，而且付了款。"我知道你再也不会穿这衣服了。"阿米莉娅当时说。

"这种颜色不容易穿好，"丹尼尔说，"不过你穿上很棒。雅尼纳，对吗？"

她点点头。

"伴娘雅尼纳。我应该问一下你是做什么的吗？"丹尼尔说，"或者这么问是乏味的派对套话？"

"我是个编辑。"雅尼纳说。

"性感又聪明。你编过什么书？"

"几年前，我编的一本关于哈丽雅特·塔布曼①的绘本获得了凯迪克荣誉奖②。"

"不简单。"丹尼尔说，尽管事实上他感到失望。他正在为自己寻找一家新的出版社。他的作品销量大不如前，他认为原来

---

① 哈丽雅特·塔布曼（Harriet Tubman，1822–1913），美国黑人废奴女勇士。她曾担任地下活动组织人，协助无数的黑奴奔向自由。
② 凯迪克奖是美国最具权威的图画书奖。

的出版社为他做得不够多。他想在被抛弃前，先抛弃他们。"那是头奖，对吧？"

"没有获头奖，是荣誉奖。"

"我打赌你是位好编辑。"他说。

"有何根据？"

"嗯，你的书没有得头奖，你并没有让我以为得了头奖。"

雅尼纳看了看手表。

"雅尼纳在看手表，"丹尼尔说，"她对老作家感到了厌烦。"

雅尼纳微笑了。"删掉第二句。读者会知道的。表现出来，别讲出来。"

"你要是这样说，我就要喝一杯了。"丹尼尔朝酒保示意，"伏特加，灰雁伏特加①，如果有的话。兑点赛尔脱兹矿泉水。"他转向雅尼纳。"你呢？"

"一杯桃红葡萄酒。"

"'表现出来，别讲出来'，完全是一派胡言，伴娘雅尼纳，"丹尼尔教导她，"这句话来自悉德·菲尔德②关于编剧的书，但是跟长篇写作一点关系都没有。长篇小说都是要讲出来的，至少写得最好的都是。长篇小说可不能模仿剧本。"

---

① 一种法国伏特加品牌，被誉为世界上口感最好的伏特加。
② 悉德·菲尔德（Syd Field，1935-2013），享誉全球的著名编剧、制片人、教师、演讲人，也是诸多畅销书的作者。他的一系列电影编剧写作教程自出版以来已被译成二十四种语言，并被全球超过四百所大学选作教材。

"我上初中时读过你的书。"雅尼纳说。

"哦，别跟我说这个。让我感觉自己已经七老八十了。"

"我妈最喜欢那本书。"

丹尼尔做了个被击中心脏的哑剧动作。伊斯梅轻轻拍了拍他的肩膀。"我要回家了。"她在他耳边低语。

丹尼尔跟着她出来朝汽车走去。"伊斯梅，等一下。"

伊斯梅开车，因为丹尼尔醉得开不了车。他们住在克里弗斯，艾丽丝岛最贵的地段。每座房子都有风景可看，通往那里的路是上山路，拐来拐去，有很多盲点，照明不佳，路边有黄色的警示标志，提醒人们小心驾驶。

"你那个弯拐得太急，亲爱的。"丹尼尔说。

她想过把车开出路面，开进大海，这个念头让她感到高兴，比她一个人自杀更高兴。那一刻，她意识到自己不想死，只是想让丹尼尔死，或者至少消失。对，消失。她可以接受消失。

"我不再爱你了。"

"伊斯梅，你在胡闹。你参加婚礼总是这样。"

"你不是好人。"伊斯梅说。

"我复杂，也许我不好，但我肯定不是最糟糕的。根本没理由结束一桩普通得完美的婚姻。"丹尼尔说。

"你是蚱蜢，我是蚂蚁。我当蚂蚁当累了。"

"这样打比方很小孩子气。我肯定你能打个更好的比喻。"

伊斯梅把车停到路边，手在颤抖。

"你很糟糕，更糟糕的是，你把我也变糟糕了。"她说。

"我不知道你在说什么。"一辆车从他们旁边呼啸而过，近得差点擦上这辆越野车的车门。"伊斯梅，把车停在这里太危险了。想吵架的话，开车回家好好吵。"

"每次看到她跟A.J.和阿米莉娅在一起，我都感觉不舒服。她应该是我们的。"

"什么？"

"玛雅，"伊斯梅说，"如果你做了正确的事，她就是我们的。可是你，你永远不会做任何棘手的事。我还惯着你那样。"她死死地盯着丹尼尔，"我知道玛丽安·华莱士是你的女朋友。"

"不是。"

"别撒谎了！我知道她来这儿，要在你家的前院自杀。我知道她把玛雅留给了你，可是你要么是太懒，要么太懦弱，没有认她。"

"你如果觉得是那样，干吗不做点什么呢？"丹尼尔问。

"因为那不是我的活！我当时怀着孕，你出了轨，帮你擦屁股可不是我的义务！"

又一辆车疾驰而过，差点跟他们擦撞。

"可是如果你能勇敢地跟我说这件事，我会收养她的，丹尼尔。我会原谅你，接纳她。我等着你说，可是你从来不说。我等了好多天，好多个星期，然后是好多年。"

"伊斯梅，你愿意相信什么就相信什么，但玛丽安·华莱士不是我的女朋友。她只是我的书迷，来参加朗诵会。"

"你以为我有那么蠢？"

丹尼尔摆摆脑袋。"她只是个来参加朗诵会的女孩，我跟她睡过一次。我怎么肯定那个孩子是我的？"丹尼尔想抓住伊斯梅的手，但是她抽开了。

"真有意思，"伊斯梅说，"我对你的最后一丁点儿爱也没有了。"

"我还爱你。"丹尼尔说。突然，后视镜上出现了车头灯光。

车是从后面撞上来的，把这辆车撞到路中间，结果它横在路上，把两个方向的路都占了。

"我觉得我没事，"丹尼尔说，"你还好吧？"

"我的腿，"她说，"可能断了。"

又看到了车头灯，这次是从另一侧路面过来。"伊斯梅，你必须开动车子。"他转过身，刚好看到了那辆卡车。一个逆转，他想。

在丹尼尔那部著名的长篇小说处女作的第一章，主角遭遇了一次灾难性的车祸。那一部分丹尼尔写得很艰难，因为他想到他对可怕车祸的全部了解，都来自他读过的书、看过的电影。那段描述他写了肯定有五十遍才定稿，还一直觉得不满意。那是一系列现代派诗人风格的断片。也许像阿波利奈尔[1]或者布勒东[2]，但也根本不足够好：

> 灯光，亮得能扩大地的瞳孔。
>
> 喇叭，不够响亮且太迟。
>
> 金属像纸巾一样皱起。
>
> 身上不疼，只是因为身体没了，已在异处。

对，在撞击之后、死亡之前，丹尼尔想，就是那样。那一段并不像他以为的那么糟糕。

---

① 纪尧姆·阿波利奈尔（Guillaume Apollinaire，1880-1918），法国著名诗人、小说家、剧作家和文艺评论家，其诗歌和戏剧在表达形式上多有创新，被认为是超现实主义文艺运动的先驱之一。
② 安德烈·布勒东（André Breton，1896-1966），法国诗人和评论家，超现实主义创始人之一。

第二部

《与父亲的对话》

1972/格蕾斯·佩利[1]

垂死的父亲跟女儿争论何为讲故事的"最佳"方式。你会喜欢这一篇的,玛雅,我能肯定。也许我会下楼一趟,立马把它塞进你手里。

——A.J.F.

---

[1] 格蕾斯·佩利(Grace Paley, 1922-2007),美国短篇小说作家、诗人。

玛雅创意写作课的作业，是写一个短篇——关于一位希望了解更多的人。"对我来说，我的生父是个幻象。"她写道。她觉得第一句不错，但是往下该怎么写？写了两百五十个字之后，整个上午就浪费了，她认输了。毫无内容可写，因为她对那个人一无所知。对她而言，他真的是个幻象。这篇作业从构思就失败了。

　　A.J.给她送来了烤乳酪三明治。"写得怎么样了，小海明威？"

　　"你从来不敲门吗？"她说。她接过三明治，关上门。她以前喜欢住在书店上面，但是现在她十四岁了，而且阿米莉娅也住在这里，这个住处就感觉小了，而且嘈杂。她整天都能听到楼下顾客的声音。就这种条件，让人怎么写东西？

　　实在走投无路了，玛雅就写阿米莉娅的猫。

　　"'忧郁坑'从来没想到自己会从普罗维登斯搬到艾丽丝

岛。"

她修改了一下："'忧郁坑'从来没想到自己会住在一家书店的上面。"

噱头。创意写作老师巴尔博尼先生会那样说。她已经以雨的视角和一本图书馆旧书的视角各写了个短篇。"挺有趣的概念，"巴尔博尼先生在那个图书馆旧书的故事上面写道，"不过下次你可以尝试写一个人物。你真的想让拟人化写作成为你的套路吗？"

在下决定之前，她不得不先去查查"拟人化写作"是什么意思，不，她不想让那成为她的套路。她根本不想有什么套路。然而，如果这有点是她的套路，那能怪她吗？她的童年都是在看书和想象顾客们的生活中度过的，有时是为没有生命的物品如茶壶或者书签旋转架想象它们的生活。这种童年不算孤独，然而她很多亲密朋友多少有点不够真实。

过了一会儿，阿米莉娅敲门。"你在写东西吗？可以休息一下吗？"

"进来吧。"玛雅说。

阿米莉娅"扑通"一声坐到床上。"你在写什么？"

"我不知道。问题就在这里。我还以为我想好了怎样写呢，但是行不通。"

"哦，那是个问题。"

玛雅解释了一下作业。"要写一个对你重要的人。某个很可能已经死了的人，要么某个你希望有更多了解的人。"

"也许你可以写写你的妈妈？"

玛雅摇摇头。她不想伤害阿米莉娅的感情，但是那似乎有点明显。"我对她，就跟我对生父一样，知之甚少。"她说。

"你跟她生活了两年。你知道她的名字，还有她以前的故事。也许可以从此入手。"

"我对她想了解的都了解了。她有过机会，可是她把什么都搞砸了。"

"不是那样的。"阿米莉娅说。

"她放弃了，不是吗？"

"她很可能有苦衷。我肯定她尽了全力。"阿米莉娅的妈妈两年前去世，尽管以前两人的关系时而紧张，阿米莉娅还是出乎意料地想她想得心痛。例如，她的妈妈一直到去世前，每隔一个月都会给她寄来新内衣。她这一辈子都不用买内衣了。最近，她不知不觉中站在一家TJ麦克斯商店①的内衣区，当她在内裤箱里翻拣时，她哭了起来：再也没有人会那样爱我了。

"某个已经去世的人？"A.J.吃晚饭时说，"丹尼尔·帕里什怎么样？你跟他曾是好朋友。"

"那是小时候。"玛雅说。

"不是他让你决心当一名作家的吗？"A.J.说。

玛雅翻翻眼珠子。"不是。"

---

① 美国名牌折扣连锁店。

"她小时候迷恋过他。"A.J.对阿米莉娅说。

"爸——爸！不是那样的。"

"你在文学上最初的迷恋很重要，"阿米莉娅说，"我当时迷恋的是约翰·欧文[1]。"

"你撒谎，"A.J.说，"是安·M.马丁[2]。"

阿米莉娅大笑着又给自己倒了杯葡萄酒。"是啊，很可能你说得对。"

"我挺高兴你们都觉得这很好玩，"玛雅说，"我很可能会失败，很可能结局就跟我妈妈一样。"她从桌子前站起来，跑向她的房间。他们的住处不适合横冲直撞，她的膝盖撞到一个书架。"这个地方太小了。"她说。

她进了自己的房间，"砰"的一声关上了门。

"我应该跟过去吗？"A.J.悄声说。

"不，她需要空间。她到了青春期了，让她去生会儿闷气吧。"

"也许她说得对，"A.J.说，"这个地方太小了。"

婚后他们就一直在网上看房子。现在玛雅已经十几岁了，阁楼上这个只有一个卫生间的住处就神奇地相应缩小了。有一半时间，A.J.发现自己得使用书店里的公共卫生间，以避免跟玛雅

---

① 约翰·欧文（John Irving，1942- ），当代美国最知名的小说家之一，被美国文坛泰斗冯尼古特誉为"美国最重要的幽默作家"。
② 安·M. 马丁（Ann M. Martin，1955- ），美国童书作家。

和阿米莉娅抢着用。顾客可要比这两位客气。另外，生意还不错（或者说至少是稳定吧），他们搬走的话，他可以把住处扩展为童书区，有一块讲故事的区域，还可以放礼物和贺卡。

以他们在艾丽丝岛上出得起的价格，能买得起的都是起步房[1]，A.J.感觉自己已经过了买起步房的那个岁数。古怪的厨房和平面布置图，房间太小，暗示地基问题的不祥征兆。在此之前，A.J.多少带着遗憾想起《帖木儿》的次数屈指可数。

那天夜里晚些时候，玛雅发现她的门下面有张纸条：

玛雅，

要是你写不下去，读书是有帮助的：

安东·契诃夫[2]的《美人》，凯瑟琳·曼斯菲尔德[3]的《玩具屋》，J.D.塞林格[4]的《逮香蕉鱼的最佳日子》，ZZ·帕克[5]的《布朗尼蛋糕》或《别处喝咖啡》，艾米·亨佩尔[6]的《在艾尔·乔森入葬的墓地》，雷蒙德·卡佛的《肥》，厄内斯特·海明威的《印第安人的营地》。

---

① 指首次买房者能买得起的低价小房子。
② 安东·契诃夫（1860-1904），俄国世界级短篇小说巨匠。
③ 凯瑟琳·曼斯菲尔德（Katherine Mansfield，1888-1923），出生于新西兰，后定居英国，短篇小说作家，新西兰文学的奠基人，被誉为一百多年来新西兰最有影响的作家之一。
④ J.D.塞林格（J.D. Salinger，1919-2010），美国作家，其作品《麦田里的守望者》被认为是二十世纪美国文学的经典作品之一。
⑤ ZZ·帕克（ZZ Packer，1973- ），美国作家，尤以短篇小说著称。
⑥ 艾米·亨佩尔（Amy Hempel，1951- ），美国短篇小说作家。

我们楼下应该都有。要是你有哪篇找不到，尽管问，不过你比我更清楚它们都在哪儿。

爱你的，

爸爸

她把那份单子塞进口袋下了楼，书店已经结束营业。她转动书签旋转架——喂，你好，旋转架！——然后往右急转，到了成年读者文学区。

玛雅把短篇故事交给巴尔博尼先生时感到紧张，还有些许兴奋。

"《海滩一日》。"他读标题。

"是从沙子的角度写的，"玛雅说，"这是艾丽丝岛上的冬天，沙子怀念那些游客。"

巴尔博尼先生换了一下坐姿，黑色紧身皮裤发出吱吱响声。他鼓励他们强调正面因素，同时阅读时带着批评性和富于见识的眼光。"嗯，听上去好像里面已经有引人遐思的描写。"

"我开玩笑呢，巴尔博尼先生。我正在努力不再拟人化写作。"

"我期待读一读。"巴尔博尼先生说。

过了一周，巴尔博尼先生宣布他要朗读一个短篇，每个人都坐直了一点。被选中的人会很兴奋，就算会被批评。能被批评也令人兴奋。

"觉得怎么样？"读完后，他问全班同学。

"嗯，"萨拉·皮普说，"恕我直言，对白有点糟糕。例如我明白那个人的意图，作者为什么不写得更简洁些呢？"萨拉·皮普在她的博客"佩斯利独角兽书评"上撰写书评，她总是吹嘘出版社免费送书给她。"另外为什么用第三人称？为什么用现在时态？在我看来，作品显得孩子气。"

比利·利博尔曼——他写的是被人误解的男孩主人公克服了超自然和父母的障碍——说："我根本没明白最后到底应该发生什么事？让人糊涂。"

"我觉得那是晦涩，"巴尔博尼先生说，"记得上星期我们谈到过晦涩吗？"

玛吉·马卡基斯——她之所以选读这门课，是因为数学和辩论课在时间安排上有冲突——说她喜欢这篇，但是她注意到故事中金钱因素的不一致之处。

阿布纳·肖切不喜欢这篇，基于这几方面：他不喜欢里面有角色撒谎的故事（"我真是受够了不可靠的叙述者"——这一概念两星期前介绍给了他们），更糟糕的是，他觉得根本没有什么情节。这没有伤害到玛雅什么感情，因为阿布纳的所有短篇最后都以同样的转折结束：一切都是一个梦。

"这一篇里，有什么你们喜欢的地方吗？"巴尔博尼先生说。

"语法。"萨拉·皮普说。

约翰·弗内斯说:"我喜欢它如此忧伤。"约翰有着长长的褐色眼睫毛,像流行音乐偶像那样梳着大背头。他写的短篇是关于他奶奶的手,甚至把铁石心肠的萨拉·皮普感动得流了泪。

"我也是,"巴尔博尼先生说,"作为读者,你们不喜欢的很多东西都会打动我。我喜欢它略带正式的风格和其中的晦涩。我不同意关于'不可靠的叙述者'这样的评论——我们也许得重新讲讲这个概念。我也不觉得金钱的因素处理得不好。综合看来,我觉得这一篇和约翰的《奶奶的手》,是我们班这个学期最好的两个短篇。这两篇将代表艾丽丝镇中学参加县里的短篇小说竞赛。"

阿布纳不高兴地咕哝道:"你还没说另外那篇是谁写的。"

"对,当然。是玛雅。大家为约翰和玛雅鼓掌。"

玛雅尽量不让自己显得很得意。

"真棒,对吧?巴尔博尼先生挑了我们俩。"下课后约翰说。他跟着玛雅到了她的储物柜那里,而玛雅搞不清楚这是为什么。

"是啊,"玛雅说,"我喜欢你的短篇。"她的确喜欢他的短篇,但是她真的想获奖。第一名是亚马逊的一百五十美元礼券,还有座奖杯。

"你如果得了第一会买什么?"约翰问。

"不是书。书我爸爸会给我。"

"你真幸运,"约翰说,"我真希望住在书店里。"

"我住在书店上面，不是里面，另外也没那么棒。"

"我敢说的确棒。"

他拨开遮住眼睛的褐色头发。"我妈妈想知道你愿不愿意跟我们拼一辆车去参加颁奖典礼。"

"可是我们今天才知道有这件事呀。"玛雅说。

"我了解我妈妈。她总是喜欢拼车分摊费用。问问你爸爸。"

"问题是，我爸爸会想去，而他不会开车。所以很有可能我爸爸会让我的教母或者教父开车送我们。另外你妈妈也会想去。所以我不能肯定拼车行不行得通。"她觉得自己已经讲了半个钟头的话了。

他朝她微笑，那让他往后梳的大背头有点起伏。"没问题。也许我们可以换个时间开车带你去其他什么地方。"

颁奖仪式在海恩尼斯的一所中学举行。尽管是体育馆（各种球类的味道还能闻到），仪式并没有开始的时候，每个人却都压低了声音说话，好像是在教堂里。某个重要的、跟文学有关的活动即将在这里举行。

来自二十所中学的四十篇参赛作品，只有前三名会被朗读。玛雅在约翰·弗内斯面前练习过读她的短篇。他建议她多换气，放慢速度。她一直在练习换气和朗读，这并不像人们以为的那么容易。她也听他读过。她给他的建议，是用他正常的声音读。

他一直用那种有点假的播报新闻的声音在读。"你知道你喜欢的。"他这样说过。现在他一天到晚用这种假假的声音跟她说话，很烦人。

玛雅看到巴尔博尼先生在跟一个人说话，那只可能是别的学校的一位老师。她穿着老师的衣服——一条碎花裙和一件绣了几片雪花的米色开襟羊毛衫，不论巴尔博尼先生说什么，她都用力点头。当然，巴尔博尼先生穿着他的皮裤，因为他出来了，还穿了件皮夹克——总体说来，是一身皮装。玛雅想带他去见爸爸，因为她想让A.J.听听巴尔博尼先生夸奖她。权衡之下，她不想让A.J.令她难堪。上个月在书店，她曾把A.J.介绍给她的英语老师斯迈思太太，A.J.把一本书塞进那位老师的手里，一边还说："你会喜欢这本长篇小说的，情色描写很细腻。"玛雅当时窘得要死。

A.J.打着领带，玛雅穿着牛仔裤。她本来穿的是阿米莉娅为她挑选的一条裙子，但是她觉得穿裙子会显得她太过在乎。阿米莉娅这个星期去了普罗维登斯，会过来跟他们碰头，不过她很可能会晚到。玛雅知道不穿裙子会伤她的心。

有人用一根接力棒在讲台上敲。穿着雪花羊毛衫的老师欢迎他们参加艾兰县中学短篇小说竞赛。她称赞所有的参赛作品风格多样、触人心弦。她说她很喜欢自己的工作，希望每个人都能获奖。然后她宣布了进入最后决选的第一篇。

当然，约翰·弗内斯会进入最后决选。玛雅往后靠着坐在椅子上听。故事比她印象中的还要好。她喜欢描写那位奶奶的手像是纸巾的那一句。她望向A.J.，想看他对这篇有什么反应。他的眼神显得冷漠，玛雅认出那是厌倦。

第二个短篇是布莱克哈特中学弗吉尼亚·基姆的作品。《旅程》是关于一个从中国收养的孩子。A.J.点了几次头。她看得出跟《奶奶的手》比起来，他更喜欢这篇。

玛雅开始担心自己根本不会被选中。她为自己穿了牛仔裤而高兴。她转过头看从哪里能最快出去。阿米莉娅站在礼堂的门口，她冲玛雅竖起两根大拇指。"裙子，那条裙子呢？"阿米莉娅不出声地做口形说。

玛雅耸耸肩，扭头接着听《旅程》。弗吉尼亚·基姆穿了一条黑色天鹅绒裙子，有一个小飞侠式的领子。她的声音很轻，有时比耳语大声不了多少。似乎她想让大家都不得不往前探着身子听。

不幸的是，《旅程》这篇没完没了，是《奶奶的手》的五倍长。过了一会儿，玛雅不再听了。玛雅想很可能飞到中国所花的时间还要短一点。

如果《海滩一日》不是前三名，也会得到T恤衫，招待会上还有饼干吃。但是如果没有取得名次，谁还想待到开招待会呢？

如果取得名次，她不会因为不是第一名而很恼火。

如果约翰·弗内斯得到第一名，她会尽量不去讨厌他。

如果玛雅得了第一名，也许她会把礼券捐给慈善团体，例如给贫穷的孩子或者孤儿院。

如果她得不到名次，也没关系。她写那个短篇又不是为了得奖，甚至不是为了完成家庭作业。如果她只是想要完成作业，她可以写写"忧郁坑"。创意写作的评分不过是及格和不及格。

获第三名的短篇宣布了，玛雅抓紧了A.J.的手。

《逮香蕉鱼的最佳日子》

1948/J.D.塞林格

如果什么东西是好的，且普遍被认为如此，这并不是个讨厌它的好理由。（旁注：我花了整整一下午的时间来写这个句子。我的脑子一直在琢磨这个短语："普遍被认为。"）

你参加县里短篇小说竞赛的《海滩一日》让我有点想到塞林格的短篇。我提到这个，是因为我觉得你应该是第一名。获第一名的那篇——我想题目是《奶奶的手》——跟你那篇相比，在形式和叙事上都要简单得多，在感情上更是如此。振作起来，玛雅。作为一个卖书的，我可以向你保证，获奖对销售来说多少有其重要性，但就质量来说很少有关。

——A.J.F.

又及：你这个短篇中最让我感到有希望的，是它体现出了移情作用。为什么人们会做他们所做的事？这是杰出作品的标志。

又又及：如果让我提意见，你也许可以早一点写到游泳。

又又又及：另外，读者知道什么是ATM卡。

海滩一日

作者：玛雅·帖木儿·费克里
指导教师：爱德华·巴尔博尼，艾丽丝镇中学
九年级

玛丽快迟到了。她自己住一间房，可是跟其他六个人共用一个卫生间，卫生间好像总是有人占着。她从卫生间回来时，临时保姆坐在她的床上。"玛丽，我已经等你五分钟了。"

"对不起，"玛丽说，"我想洗个澡，可是进不了卫生间。"

"已经十一点了，"临时保姆说，"你给我的钱只让我待到中午，我十二点一刻还需要去到另一个地方，所以你最好别回来晚了。"

玛丽向临时保姆道了谢。她吻了吻宝宝的头。"听话啊。"她说。

玛丽跑过校园去英语系。她跑上楼梯。她赶到

时，她的老师已经要走了。"玛丽，我正要走，想着你不会来了呢。请进。"

玛丽进了办公室。那位老师拿出玛丽的作业放到办公桌上。"玛丽，"老师说，"你以前一直是得A的，现在你却是每门课都不及格。"

"对不起，"玛丽说，"我以后会努力做得更好。"

"你的生活出了什么变故吗？"老师问，"你以前可是我们最好的学生之一。"

"没有。"玛丽说。她咬着嘴唇。

"你上这所学院有奖学金。可你已经面临麻烦，因为你已经有一阵子成绩不好了，要是我跟学院讲了，他们很可能会取消你的奖学金，或者至少让你休学一段时间。"

"求您别说！"玛丽恳求道，"我没地方可去。除了奖学金我没有别的经济来源。"

"这是为你好，玛丽。你应该回家调整好自己。还有两星期就到圣诞节了。你的父母会理解的。"

玛丽晚了十五分钟才回到宿舍。玛丽进屋时，临时保姆皱着眉。"玛丽，"临时保姆说，"你又迟到了！你一旦迟到了，我要做的事也会迟到。对不起，我很喜欢这个宝宝，但是我觉得我不能再帮你带孩子了。"

玛丽从临时保姆那儿接过孩子。"好吧。"她说。

"另外，"临时保姆补充说，"之前三次看孩子的钱你还没有付我呢。每小时十美元，所以是三十美元。"

"我可以下次付你吗？"玛丽问，"我本来想回来时顺路去一下自动柜员机（ATM）那里，可是我没有时间。"

临时保姆做了个鬼脸。"只用放在信封里，信封上写我的名字，留在我的宿舍就行。我真的想在圣诞节前收到这笔钱，我要买礼物。"

玛丽同意了。

"再见，小宝宝，"临时保姆说，"圣诞节快乐。"

宝宝轻轻地咕哝着。

"你们俩假期有什么特别的计划吗？"临时保姆问。

"我可能会带她去看我妈妈。我妈妈住在康涅狄格州的格林尼治，她总是会弄一棵很大的圣诞树，做美味的晚餐，还有很多很多给我和迈拉的礼物。"

"听着真不错。"临时保姆说。

玛丽把宝宝背在背巾里，走路去了银行。她用她的ATM卡查了她的账户余额，里面有75.17美元。她取了四十美元，然后进银行换零钱。

她把三十美元放进写有临时保姆名字的信封里。她买了地铁票，坐到了终点站。那一带不像玛丽所上的学院一带那样漂亮。

玛丽沿着那条街走到一座破败的房子前，房前有粗钢丝网栅栏。院子里有条狗，被拴在一根柱子上，它朝宝宝吠叫，宝宝哭了起来。

"别怕，宝宝，"玛丽说，"那条狗咬不到你。"

她们进了屋。屋内很脏，到处都是小孩子，他们也脏。那些孩子们吵吵闹闹，年龄大小不一。他们有的坐着轮椅，有的身有残疾。

"嗨，玛丽，"一个残疾女孩说，"你来这儿干吗？"

"我来看妈妈。"玛丽说。

"她在楼上。她不舒服。"

"谢谢。"

"玛丽，那是你的宝宝吗？"那个残疾女孩问。

"不是。"玛丽说。她咬着嘴唇。"我只是在帮一个朋友照看。"

"哈佛大学怎么样？"那个残疾女孩问。

"很棒。"玛丽说。

"我敢说你每科都是A。"

玛丽耸耸肩。

"你总是那么谦虚，玛丽。你还在游泳队吗？"

玛丽又耸耸肩。她上楼去看"妈妈"。

"妈妈"是个胖得病态的白人妇女。玛丽是个瘦得皮包骨头的黑人女孩。"妈妈"不可能是玛丽的生母。

"嗨，妈妈，"玛丽说，"圣诞快乐。"玛丽吻了吻那个胖女人的脸颊。

"嗨，玛丽，名牌大学生小姐啊，没想到你会回到你的寄养家庭。"

"是啊。"

"那是你的宝宝？""妈妈"问。

玛丽叹了口气。"是啊。"

"真可惜，""妈妈"说，"像你这么聪明的女孩把自己的生活搞得一团糟。不是跟你说过千万别上床吗？不是跟你说过永远要采取保护措施吗？"

"是的，妈妈。"玛丽咬着嘴唇，"妈妈，我和宝宝在这里住一段时间可以吗？我已经决定休学一段时间，把我的生活调整好。那对我很有帮助。"

"哦，玛丽。真希望我能帮上忙，可这里已经住满了人。我没有房间可以给你住。对我来说，你年龄大了，马萨诸塞州不会再为了你付我支票的。"

"妈妈，我没有别的地方可以去了。"

"玛丽，我觉得你应该这样做。你应该联系宝宝的父亲。"

玛丽摇摇头。"我真的没那么了解他。"

"那样的话，我觉得你应该把宝宝送给别人收养。"

玛丽又摇摇头。"我也不能那样做。"

玛丽回到宿舍。她为宝宝收拾了一个袋子，把一个艾摩填充玩具塞进袋子。住在楼下走廊的一个女生进了玛丽的房间。

"嗨，玛丽，你要去哪儿？"

玛丽露出灿烂的笑容。"我想要去一趟海边，"她说，"宝宝很喜欢海滩。"

"现在去海滩不是有点冷吗？"那个女孩问。

"不算很冷，"玛丽说，"我和宝宝会穿上我们最暖和的衣服。另外，冬天的海滩真的很不错。"

那个女生耸耸肩。"也许是吧。"

"我小时候，我父亲一年四季都会带我去海滩。"

玛丽把那个信封放到临时保姆的宿舍。在火车站，她用信用卡购买去艾丽丝岛的火车票和船票。

"小宝宝不需要买票。"检票的人告诉玛丽。

"好的。"玛丽说。

到艾丽丝岛后，玛丽看到的第一个地方是一家书店。她走进书店，好让自己和宝宝可以暖和一下。柜台那里有个男人，他举止显得不耐烦，穿了一双匡威运动鞋。

书店里在播放圣诞音乐。那首歌是《祝你过一个小小的快乐圣诞节》。

"这首歌让我听得很悲伤，"一位顾客说，"这是我听过的最悲伤的歌曲。怎么会有人写这样一首悲伤的圣诞歌曲？"

"我在找东西读。"玛丽说。

那个男人稍微没那么不耐烦了。"你喜欢哪类书？"

"哦，各类书，但我最喜欢的，是那种里面有角色遇到困难，不过最后克服了困难的书。我知道生活并非如此，也许就因为这一点，才是我最喜欢看的。"

那位卖书的说他有本绝对适合她的书，可是等他取来那本书时，玛丽已经不在了。"小姐？"

他把那本书放在柜台上，以备玛丽决定回来。

玛丽在海滩上，但是宝宝并没有跟她在一起。

她曾是游泳队的，表现出色，曾在中学时获得过州里的冠军。那天，海浪滔滔，海水冰凉，而玛丽早已疏于练习。

她游了出去，游过灯塔，她没有再游回来。

完

"恭喜。"招待会上，玛雅对约翰·弗内斯说。她手里紧紧抓着卷起来的T恤衫。阿米莉娅拿着玛雅的获奖证书：第三名。

约翰耸了耸肩，他的头发上下起伏了一下。"我本来觉得你应该得第一名，不过他们选了来自艾丽丝镇中学的两篇进终选，挺酷的。"

"也许是巴尔博尼老师教得好。"

"你愿意的话，我们可以平分我的礼券。"约翰说。

玛雅摇了摇头。她不想那样。

"你本来会买什么？"

"我本来是要捐给慈善团体，给贫穷的孩子。"

"真的？"他用上了他那种播报新闻的声音。

"我爸爸不是很喜欢我们在网上买东西。"

"你没有生我的气，对吧？"约翰说。

"没有。我为你感到高兴。加油！"她捶了一下他的肩膀。

"哎哟。"

"回头见。我们还要赶回艾丽丝岛的汽车渡轮。"

"我们也要，"约翰说，"我们有很多时间可以一起出去玩。"

"我爸爸的书店里有事情要处理。"

"学校里见。"约翰说，他又用上了那种播报新闻的语气。

回家的汽车上，阿米莉娅祝贺玛雅凭着一个精彩的短篇获得了名次，A.J.什么都没说。

玛雅认为A.J.肯定是对她感到失望，但就在他们下车前，他说："这种事情从来就不公平。人们喜欢他们所喜欢的，那样很棒，也很糟糕。事关个人趣味和某一天特定的一批人。例如，前三名中有两个女性，这样有可能让天平往男性那边倾斜。要么其中一个评委的奶奶上周去世了，这让那个短篇特别能打动他。谁都不晓得。但是我真切地知道：玛雅·帖木儿·费克里的《海滩一日》是由一位作家写出来的。"她觉得他会要拥抱她，但他只是跟她握了握手，就像他跟一位同事打招呼那样——也许是跟来到书店的一位作家。

她脑海里出现了一句话：父亲跟我握手的那天，我知道我是一名作家。

就在那个学年结束之前，A.J.和阿米莉娅付了一幢房子的订金。那房子离书店有十分钟的路程，离海边更远。尽管有四间卧室、两个卫生间和A.J.认为的一位年轻作家写作所需的安静，但谁都不会觉得那幢房子是梦想之屋。上一任主人死在那里——她不想搬走，但是过去五十年左右，她也没有做多少维修及保养。天花板低，要撕掉好几个年代的壁纸，地基不牢固，等等。A.J.称它为"十年后的房子"，意思是"再过十年，它也许真的能住了"。阿米莉娅称它为"一项工程"，她马上就着手干活。玛雅刚刚好不容易看完《魔戒》三部曲，把这座房子命名为"底袋洞"，"因为它看起来像是一位霍比特人的住所"。

A.J.吻了吻女儿的额头。他为自己培养出这样一个妙不可言的书呆子感到开心。

《泄密的心》

1843/埃德加·爱伦·坡

真的！

玛雅，也许你不知道在阿米莉娅之前，我还有过一位妻子，在我成为一个卖书的人之前，我还有过别的职业。我娶过一个名叫妮可·埃文斯的女孩，我很爱她。她死于一场车祸，之后有很长一段时间，我的很大一部分也死了，很可能直到我遇见你。

我和妮可认识时，都还在读大学。我们赶在升入研究生院前的夏天结了婚。她想当诗人，但同时还在不甚开心地攻读博士学位，研究方向是二十世纪女诗人（阿德里安娜·里奇、玛丽安·摩尔、伊丽莎白·毕肖普；她真是讨厌西尔维娅·普拉斯啊）。我当时也在攻读美国文学的博士学位，我的论文写的是埃德加·爱伦·坡的作品中对疾病的描写，一个我从未特别喜欢并逐渐真心反感的课题。妮可建议道，想要拥有文学生活，可能有更好、更快乐的方式。我说："是嘛，例如呢？"

她说："开书店。"

"说详细点。"我说。

"你知道我老家那里没有书店吗？"

"真的吗？艾丽丝岛那种地方似乎应该有一家书店。"

"我知道，"她说，"一个地方如果没有一家书店，就算不上个地方了。"

我们就这样放弃了研究生学习，取出她的托管基金，搬到了艾丽丝岛，开了这家书店，这就是小岛书店。

我们当时不知道会有什么遭遇，那还用说吗？

妮可出事后有好几年，我经常会想象要是我读完了博士，我的生活会是什么样。

不过我扯远了。

说这一篇是埃德加·爱伦·坡最知名的作品尚有争议。如果你感兴趣想读一读爸爸以前生活中所做之事的话，在一个有蜉蝣标记的箱子里，你可以找到我做的笔记和二十五页论文（大部分是关于《泄密的心》）。

——A.J.F.

"一个故事最让人感觉不舒服的是结尾松散。"副警长道格·李普曼一边说，一边从兰比亚斯准备的开胃食品中挑了四块小蛋奶火腿蛋糕。主持了多年"警长精选读书会"之后，兰比亚斯知道最重要的，甚至比手头的书还要重要的，是食品和饮品。

　　"副警长，"兰比亚斯说，"最多只能拿三块，否则就不够大家吃了。"

　　副警长把一块小蛋奶火腿蛋糕放回碟子上。"嗯，好吧，那把小提琴到底怎么了？我漏读了什么吗？一把无比珍贵的斯特拉迪瓦里①小提琴不可能真的凭空消失。"

　　"说得好，"兰比亚斯说，"还有谁？"

　　"你知道我最讨厌什么吗，"凶杀组的凯西说，"我最讨厌警方毛糙的工作。例如，要是没有人戴手套，我就会叫：闭嘴，你在破坏犯罪现场。"

---

① 斯特拉迪瓦里（Stradivari，1644？-1737），意大利提琴制造家，在型号、种类上颇多创新，其小提琴制造法成为后世的楷模。

"在迪弗的作品中，你就从来不会遇到这个问题。"调度部门西尔维奥说。

"他们要都是迪弗该多好。"兰比亚斯说。

"但是跟糟糕的警方工作相比，我更讨厌的是一切都解决得太快，"凶杀组的凯西接着说，"就算是迪弗也是如此。事情是需要时间才能琢磨出来的。有时是好几年。你得带着一个案子生活好长一段时间。"

"说得好，凯西。"

"对了，小蛋奶火腿蛋糕很好吃。"

"在好市多买的。"兰比亚斯说。

"我讨厌那些女性角色，"消防员罗西说，"女警察总是来自警察家庭，以前当过模特。而且她必定有一个缺点。"

"咬指甲，"凶杀组的凯西说，"头发乱，嘴巴大。"

消防员罗西哈哈大笑。"这是对女性执法人员的凭空想象，就是这样。"

"我说不好，"副警长戴夫说，"我喜欢那种凭空想象。"

"也许作者是想说明那把小提琴并非重点？"兰比亚斯说。

"当然，它就是重点。"副警长戴夫说。

"也许重点是想说明这把提琴怎样影响了每个人的生活？"兰比亚斯又说。

"呸。"消防员罗西说。她做了个大拇指朝下的手势，"呸，呸。"

A.J.从柜台那里听着讨论。小岛书店主办了十二个左右的读书小组，其中"警长精选"是目前为止他最喜欢的。兰比亚斯朝他叫道："支援我一下，A.J.。你并不是每次都得知道是谁偷走了小提琴。"

"按照我的经验，你要是知道的话，一本书会更让人满意，"A.J.说，"不过我自己并不介意含糊一点。"

那群人的欢呼声淹没了他"满意"后面的话。

"叛徒。"兰比亚斯大声说。

这时，风铃响了，伊斯梅进了书店。那群人继续讨论那本书，可是兰比亚斯不由自主地盯着她。她穿了一条白色的夏裙，拖地长裙突出了她纤细的腰身。她的红色头发又长长了，使她脸部的线条柔和了。他想起前妻曾在前面窗户那里种过的兰花。

伊斯梅走向A.J.。她把一张纸放在柜台上。"我终于选好了哪出戏剧，"她说，"我大概需要五十本左右《我们的小镇》[①]。"

"这是部经典。"A.J.说。

丹尼尔·帕里什去世好多年之后的这一天，"警长精选读书会"活动结束后的半小时，兰比亚斯想已经等得够久了，可以专门向A.J.打听一下。"我很不想越界，不过你去问一下你的妻姐，她有没有兴趣跟一个长相还过得去的警官约会？"

"你指的是谁？"

"我。长相还过得去那点是我开玩笑。我知道准确说来，我

---

① 美国剧作家、小说家桑顿·怀尔德（Thornton Wilder, 1897—1975）的经典话剧。

并不是特别抢手。"

"不，我是问你想让我去问谁。阿米莉娅是独生女。"

"不是阿米莉娅。我是说你的前妻姐，伊斯梅。"

"哦，对，伊斯梅。"A.J.犹豫了一下，"伊斯梅？真的？她？"

"是啊，我一直对她有点意思，从高中就开始了。倒不是说她有多注意过我。我想我们都只会越来越老，所以我现在应该把握机会。"

A.J.打电话给伊斯梅问她。

"兰比亚斯？"她问，"他？"

"他是个好人。"A.J.说。

"只是……嗯，我以前从来没跟警察约会过。"伊斯梅说。

"这话开始听着很势利。"

"我没有那意思，只是我对蓝领一直没什么感觉。"

这样说来你跟丹尼尔过得挺好嘛，A.J.想，但是没有说。

"当然，我之前的婚姻是一场灾难。"伊斯梅说。

几天后的一个晚上，她和兰比亚斯在科拉松餐馆吃饭。她点了一份海陆大餐和金汤力。不需要表现出女人味，因为她怀疑不会有第二次约会。

"胃口不错，"兰比亚斯评论道，"我要一样的。"

"那么，"伊斯梅说，"你不当警察的时候干吗？"

"嗯，信不信由你，"他腼腆地说，"我读很多书。也许你会觉得那没什么。我知道你教英语。"

"你读什么书？"伊斯梅问。

"什么都读一点。我一开始读犯罪小说，我猜这很容易想到。但是后来A.J.让我读起了别的书。文学小说，我想你会这么称呼她们。跟我喜欢看的比起来，这种小说的情节不够丰富。说来有点不好意思，可是我喜欢青少年小说，里面情节丰富，感情复杂。另外A.J.读什么，我也会读什么。他偏爱短篇小说……"

"我知道。"

"还有不管玛雅读什么，我也读。我喜欢跟他们讨论那些书。他们是读书人，你知道。我还为别的警察主持一个读书小组。也许你看到过'警长精选'的指示牌？"

伊斯梅摇摇头。

"对不起，我说话太多了。我是紧张了，我想。"

"你挺好的。"伊斯梅呷了一口她的酒，"你有没有读过丹尼尔的书？"

"读过，一本，第一本。"

"你喜欢吗？"

"不算是我的菜。可是写得很好。"

伊斯梅点点头。

"你想念你丈夫吗？"兰比亚斯说。

"不是很想念，"她过了一会儿才说，"有时想念他的幽默感。但是他最好的方面全在他的书中。我想如果我太想他，总是可以去读他的书。不过我还没有想过去读呢。"伊斯梅笑了一下。

"那你读些什么？"

"剧本，偶尔读一点诗。然后是我每年都教的书：《德伯家的苔丝》《约翰尼上战场》《永别了，武器》《为欧文·米尼祈祷》，有些学年读《呼啸山庄》《织工马南》《他们眼望上苍》或者《我的秘密城堡》。这些书就像老朋友。

"不过我选择新书只是自己看的话，我最喜欢的角色是这样的，遥远地方的一个女人，在印度，或者曼谷。有时，她离开自己的丈夫。有时她从未嫁人，因为她睿智地知道婚姻生活不会适合她。我喜欢看到她有好几个情人，喜欢看到她戴着帽子不让阳光晒到她白皙的皮肤，喜欢她去旅行和冒险，喜欢看到对于旅馆、贴着标签的行李箱、食物、衣服和珠宝的描写。有点浪漫因素，但又不过分。故事背景是在过去，没有手机，没有社交网络，根本没有互联网。理想的背景是二十世纪二十年代或者四十年代。也许当时正在打仗，但那只是背景。没有流血，有点性爱，但并不过于绘形绘色。没有孩子，我觉得孩子经常会破坏一个故事。"

"我没有孩子。"兰比亚斯说。

"我并不介意在现实生活中有。我只是不想读到他们。结尾可以是快乐或悲伤的，我不再有所谓了，只要是合情合理的。她可以安定下来，也许做点小生意，要么她可以投海自尽。最后，漂亮的封面很重要。我不关心里面有多好，但一点都不想在难看的东西上花时间。我浅薄，我想。"

"你是长得特别漂亮的女人。"兰比亚斯说。

"我普普通通。"她说。

"绝对不是。"

"长得漂亮不是追求人的好理由，你要知道。我得一天到晚跟我的学生们讲这个。"

"这话可出自一个不读封面丑陋的图书的人之口。"

"嗯，我是在提醒你。我有可能是本封面漂亮但不好看的书。"

他叹息了一声。"我知道几例这种情况。"

"例如呢？"

"我的第一次婚姻。妻子漂亮，但是刻薄。"

"所以你觉得你会同一个错误犯两次？"

"不，你这本书上架已经有好几年了，我读过情节摘要和封底引用的话。一位关心人的老师，教母，正直优秀的社区成员，妹夫及其女儿的照顾者。婚姻不幸，可能是结婚结得太早吧，但是也尽了力。"

"很概括。"她说。

"但是足够让我想读下去。"他朝她微笑，"我们可以点甜品了吗？"

"我确实有很久没做过爱了。"回她家的路上，她在车上说。

"好吧。"兰比亚斯说。

"我想我们应该做爱，"伊斯梅又明确道，"如果你想的话，我是说。"

"我的确想，"兰比亚斯说，"但是如果那意味着我没有机会跟你第二次约会，那我就不想了。我不想为最后得到你的人热身。"

她笑他，领他进了她的卧室。她脱下衣服，灯也没关。她想让他看看一个五十一岁的老女人是什么样子。

兰比亚斯轻轻吹了声口哨。

"你真可爱，但是你应该看看我以前的样子，"她说，"你肯定看到了伤疤。"

从她的膝盖到臀部，有一道长长的伤疤。兰比亚斯用拇指抚摸了一遍，那道伤疤就像玩具娃娃身上的一条缝。"对，我看到了，但它一点也没减少你的魅力。"

她的腿上有十五处骨折，她不得不换掉了右髋关节的关节窝，但是除此之外她都挺好。丹尼尔这辈子总算有一次承担起了撞击的力量。

"现在还很疼吗？"兰比亚斯问，"要我轻点吗？"

她摇摇头，让他也脱掉衣服。

第二天早上她先醒。"我去给你做早餐。"她说。他迷迷糊糊地点头，然后她吻了一下他剃过的头。

"你剃光头是因为谢顶，还是因为喜欢光头？"她问。

"都有一点。"兰比亚斯回答道。

她把毛巾放到床上后离开了卧室。兰比亚斯不慌不忙地收拾自己。他打开她的床头柜抽屉，翻了一下她的东西。她有几种看上去价格不菲的化妆品，闻着就像她身上的味道。他抹了一些在自己手上。他打开她的衣橱。她的衣服很小。有丝质裙子、熨好的棉布上衣、羊毛紧身裙和像纸一样薄的开司米开襟羊毛衫。全都是颜色偏明亮的米色和灰白色，她的衣服收拾得干干净净。他看着衣橱里最上面的一格，她的鞋子放在原装盒子里整整齐齐地摆着。在其中一摞鞋子上面，他注意到有个很小的粉红色儿童背囊。

他的警察目光锁定了那个儿童背囊，因为它有点跟那里不相协调。他知道自己不应该，但还是把它抽了下来，拉开拉链。里面的拉链袋里有蜡笔和几本涂色书。他拿起那本涂色书，封面上写着"玛雅"。涂色书下面是另外一本书，薄薄的，更像是一本小册子，而不是一本书。兰比亚斯看封面：

帖木儿

及

其他诗歌

一位波士顿人 著

封面有一道道蜡笔画过的痕迹。

兰比亚斯不知道这是怎么回事。

他的警察大脑开始转动，形成了以下问题：1）这是A.J.被偷走的《帖木儿》吗？2）为什么《帖木儿》在伊斯梅手里？3）《帖木儿》上面怎么有蜡笔画过，谁画过？玛雅？4）为什么《帖木儿》放在一个有玛雅名字的背囊里？

他正要跑下楼让伊斯梅解释，却又改变了主意。

他再花了几秒钟看着那本古老的书。

在坐着的地方，他能闻到薄煎饼的香味，他想象得出她在楼下做煎饼。她很可能系着一条白色围裙，穿了件丝质睡衣；或者只穿着围裙，别的什么都没穿。那可真让人兴奋。也许他们可以再做一次爱，不是在厨房的餐桌上。无论在电影里多么有情色味道，在厨房的餐桌上做爱还是不舒服。也许在沙发上，也许再上楼。她的床垫很软，她的床单的纱线支数肯定有几千。

兰比亚斯为自己是个好警察感到自豪，他知道自己现在应该下楼，编个借口告诉她自己为什么要走。

可那是榨橙汁的声音吗？她也在热糖浆吗？

那本书被毁坏了。

除此之外，它是很久很久以前被偷走的，到现在已经超过十年了。A.J.婚姻美满。玛雅安定下来了。伊斯梅也受过苦。

更别提，他是真的很喜欢这个女人。无论如何，这全都跟兰比亚斯无关。他把那本书放回背囊，拉好拉链，然后把背囊放回原来的地方。

兰比亚斯认为警察渐老时，要么喜欢多嘴，要么反过来。兰比亚斯已不像年轻时那么顽固了。他发现人们会做出各种各样的事，通常自有其理由。

他下楼，坐到她的餐桌前，那是张圆餐桌，铺着他见过的最白的桌布。"闻着真香。"他说。

"能给人做东西吃挺好的。你在上面待了挺久啊。"她说着给他倒了一杯鲜榨橙汁。她的围裙是青绿色，她穿着黑色健身衣。

"嗨，"兰比亚斯说，"你有没有刚好读过玛雅参加比赛的短篇小说？我还以为这孩子十拿九稳会得第一名呢。"

"还没读过。"伊斯梅说。

"基本上就是玛雅认为的她妈妈生命中的最后一天。"兰比亚斯说。

"她一直特别早熟。"伊斯梅说。

"我总是纳闷玛雅的妈妈为什么选了艾丽丝岛。"

伊斯梅把一张薄煎饼翻了个面，然后把另一张也翻了个面。"谁知道人们做事情都是怎么想的？"

《铁头》

2005/艾梅·本德[1]

需要指出的是，新生的一切并非都比老旧的糟糕。

南瓜脑子的父母有个铁脑袋的孩子。我最近对这篇想得比较多，我想原因很明显。

——A.J.F.

又及：我还发现自己在考虑托拜厄斯·沃尔夫的《脑子中的子弹》。你或许也可以去读下那篇。

---

[1] 艾梅·本德（Aimee Bender，1969— ），美国作家，短篇小说家。

A.J.的母亲圣诞节来了，她跟他一点都不像。保拉是个身材小小的白人妇女，一头长长的灰色头发，自从她十年前从电脑公司退休后，就再没有剪过。她退休后大部分时间都在亚利桑那州度过。她在石头上画画，然后做成首饰，为监狱里的人扫盲，拯救西伯比亚狗，每个星期都会尝试一家新的餐馆。她跟几个人约会，男女都有。她逐渐变成了双性恋，也没觉得有什么大不了的。她七十岁了，她信奉的是要尝试新事物，否则还不如死了。她来时带着三个包装一样、形状也一样的礼物给儿子一家，她还保证说并不是有欠考虑才让她为他们三个人选了同样的礼物。"只是我觉得这是你们都会看重并使用的东西。"她说。

　　还没有把包装纸拆完，玛雅就知道是什么东西。

　　她在学校里见过，似乎现在人手一个这玩意儿，可是她爸爸不赞成用。她放慢了拆礼物的速度，好让自己有时间想出如何回应才不会惹恼她的奶奶还有爸爸。

"电子阅读器！我想要很久了。"她很快地瞄了一眼她的爸爸。他点点头，不过稍微皱起了眉头。"谢谢奶奶。"玛雅吻了吻奶奶的脸。

"谢谢，费克里妈妈。"阿米莉娅说。她因为工作需要已经有了个电子阅读器，但是她没有讲。

A.J.一看到是什么，决定不拆礼物了。如果他留着包装，也许可以送给别人。"谢谢你，妈妈。"A.J.说，然后一言不发。

"A.J.，你噘着嘴。"他的母亲说。

"我没有。"他坚持说。

"你一定要跟上时代。"她又说。

"我干吗一定要？时代有什么了不起？"A.J.经常在想这一点，就像肉上的脂肪一样，世界上的好东西都被一点一点地割走了。首先是唱片店，接着是录像带出租店，然后是报纸和杂志，现在目光所及的处处，就连那些大型连锁书店也正在消失。在他看来，唯一一件比世界上有大型连锁书店更糟的事是世界上没有任何大型连锁书店。至少大型书店卖的是书，而不是药物和无用的废物！至少在那里上班的一些人拥有英语文学的学位，知道怎样读书和理书！至少那些大型书店能够卖一万本出版社的垃圾书，而小岛书店也能卖一百本文学小说！

"最快变老的方式，就是在技术上落伍，A.J.。"他的母亲在电脑公司工作了二十五年后，带着令人艳羡的退休金和这个观念退休了，A.J.不为所动地想。

A.J.做了次深呼吸，喝了一大口水，又做了次深呼吸。他感觉自己的脑子紧紧地顶着颅骨。他的母亲很少来，他不想破坏他们在一起的时光。

"爸爸，你有点脸红了。"玛雅说。

"A.J.，你没事吧？"他的母亲问。

他把拳头放在咖啡桌上。"妈妈，你到底明不明白那个可恨的东西正在大肆搞破坏，不只是破坏我的生意，而且更糟糕的是，还会导致多少个世纪充满活力的文学文化粗暴而快速地衰落？"A.J.问。

"你夸大其词了，"阿米莉娅说，"冷静。"

"我为什么要冷静？我不喜欢这件礼物。我不喜欢那种玩意儿，当然也不喜欢我家里一出现就是三个。我宁愿你送我女儿破坏性小点的东西，例如嗑药用具。"

玛雅咯咯笑了。

A.J.的母亲看上去就要哭了，"嗯，我当然没想让任何人不高兴。"

"没事，"阿米莉娅说，"这件礼物很可爱。我们都喜欢读书，我敢说我们都会很喜欢使用。另外，A.J.真的是夸大其词了。"

"对不起，A.J.，"他的母亲说，"我不知道你对这件事有这么大的意见。"

"你可以先问一下的！"

"别再说了，A.J.；别再道歉了，费克里妈妈，"阿米莉娅说，"这是给都爱读书的一家人的绝佳礼物。有很多书店都在想办法既卖传统的纸质书，也卖电子书。A.J.只是不想……"

A.J.打断她的话："你知道那是胡说八道，艾米！"

"你很没礼貌，"阿米莉娅说，"你不能不认清现实，表现得好像那些电子阅读器不存在似的，那根本不是处理事情的方法。"

"你们闻到了烟味吗？"玛雅问。

一秒种后，火警报警器响了。

"哦，要命！"阿米莉娅说，"牛胸肉！"她跑进厨房，A.J.跟着她。"我在手机上定了时间，可手机没有响。"

"我把你的手机调了静音，好让它别毁了圣诞节！"A.J.说。

"你做了什么？别再碰我的手机。"

"为什么不用烤炉内置的定时器？"

"因为我信不过它！如果你没有注意到，那烤炉跟这座房子里的所有东西一样，有差不多一百年了。"阿米莉娅一边大声说，一边把烧着的牛胸肉从炉子里取出来。

因为牛胸肉烤坏了，圣诞节晚餐吃的全是配菜。

"我最喜欢配菜。"A.J.的妈妈说。

"我也是。"玛雅说。

"一点儿不实在，"A.J.嘟囔道，"吃了还饿。"他感到头疼，喝了几杯红葡萄酒也无助于缓解头疼。

"谁来让A.J.把酒递过来？"阿米莉娅说，"谁来告诉A.J.他一直在霸着那瓶酒？"

"很成熟啊。"A.J.说。他又给她倒了一杯酒。

"我真等不及想试用一下，奶奶，"玛雅跟她受到打击的奶奶低语，"我等到上床睡觉时就会用。"她朝A.J.瞄了一眼，"你知道的。"

"我觉得那是个很好的主意。"A.J.的母亲也悄悄说。

那天夜里在床上时，A.J.还在谈论电子阅读器。"你知道电子阅读器真正的问题是在哪里吗？"

"我想你正要告诉我呢。"阿米莉娅说，并没有从她正在看的纸质书中抬起头来。

"每个人都觉得自己品位不错，但是大多数人并没有好品位。事实上，我个人觉得大多数人的品位都很糟糕。如果由着他们自个儿来——完全由着他们自个儿来——他们会读垃圾书，而且分不出差别。"

"你知道电子阅读器哪一点好吗？"阿米莉娅问。

"不知道，'乐观派女士'，"A.J.说，"而且我也不想知道。"

"嗯，对于我们中间那些其丈夫越来越远视的人来说，我在这里就不点名字了；对于我们中间那些其丈夫正在迅速步入中年且视力下降的人来说；对于我们中间那些其伴侣是可悲的中年男人……"

"说重点，艾米！"

"电子阅读器可以让这些运气糟透的人想把正文放多大就放多大。"

A.J.一言不发。

阿米莉娅放下书，得意地微笑着看着丈夫，然而等她再留意去看，那一位已经呆住了。A.J.正遭受他的间歇性发作。这些发作让阿米莉娅感到不安，虽然她提醒自己不用担心。

过了一分钟半的时间，A.J.恢复过来。"我一直有点远视，"他说，"这跟步入中年无关。"

她用纸巾擦去他嘴角的口水。

"天哪，我刚才失去意识了吗？"A.J.问。

"是的。"

他从阿米莉娅手里抓过纸巾。他不是喜欢被人如此照顾的那种人。"有多久？"

"大约有九十秒，我想。"阿米莉娅顿了一下，"时间过长还是正常？"

"也许有点久，但从根本上说来是正常的。"

"你觉得要去检查一下吗？"

"不。"A.J.说。"你知道从我还是少孩时起就会这样。"

"少孩？"她问。

"小孩。我说什么了？"A.J.下床朝卫生间走去，阿米莉娅跟着他。"拜托，艾米，给我点空间。"

"我不想给你空间。"她说。

"好吧。"

"我想让你去看医生。感恩节以来已经发作三次了。"

A.J.摇摇头。**我的健康保险很垃圾，亲爱的艾米**。不管怎样，罗森医生会说跟我多年以来的毛病一模一样。我会在三月份年度体检时去看医生，像一贯的那样。"

阿米莉娅进了卫生间。"也许罗森医生会给你开点新药？"她挤到他和卫生间镜子之间，把她大大的屁股放到新的双洗手池台面上，那是他们上个月才安装的。"你很重要，A.J.。"

"我又不是什么总统呢。"他回答道。

"你是玛雅的爸爸，是我生命中的爱人，还是这个社区的文化传播者。"

A.J.翻翻眼珠子，然后吻住"乐观派女士"阿米莉娅的嘴。

圣诞节和新年都过去了；A.J.的母亲愉快地回了亚利桑那州；玛雅又去上学了；阿米莉娅也回去工作了。A.J.想，节日假期真正的礼物，是它有结束之时。他喜欢按部就班，喜欢早上做早餐，喜欢跑步去上班。

他穿上跑步的衣服，应付地做了几个拉伸动作，把束发带一下子拉到耳朵后面，把背包带扣好，准备跑步去书店。现在他不再住在书店上面，他的跑步路线跟他以前的跑步路线方向相反，所谓以前，包括妮可还活着、玛雅还很小和他跟阿米莉娅结婚后的头几年。

他跑过了伊斯梅家的房子，以前她跟丹尼尔住在那里，现在跟兰比亚斯一起住，真是不可思议。他也跑过了丹尼尔丧命的地点。他跑过了以前的舞蹈房。那位舞蹈老师叫什么名字？他知道她前不久搬去了加利福尼亚，舞蹈房那里没人。他想知道以后谁会来教艾丽丝岛的小姑娘们跳舞呢？他跑过了玛雅的小学，跑过了她的初中，跑过了她的高中。高中。她有了个男朋友，那个姓弗内斯的男孩会写东西。他听到他们整天都在争论。他抄近路穿过一块田野，快要穿过去到达威金斯船长街时，他失去了知觉。

当时室外只有零下五六摄氏度。他醒来时，手部挨着冰的地方变青了。

他站起来，在外套上捂热双手。他从来没有在跑步时昏厥过去。

"奥伦斯卡夫人。"他说。

罗森医生给他作了全面检查。相对他的年龄而言，A.J.挺健康的，但是他的眼睛有点奇怪之处，让医生停了下来。

"你还有别的问题吗？"她问。

"嗯……也许只是变老了，但是最近我好像时不时就会有口误。"

"口误？"她说。

"我能意识到，没那么严重，可我偶尔会把一个词说成别的，例如把'小孩'说成'少孩'。还有上个星期，我把《愤怒的葡萄》说成了《垃圾葡萄柚》。显然，这样会给我的工作带来一些问题。我相当确信我当时说的话没错。我妻子觉得也许有抗发作的药物能管点用？"

"失语症，"她说，"我不喜欢这个词的发音。"鉴于A.J.的发病史，医生决定送他去波士顿的一位脑科专家那里。

"莫莉怎么样？"为了转移话题，A.J.问。到现在，这个莽撞无礼的女店员为他打工已经是六七年前的事了。

"她刚刚被录取到……"这位医生说了个写作项目的名称，但是A.J.没有认真听。他在想着自己的大脑。他觉得这挺怪，他得使用也许有问题的东西来考虑有问题的东西。"……觉得自己就要写出伟大的美国长篇小说了。我想我要怪到妮可和你的头上。"医生说。

"全责。"A.J.说。

多形性胶质母细胞瘤。

"你介意帮我写下来吗？"A.J.问道。这次约诊，他是一个人来的。在确定病情之前，他不想让任何人知道。"我想之后上谷歌搜索一下。"

这种肿瘤极为罕见，马萨诸塞州总医院的肿瘤学家从未见到过一个病例，除了在学术出版物和电视剧《实习医生格蕾》中。

"出版物中提到的那个病人怎么样了？"A.J.问。

"死了。活了两年。"那位肿瘤学家说。

"那两年过得好吗？"

"我会说第一年挺好。"

A.J.想再听听另一种意见。"电视剧里呢？"

肿瘤学家哈哈笑了，像链锯一般喧嚣的笑声，成为房间里最响亮的声音。瞧瞧，肿瘤，还能令人捧腹。"我认为我们不应该根据晚间肥皂剧来进行预测，费克里先生。"

"怎么了？"

"我相信病人做了手术，活了一两集，认为自己没有危险了，就向他当医生的女朋友求婚。后来显然是心脏病发作，跟脑瘤毫无关系，下一集就死了。"

"哦。"

"我的妹妹是电视编剧，我相信电视编剧称之为'三集曲'。"

"这么说，我应该指望活三集电视剧到两年之间。"

肿瘤学家链锯般的笑声又响了起来。"好，关键是要有幽默感。我要说你这样估计听着是正确的。"肿瘤学家想马上安排做手术。

"马上？"

"你的症状被你发病所掩盖，费克里先生。扫描显示肿瘤已经长得很大了。我要是你，就不会再等。"

手术的费用几乎跟他们买房的订金一样高。尚不清楚A.J.微薄的小企业主保险会支付多少。"如果我做手术，能给我买来多少时间？"A.J.问。

"取决于我们能取出多少。如果能清除得很干净，那就是十年。如果做不到，也许是两年。你长的这种肿瘤有复发倾向，十分讨厌。"

"如果你成功地清除了那玩意儿，我会不会成为植物人？"

"我们不喜欢使用像'植物人'那样的术语，费克里先生。不过它长在你左脑的前叶上。你可能会偶尔出现言语失误，失语症越来越严重，等等。可是我们不会取出那么多，以至于让你很大程度上不是你自己了。当然，如果不治疗，肿瘤会长得直到你的大脑语言中枢基本上完全失灵。不管怎么样，无论我们治疗还是不治疗，这种情况最终都很有可能发生。"

古怪的是，A.J.想到了普鲁斯特[①]。尽管他假装通读了《追忆似水年华》，其实他只读了第一卷。光读第一卷就有些吃力，此刻他想到的是，至少我再也不用去读剩下的几卷了。"我得跟我的妻子和女儿商量一下。"他说。

---

① 马塞尔·普鲁斯特（Marcel Proust，1871-1922），法国作家，七卷本的《追忆似水年华》为他的代表作。

"对，当然要，"那位肿瘤学家说，"但是别耽误得太久。"

先是坐火车，然后是坐渡轮，在回艾丽丝岛的一路上，A.J.都在考虑玛雅上大学的费用和阿米莉娅是否有能力支付他们买了不到一年的那幢房子的分期付款。等到他走在威金斯船长街上时，他想好了如果做手术会让他最亲近最心爱的人一文不名，他宁可不做手术。

A.J.暂时不想回家面对他的家人，他就打电话给兰比亚斯，两个人在酒吧见面。

"给我讲一个好的警察故事。"A.J.说。

"是要听关于一个好警察的故事呢，还是涉及到警察的有趣的故事？"

"都行，随你。我想听点有意思的东西，好让我分散一下心思，不去想自己的问题。"

"你有什么问题？完美的妻子，完美的孩子，生意也不错。"

"我晚点再跟你说。"

兰比亚斯点点头。"好吧，让我想想。也许是十五年前的事了，有这么一个孩子，在艾丽丝镇上学。他有一个月没去学校了。每天他都告诉他的父母他去上学了，而每天他都没有出现。就算他们把他留在学校，他也会溜走去别的地方。"

"他去哪儿？"

"对。父母想着他肯定是惹了什么很大的麻烦。他是个难对付的孩子，跟一群难缠的人混在一起。他们全都成绩差，穿低腰裤。他的父母在海滩上经营一个小吃摊，所以家里也没多少钱。反正，他的父母束手无策，于是我就决定跟踪这个小孩一整天。这个小孩去上学，第一节下课后，他就走了。我尾随在他后面，最后我们到了一座建筑前，以前我从来没有进去过。我当时在主街和帕克街的路口。你知道我在哪里吗？"

"那是图书馆。"

"猜对了。你知道当时我从来不怎么读书。我就跟着他上了台阶，进了后面的一间图书馆研究室，我当时想着，他很可能要在那里嗑药什么的。绝佳的地点，对吧？与世隔绝。可是你知道他拿了什么吗？"

"书，我想应该是这样。那是显然的，不是吗？"

"他拿了本厚厚的书。他把《无尽的玩笑》读了一半。你听说过这本书吗？"

"哎，这是你编出来的。"

"那个男孩在读《无尽的玩笑》。他说他没法在家里读，因为他有五个弟弟妹妹要照看。他没法在学校里看，因为他的朋友会笑话他。所以他逃学，去安安静静地读。那本书需要很专心地阅读。'听着，hombre①，'他说，'学校对我而言一无是处。

---

① 西班牙语，"老兄"的意思。

一切都在这本书里。'"

"我知道了，他是拉美人，因为你用了'hombre'这个词。艾丽丝岛上有很多拉美人吗？"

"有几个。"

"那你怎么办呢？"

"我把他拎回学校。校长问我该怎样惩罚那个孩子。我问那个孩子他觉得还需要多久才能看完那本书。他说：'两星期左右吧。'我就建议他们以行为不良为由，让他停学两个星期。"

"这绝对是你编出来的。"A.J.说。"承认吧。这个问题少年才不会跷课去读《无尽的玩笑》。"

"他的确是的，A.J.，我向上帝发誓。"但是兰比亚斯接着就放声大笑，"你看上去情绪低落啊，我想给你讲个能振奋一点你精神的故事。"

"谢谢。非常感谢。"

A.J.又要了杯啤酒。

"你想告诉我什么？"

"有意思的是你会提到《无尽的玩笑》。对了，你为什么单单选了那本书？"A.J.说。

"我总是在书店里看到它，在书架上占了好大一片地方。"

A.J.点点头。"我曾经为这本书跟我的一个朋友大吵一架。他很喜欢这本书，我却很讨厌。但是关于这场争论，最滑稽的，我现在要向你坦白的是……"

"什么？"

"我一直没有读完那本书。" A.J.笑了起来，"那本书，还有普鲁斯特都可以继续待在我的未读完书单上，感谢上帝。对了，我的大脑坏掉了。"他取出那张纸条读道："多形性胶质母细胞瘤。它会把你变成植物人，然后你就死了。不过至少来得快。"

兰比亚斯放下啤酒，"肯定可以做手术什么的。"他说。

"是可以，但是要花一大堆钱。而且不管怎么样，只是推迟死亡而已。我不会只是为了多活几个月，就让艾米和玛雅一贫如洗。"

兰比亚斯喝完啤酒，向酒保示意再来一杯。"我觉得你应该让她们自己决定。"兰比亚斯说。

"她们会感情用事的。" A.J.说。

"那就让她们感情用事。"

"对我来说，正确的做法，我觉得，就是把我的破大脑给一枪崩了。"

兰比亚斯摇摇头，"你会那样对玛雅吗？"

"对她来说，有一个脑死亡的父亲会好过没钱上大学吗？"

那天夜里上床关灯之后，兰比亚斯把伊斯梅拉向自己。"我爱你，"他告诉她，"我想让你知道，你过去也许做过什么，但我不会计较。"

"好吧，"伊斯梅说，"我快睡着了，不知道你在讲什么。"

"我知道衣橱里的那个包，"兰比亚斯悄声说，"我知道里面有那本书。我不知道它怎么会到了那里，也不需要知道。但只有这样做才正确，那就是还给合法的主人。"

过了好久，伊斯梅说："那本书已经毁了。"

"即使是一本受损的《帖木儿》，可能也值点钱，"兰比亚斯说，"我在克里斯蒂拍卖行的网站上搜过，上一本在市场上卖了五十六万美元。所以我想也许受损的一本会值五万美元左右。A.J.和艾米需要这笔钱。"

"他们为什么需要这笔钱？"

他跟她说了A.J.肿瘤的事，伊斯梅用手捂住了脸。

"照我看，"兰比亚斯说，"我们把那本书上的指纹抹掉，放进信封里还回去。谁都不用知道它来自何处，来自于谁。"

伊斯梅打开床头灯。"这件事你已经知道多久了？"

"从我在你家第一次过夜后就知道。"

"而你无所谓？你为什么不告发我？"伊斯梅的眼神凌厉。

"因为那跟我无关，伊西。我不是作为警察被邀请到你家的。我无权翻看你的东西。我想里面肯定有什么故事。你是个好女人，伊斯梅，你也过得不容易。"

伊斯梅坐了起来，她双手颤抖。她走到衣橱前把那个包拉了下来。"我想让你知道发生了什么事。"她说。

"我不需要知道。"兰比亚斯说。

"求你了，我想让你知道。也别打岔。你打岔的话，我就没办法全讲出来了。"

"好吧，伊西。"他说。

"玛丽安·华莱士第一次来见我时，我当时怀孕五个月。她带着玛雅，那个宝宝两岁上下。玛丽安·华莱士很年轻，很漂亮，个头很高，金褐色的双眼透着疲惫。她说：'玛雅是丹尼尔的女儿。'我说——我并没有为此感到自豪——'我怎么知道你不是在撒谎？'我看得一清二楚她没在撒谎。我毕竟了解自己的丈夫，知道他那种人。从我们结婚那天起他就出轨，在结婚之前很可能也是如此。可是我很喜欢他的书，或者说至少是第一本吧。我感觉在他内心深处，写了那本书的那个人肯定在那里。你不可能写了那么出色的一本书，却有如此丑陋的一颗心。可事实就是那样，他是个出色的作家，人品却很糟糕。

"但是我不能把这全怪到丹尼尔头上。我不能把我在其中所扮演的角色也怪到他头上。我朝玛丽安·华莱士尖叫。她二十二岁了，但看起来还像个孩子。'找上门来说有了丹尼尔的孩子，你以为你是第一个这样的骚货？'

"她道歉，不停地道歉。她说：'这个孩子并不是非得出现在丹尼尔·帕里什的生活中'——她一直连名带姓地称呼他。她是个书迷，你要明白。她尊敬他。'这个孩子并不是非得出现在丹尼尔·帕里什的生活中。我们再也不会麻烦你们了，我向上帝发誓。我们只需要一点钱来起步，继续过活。他说过他会帮忙，而现在我哪儿都找不到他。'这话我听着有道理。丹尼尔一直到处跑来跑去——在瑞士的一所学校当驻校作家，一趟趟去洛杉矶，但是都没有什么结果。

"'好吧，'我说，'我会尽量联系上他，看看我能做点什么。要是他承认你讲的是真话——'可我当时已经知道是真话，兰比亚斯！'要是他承认你讲的是真话，也许我们可以做点什么。'那个女孩想知道她怎样联系我最好，我跟她说我会联系她。

"那天晚上我跟丹尼尔通了电话。聊得挺好，我没有提玛丽安·华莱士的事。丹尼尔很关心我，并且开始为我们自己孩子的出生做一些计划。'伊斯梅，'他说，'宝宝一出生，我就会变个人。'这话我以前就听他说过。'不，我是认真的，'他坚称，'我绝对会少去外地，要待在家里，写更多，照顾你和这个土豆。'他总是很会说话，我也想去相信从这个晚上开始，我婚姻中的一切都会改变。我就在彼时彼刻决定了我会去处理玛丽安·华莱士这个问题。我会想办法收买她。

"这个镇上的人们总是以为我家有钱，比实际的更有钱。我和妮可的确各自有笔小小的托管基金，但也不是特别多。妮可用她的托管基金买了书店，我用我的买了这幢房子。我这边剩下来的钱，我丈夫花得很快。他的第一本书畅销，但是后面的书就没那么畅销，他还老是生活讲究，收入却不稳定，我只是个中学老师。我和丹尼尔总是看上去有钱，可实际上穷。

"山下呢，我妹妹死了一年多，她的丈夫正在一步步把自己喝死。出于对妮可的义务，我会在有些晚上去看看A.J.怎么样。我自己开门进去，抹掉他脸上沾的呕吐物，把他拖上床。有天夜里，我进去了。A.J.像通常那样不醒人事，而《帖木儿》就放在桌子上。在此，我应该提提他发现《帖木儿》的那天，是我跟他一起去的。他从来没提过要分给我一点钱，但可能那样做才像话。要不是因为我，这个小气的家伙根本就不会去那个资产拍卖会。我就把A.J.弄到床上，去客厅把那个烂摊子清理干净，我把什么都擦掉了，最后所做的，也没有怎么去想，就是把那本书塞进了我的袋子。

　　"第二天，每个人都在找《帖木儿》，可是我不在岛上。那天我去了剑桥，去了玛丽安·华莱士的宿舍，把那本书扔到她的床上。我告诉她：'听着，你可以把这个卖了，它值很多钱。'她怀疑地看着那本书，说：'来路有问题吗？'我说：'不，它是丹尼尔的，他想送给你，但是你绝对不能讲你是从哪儿得到的。拿去拍卖行或者找个珍本书经销商，就说你是在什么地方的旧书箱里找到的。'我有段时间再没有玛丽安·华莱士的消息，我想也许就那样结束了。"伊斯梅的声音低了下来。

　　"但是事情并没有结束，对吧？"兰比亚斯问。

　　"对。就在圣诞节前，她带着玛雅还有那本书又来到我家。她说她去找了波士顿地区所有的拍卖行和经销商，没有一家想经手这本书，因为它没有来源证明，而且警方在打电话询问一本失窃的《帖木儿》。她从包里取出那本书递给我，我扔回给她。'我拿这本书有什么用？'玛丽安·华莱士只是摇着头。那本书掉到地上，那个小女孩把它捡起来开始翻看，但是根本没有人注意她。玛丽安·华莱士大大的琥珀色眼睛里涌满了泪水，她说：'您读过《帖木儿》了吗，帕里什太太？它写得很悲伤。'我摇头。'这首诗是关于一个突厥征服者，他为了得到权力，用自己生命中的爱人——一个可怜的乡下女孩——做了笔交易。'我说：'你觉得我们这里就是这种情况？你想象自己是个可怜的乡下女孩，我是卑鄙的妻子，把你和你生命中的爱人拆散？'

'不。'她说。就在那时，那个小孩哭了起来。玛丽安说最糟糕的，是她知道自己在干什么。丹尼尔去她就读的学校开过朗诵会，她很喜欢那本书，她跟他睡觉时，已经读过上百万遍他的作者小传，也完全知道他是有妇之夫。'我犯了很多错误。'她说。'我帮不了你。'我说。她摇摇头，抱起那个孩子。'我们不会再妨碍您了，'她说，'圣诞快乐。'

"她们就走了。我很受触动，我就进厨房，给自己泡了点茶。等我从厨房出来进客厅时，注意到那个小女孩把背囊落下了，《帖木儿》在背囊旁边的地板上。我捡起那本书，想着我只用第二天或者第二天晚上溜进A.J.的住处，把书还回去就行。这时我注意到书上有蜡笔的画痕。那个小女孩毁了它！我拉开背囊的拉链把书放进去，把背囊放进衣橱。我没有刻意藏得很好，想着也许丹尼尔会发现并问及此事，但是他从来没有。他从来不关心。那天夜里，A.J.打电话来问该给小孩子吃什么东西。玛雅在他家里，我同意赶过去。"

"第二天，玛丽安·华莱士被冲到了灯塔那里。"兰比亚斯说。

"对，我等着看丹尼尔会说什么，看他会不会认出那个女孩，认那个小孩是他的。但是他没有。而我，懦弱如我，也一直再没有提起这件事。"

兰比亚斯搂过她。"这一切都没有关系，"过了一会儿他说，"就算那是犯罪的话……"

"那的确是犯罪。"她坚称。

"就算那是犯罪的话，"他又说了一遍，"对这件事有一点点了解的人都死了。"

"除了玛雅。"

"事实证明玛雅过得很好。"兰比亚斯说。

伊斯梅摇摇头。"是这样的，对吗？"

"照我看，"兰比亚斯说，"你偷那本书时，算是救了A.J.费克里一命。至少我是这么觉得的。"

"你算是哪门子警察啊？"伊斯梅问。

"老式的。"他说。

第二天夜里，就像过去十年里每个月的第三个星期三一样，"警长精选读书会"在小岛书店举行活动。一开始是警察们不情不愿地参加，但是一年年过去，这个小组越来越受欢迎。到如今，它是小岛书店举办的参与人数最多的图书聚会。读书会中还是警察最多，不过他们的妻子甚至他们的孩子——在他们岁数够大时——也会参加。几年前，兰比亚斯定了一条"缴械在外"的规矩，在此之前，《尘雾家园》[①]引起了特别激烈的争论，以至于有位年轻的警察拔枪对准了另外一位警察。（兰比亚斯后来对A.J.反思说那本书选得不对。"那本书里有个有趣的警察角色，但是有太多地方是非不明。从现在起，我要坚持选择轻松一点的那类。"）除了那场事故，这个小组中一直没有出现暴力，当然书中的内容除外。

按照他的惯例，兰比亚斯提前到书店来准备"警长精选读书会"活动，也跟A.J.聊聊天。"我看到这个放在门口。"兰比亚斯进门时说。他把一个内有衬垫的马尼拉纸信封交给他的朋友，信封上写着A.J.的名字。

"无非又是一本样书而已。"A.J.说。

"别那样说，"兰比亚斯开玩笑道，"里面有可能是一本超级畅销书。"

"是啊，我肯定。这很可能是伟大的美国长篇小说。我会把它加到我那一堆书里：'在我的大脑失灵前要读的东西。'"

A.J.把那个包裹放在柜台上，兰比亚斯看着它。"这种事从

---

① 美国作家、短篇小说家安德烈·迪比三世（Andre Dubus III，1959- ）的代表作品。

来说不准。"兰比亚斯说。

"我就像是个在约会阶段待了太久的女孩。我已经有过太多次失望，得到过太多次'非我莫属'这样的允诺，但从来都不是。你当警察，难道不会变成那样吗？"

"哪样？"

"愤世嫉俗，我想，"A.J.说，"你难道没有变得整天都想看到人们身上最糟糕的方面？"

兰比亚斯摇摇头。"没有。我见到的人们身上好坏参半。"

"好吧，给我说几个这样的人。"

"像你这样的人，我的朋友。"兰比亚斯清清喉咙，A.J.无言以对。"有什么不错的我还没有读过的犯罪小说？我需要为'警长精选'新挑几本。"

A.J.走到犯罪小说那一区。他望向那一排书脊，大多数都是黑、红两色，全都印着大写的银色和白色字，偶尔会有荧光色来打破这种单调。A.J.想到这类犯罪类型小说的方方面面都多么类似啊。为什么一本书会跟别的书不一样呢？它们是不一样的，A.J.总结道，因为它们的确不一样。我们得多看看书的内容。我们得去相信。我们时常接受失望，这样我们才能不断地重整旗鼓。

他选了一本书，伸过去递给他的朋友。"也许这本？"

《当我们谈论爱情时我们在谈论什么》

1980/雷蒙德·卡佛

　　两对夫妇越喝越醉；讨论什么是爱，什么不是爱。

　　有个问题我考虑了很多，那就是为什么我们写我们不喜欢、讨厌、承认有缺点的事物，要比写我们喜爱的事物容易得多★。这是我最喜欢的一个短篇，玛雅，然而我还无法讲出原因何在。

　　（你和阿米莉娅也是我最喜欢的人。）

——A.J.F.

　　★当然，这也解释了互联网利弊的很多方面。

"拍卖品2200号。今天下午拍卖会最后一刻增加的拍品，对于古旧书收藏者来说，这是个极其难得的机会。埃德加·爱伦·坡所著的《帖木儿及其他诗歌》。坡十八岁时写的这篇，署名为'一位波士顿人'，当时只印了五十本。在任何稍具规模的珍本书收藏中，《帖木儿》都会是王冠上的珍珠。这一本书脊有一点破损，封面有蜡笔的痕迹。这些污损根本不会影响这件物品的美和罕有性，这一点怎么强调都不过分。两万美元起拍。"

　　这本书卖了七万两千美元，略超过心理价位。扣除手续费和税金之后，刚好够支付A.J.动手术和第一轮放射治疗病人自付的部分。

　　甚至在从克里斯蒂拍卖行收到支票之后，A.J.对是否进行治疗还有疑虑。他仍然在想那笔钱用于玛雅上大学更好。"不，"玛雅说，"我聪明。我会申请到奖学金的。我会写一篇世界上最悲伤的入学文章，讲我怎么是个被单亲妈妈遗弃在书店的孤女，讲收养了我的养父怎样患了世界上最罕见的脑瘤，可是看看我吧，一名堂堂正正的社会成员。大家都吃这一套，爸爸。"

"你可真是厚脸皮啊，我的小书呆子。" A.J.笑他创造出来的这个怪物。

"我也有钱。"他的妻子坚持说。最根本的是，A.J.生命中重要的女人都想让他活下去，他预定了手术。

"坐在这里时，我不由自主会想到《迟暮花开》事实上全是胡编滥造。"阿米莉娅恨恨地说。她站起来走到窗前，"你想让百页窗拉起来还是放下？拉起来呢，你就有点自然光和对面儿童医院可爱的风景。放下来呢，你可以欣赏荧光灯下我惨白的肤色。随你。"

"拉起来吧，" A.J.说，"我想记着最好的你。"

"你记得弗里德曼写过你无法真正描写一间病房吧，写到当你所爱的人在里面住着时，一间病房会怎样让你痛苦得无法描写，诸如此类的废话？我们以前怎么会认为那样写得有诗意？被以前的我们恶心到了。在我人生的这个阶段，我是跟那些一开始就从来不想看那本书的人站在一起，我跟在封面放了花和那双脚的那位设计师站在一起。因为你知道吗？你完全能够描写一间病房。它是灰白色的。那幅画是你所见过的最难看的画，就好像是假日酒店不要的东西。一切闻着都像是有人在企图掩盖尿味。"

"你以前很喜欢《迟暮花开》，艾米。"

她还没有跟他说过利昂·弗里德曼的事。"可我不想在我四十几岁时，就活在这本书愚蠢的情节中。"

"你觉得我真的应该做这个手术吗？"

阿米莉娅翻翻眼珠子，"是的，我觉得你应该。首先，再有二十分钟就要做手术了，所以不管怎样，我们很可能拿不回我们的钱。第二，你已经剃了光头，你的样子像是个恐怖分子。我看不出现在打退堂鼓还有什么道理。"阿米莉娅说。

"为了大有可能是很糟糕的两年，花这钱真的值得吗？"他问阿米莉娅。

"值得。"她边说边抓过了他的手。

"我记得曾有一个女人告诉我情趣相投的重要性。我记得曾有个女人说她跟一位名副其实的美国英雄分手了，因为他们话不投机。那也可能发生在我们身上，你要知道。"A.J.说。

"那种情况完全不一样。"阿米莉娅坚持说。过了一秒，她叫了起来："操！"A.J.以为肯定出了什么严重的事，因为阿米莉娅从来不讲粗口。

"怎么了？"

"嗯，问题是，我很喜欢你的大脑。"

他笑她，她有点在哭。

"噢，别哭了，我不需要你的同情。"

"我不是为你哭，我在为我自己哭。你知道我花了多久才找到你？你知道我经历了多少次糟糕的约会？我不能——"她这时已经泣不成声了——"我不能再上婚恋网站了，真的不能。"

"'大鸟'——永远要往前看。"

"'大鸟'。这是怎么……？我们走到这一步，你不可以起外号！"

"你会遇到某个人的，我就遇到了。"

"混蛋。我喜欢你，我习惯了你，你是唯一，你这个混蛋。我不想再去认识新的人。"

他吻了她，接着她把手伸进他的病号服里，捏了一下他的裆部。"我很喜欢跟你做爱，"她说，"如果手术做完后你成了个植物人，我还能不能跟你做爱？"她问。

"当然可以。"A.J.说。

"你不会看低我？"

"不会。"他顿了一下，"我们谈着谈着拐到了这儿，我说不上来是不是感觉自在。"他说。

"你认识我四年，然后才约我出去。"

"没错。"

"我们认识的那天，你对我很差劲。"

"也没错。"

"我算是完蛋了。我怎么可能还会找别人呢？"

"你好像对我的大脑特别不关心。"

"你的大脑完蛋了。我们都知道。但是我怎么办呢？"

"可怜的艾米。"

"是啊，以前我是个书店老板的老婆，那就够可怜的。很

254

快，我就会是书店老板的寡妇。"

她吻遍他那个有毛病的脑袋上的每个地方。"我以前喜欢这个头脑，我现在也喜欢这个头脑！这是个非常好的头脑。"

"我也喜欢。"他说。

护工来把他推走。"我爱你。"她听天由命地耸耸肩，"我想留给你什么更聪明的话，但是我只知道那一句。"

苏醒后，他发现多少说来，他仍然能想起单词。他过了一阵子才找到，但是它们在那儿。

血。

止痛片。

呕吐。

桶。

痔疮。

腹泻。

水。

水泡。

尿布。

冰。

手术之后，他被送到医院的一幢单体侧楼里进行了为期一个月的放射治疗。他的免疫系统因为放射治疗而被削弱很多，不能接受探视。这是他有生以来最孤独的一段时间，比妮可去世后的那一段时间还要孤独。他希望自己能喝醉，但是他被辐射过的胃部不可能受得了。这是有玛雅之前和有阿米莉娅之前的生活。一个人无法自成孤岛，要么至少，一个人无法自成最理想的孤岛。

他没有呕吐或者在半睡半醒中烦躁时，会拿出电子阅读器，那是他的母亲去年送他的圣诞礼物。（护士认为电子阅读器比纸质书更卫生。"他们应该把那句印在包装盒上。"A.J.打趣道。）他发现自己无法保持清醒来读完一整部长篇小说，短篇小说要好一点。反正他一直更喜欢短篇小说。读书时，他发现想给玛雅新列一份短篇清单让她去读。她将会成为一名作家，他知道。他不是作家，但对这行有所了解，他想要确保自己能告诉她自己所了解的。"玛雅，长篇小说当然有迷人之处，但是在非诗体文字世界中，最雅致的当属短篇小说。掌握了怎样写短篇小说，你就掌握了整个世界。"就在他沉沉睡去之前，他这样想道。我应该把这写下来，他想。他伸手去拿笔，但是在他靠着休息的马桶附近哪儿都没有。

放射治疗结束时，肿瘤学家发现他的肿瘤既没有缩小，也没有长大。他给了A.J.一年时间。"你的说话能力和其他一切都很有可能会退化。"A.J.觉得医生的说话声音活泼得不合时宜。无所谓了，可以回家了，A.J.挺高兴的。

《书店老板》

1980/罗尔德·达尔

　　关于一位在让顾客花钱方面有一套非常规做法的书店老板的甜腻小文。在人物方面，这篇还是像达尔通常的作品那样，写了几位怪人。情节方面，转折出现得晚，不足以弥补这个短篇的缺点。实际上，《书店老板》不应该出现在这份单子上——反正它不属于达尔最出色的作品，当然绝不能跟《待宰的羔羊》相比——然而我把它列上了。我明知道它是平平之作，还把它列了上来，这如何解释？答案是这样：你的爸爸跟角色有共鸣，这一篇对我另有意义。这行做得越久（卖书，对，那当然，但也是谋生，希望这么说不会太伤感），我就越相信这一点是所有的意义所在：跟人沟通，我亲爱的小书呆子。只有沟通。

——A.J.F.

这很简单，他想，玛雅，他想说，我已全都琢磨出来了。

但是他的大脑不让他说。

你找不到的词，就去借。

我们读书而后知道自己并不孤单。我们读书，因为我们孤单；我们读书，然后就不孤单，我们并不孤单。

我的生活在这些书里，他想告诉她，读这些书吧，了解我的心。

我们并不完全是长篇小说。

他几乎就要想到一直在想的比喻。

我们并不完全是短篇小说。此时，他的生活似乎跟那最接近。

到了最后，我们是作品全集。

他已经读得够多的了，知道没有一部全集里的每个故事都是完美的。有些成功了，有些差点。幸运的话，会有一部出色之作。到最后，不管怎样，人们会记住那些出色之作，而对出色之作，他们也不会记得很久。

不，不会很久。

"爸爸。"玛雅说。

他尽量想听明白她在说什么。嘴唇动，还有声音，会是什么意思呢？

幸好她又说了一遍："爸爸。"

对，爸爸，我是爸爸，我成了爸爸。玛雅的父亲，玛雅的爸爸。不简单的词，不简单的小小的大词。不简单的词，不简单的世界！他在哭。他的心里如此充溢，却没有话语来释放。我知道话语有什么用，他想。话语让我们感觉得少一点。

"不，爸爸，请别这样。没事的。"

她搂住他。

阅读已经变得困难。他很努力的话，还能勉强读完一个短篇，但已经不可能再读长篇了。跟说话比起来，写字要容易一点，倒不是写字容易。他每天写一段，给玛雅的一段话，不算多，但他只能做到这样了。

他想告诉她一些很重要的事。

"痛吗？"她问。

不，他想。大脑没有痛觉，所以不疼。到头来，大脑失灵的过程是个奇怪的无痛过程，他觉得那应该更痛才对。

"你害怕吗？"她问。

不害怕死，他想，但是有点害怕我所处的这一阶段。每一天，我都少了一点。今天，我没有言语但有思想，明天，我将是没有思想的躯体。就这样发展下去。但是玛雅，你现在在这里，所以我很高兴也在这里，即使没有书和话语，即使没有我的大脑。你究竟怎样来说这个？究竟从何说起呢？

玛雅盯着他看，这时她也哭了起来。

"玛雅，"他说，"只有一个词是重要的。"他望着她，看她是否明白他的话。她皱着眉。他看得出自己并没有讲清。该死。他最近讲出来的话大多含糊不清。如果他想让别人听明白，最好把自己限于用一个单词来回答，但是有些事情一个单词解释不清楚。

他会再试试，他永远不会放弃尝试。"玛雅，我们会成为我们所爱的那样。是爱成就了我们。"

玛雅在摇头。"爸爸，对不起，我听不明白。"

"我们不是我们所收集的、得到的、所读的东西，只要我们还活着，我们就是爱，我们所爱的事物，我们所爱的人。所有这些，我认为真的会存活下去。"

她还在摇头。"我听不懂你的话，爸爸。我希望我能。你想让我找艾米吗？要么也许你可以打出来？"

他在冒汗。交谈不再是有趣的，以前曾经很容易。好吧，他想。如果必须用一个单词，那就必须用一个单词吧。

"爱？"他问。他祈祷自己说得对。

她皱起眉头，努心去辨读他的表情。"手套？"她问，"是你的手冷吗，爸爸？"

他点点头，她把他的手放在她手里。他的手本来冷，这时暖和了，他想好了今天说得够接近了。也许明天，他就能知道该怎么说了。

在书店老板的葬礼上，每个人的脑子都有同一个问题，那就是小岛书店将会何去何从。人们对他们的书店有感情，比A.J.费克里想到的还要深。是谁把《时间的皱折》①放到你十二岁的女儿指甲被咬短的手里，是谁卖给你Let's Go②系列当中的夏威夷旅行指南，是谁坚持说你品位挑剔的姑妈肯定会喜欢《云图》③？这些都是重要的。另外，他们喜欢小岛书店，尽管他们并非总是对这家书店特别忠实，尽管他们也有时购买电子书、在网上购书，他们喜欢一提起这个镇，就说小岛书店就在主要商业区的中央，是下了渡轮后去到的第二或者第三个地方。

在葬礼上，他们走到玛雅和阿米莉娅面前（当然是尊尊敬敬地）悄声说："A.J.是永远无法被代替的，可是你们会找别人来经营这家书店吧？"

阿米莉娅不知道该怎么办。她爱艾丽丝岛，爱小岛书店，但

---

① 美国青少年文学作家玛德琳·英格（Madeleine L'engle，1918-2007）的成名作。
② Let's Go系列旅行指南，是最省钱的旅行指南。这个系列的足迹已经遍布各大洲，每一个地方的省钱攻略都被参透、分享。它的最大优势是每年都在更新。
③ 英国作家大卫·米切尔（David Mitchell，1969- ）代表作品。

是她对经营书店没有经验。她一直在这一行的出版社里工作，她现在甚至更需要稳定的支票和医疗保险，因为她要对玛雅负责。她考虑让书店继续开着，星期一到星期五让别人开，但是这个计划不可行。来回的交通就受不了，真正应该做的是完全搬离这个小岛。在经过了一个星期的苦恼、失眠和思来想去之后，她决定关掉书店。书店——至少是开书店的这座房子和地皮——值不少钱。（妮可和A.J.好多年前就买了下来。）艾米莉娅很爱小岛书店，可是她没法开。有一个月左右，她努力想卖掉书店，但是没有买主。她把这座房子放到了市场上。到夏天结束时，小岛书店就会关门。

"一个时代的结束。"在本地的一家小餐馆吃鸡蛋时，兰比亚斯对伊斯梅说。这则消息让他伤透了心，但是不管怎样，他很快就要离开艾丽丝岛了。到明年春天，他就会当满二十五年警察，他已经存了很多钱，他想象自己买一条船在佛罗里达群岛那边生活，就像埃尔莫·伦纳德某本长篇中的退休警察那样。他一直在努力劝说伊斯梅跟他一起去，他觉得已经快说动她了。最近，她所提出的反对理由越来越少，尽管她是那种喜欢冬天的古怪的新英格兰人。

"我曾希望他们能找到别人来经营书店，但问题是，不管怎么样，没有了A.J.、玛雅和阿米莉娅，小岛书店就不是原来的小岛书店了，"兰比亚斯说，"不会有一样的感情。"

"没错，"伊斯梅回答道，"挺让人不舒服的。他们很可能会把它变成一家'Forever 21'。"

"什么是'Forever 21'？"

伊斯梅笑他："你怎么会不知道？你总在读的青少年小说中难道一次都没有提到吗？"

"青少年小说不是那样的。"

"是一家服装连锁店。事实上，那样我们会很幸运。他们很可能会把它改成一家银行。"她呷着她的咖啡。"要么一家食品杂货店。"

"也许开一家坚宝果汁店，"兰比亚斯说，"我喜欢坚宝果汁店。"

伊斯梅哭了起来。

那位侍者在这张桌前停下脚步，兰比亚斯示意她应该清理盘子。"我了解你的感觉，"兰比亚斯说，"我也不喜欢，伊西。你知道有一件事情很滑稽吗？在认识A.J.和开始去小岛书店之前，我从来不怎么读书。小时候，老师觉得我读书慢，所以我一直没有找到窍门。"

"你跟一个小孩说他不喜欢读书，他就会相信你的话。"伊斯梅说。

"英语主要得的都是C。A.J.收养了玛雅之后，我想找个借口进书店看看他们怎么样，所以一直他给什么我就读什么，然后我开始喜欢读书。"

伊斯梅哭得更厉害了一点。

"结果发现，我真的喜欢书店。你知道，我在工作中认识很多人。有很多人来过艾丽丝岛，特别是夏天时。我见过电影界的人来度假，我也见过音乐界和新闻界的人。但是图书业的人跟其他人都不一样，这是绅士淑女的行业。"

"没那么夸张。"伊斯梅说。

"我不知道，伊西。我跟你说。书店里吸引该来的人来，像A.J.和阿米莉娅那样的好人。我喜欢跟喜欢讨论书的人讨论书。我喜欢纸，我喜欢纸的手感，我喜欢书插在裤子后兜里的感觉。我还喜欢新书的味道。"

伊斯梅吻了他一下。"你是我所见过的最有趣的警察。"

"我担心艾丽丝岛如果没有书店会是什么样。"兰比亚斯说着喝完了咖啡。

"我也是。"

兰比亚斯身子倾过桌子，吻了她的脸颊。"嗨，我有个疯狂的想法。如果我和你不去佛罗里达，而是把那个地方接过来怎么样？"

"在这种经济环境下，那的确是个疯狂的想法。"伊斯梅说。

"是啊，"他说，"很可能是这样。"侍者问他们想不想点甜品，伊斯梅说她什么都不想要，但是兰比亚斯知道她总是会分吃一点他的。他要了一块樱桃馅饼，配两把叉子。

"可是，你知道，如果我们这么做又怎样？"兰比亚斯继续说，"我有存款，也很快能收到丰厚的退休金，你也是。A.J.说夏天来的人总是会买很多书。"

"夏天来的人现在有电子阅读器了。"伊斯梅说。

"确实。"兰比亚斯说道。他决定还是不谈这个话题了。

当他们馅饼吃到一半时，伊斯梅说："我们可以也开一个咖啡角，那样大概能有助于保本。"

"是啊，A.J.以前常常那么说。"

"另外，"伊斯梅说，"我们把地下室变成一个可以演戏的地方。那样的话，为作者办活动就不用就在书店的正中央举办了，甚至人们有时候也许可以租这个地方演戏或者开会。"

"你的戏剧背景对那会很有帮助。"兰比亚斯说。

"你确定要接手吗？我们并不是特别年轻了，"伊斯梅说，"说好的告别冬季呢？说好的佛罗里达呢？"

"我们可以等到老了再搬去那里。现在我们还不老，"兰比亚斯顿了一会儿说，"我这一辈子都在艾丽丝岛，这是我所了解的唯一一个地方。这里不错，我准备让它继续这样。没有书店的地方算不上是个地方，伊西。"

把书店卖给伊斯梅和兰比亚斯几年后，阿米莉娅决定离开奈特利出版社。玛雅很快就要高中毕业了，阿米莉娅也对频繁出差感到厌烦。她在缅因州的一个大型零售商那里找到一份图书采购的工作。她离开之前，就像她的前任哈维·罗兹以前所做的，阿米莉娅为她所有订货频繁的客户写了笔记。她把小岛书店留到了最后。

"小岛书店，"她写道，"老板：伊斯梅·帕里什（以前是学校教师）和尼可拉斯·兰比亚斯（以前是警长）。兰比亚斯是个了不起的销售，特别是在犯罪小说和青少年小说方面。帕里什——她以前负责学校里的戏剧俱乐部——可以指望她举办一流的作者活动。这家书店里有个咖啡角、一个舞台，网上销售的表现也很不错。所有这些，都建立在A.J.费克里所打下的基础上，这位前老板的品位倾向于文学类。这家书店里仍然有很多文学小说，但是他们不会进卖不动的书。我全心全意地爱着小岛书店。我不相信有上帝，我没有宗教信仰，但这家书店对我来说，是最接近我这辈子所知道的教堂的地方。这是个神圣的地方，有了这样的书店，我有这样的把握说，图书销售业还会继续存在很长一段时间。——阿米莉娅·洛曼"

　　阿米莉娅对最后几句感到不好意思，就把"他们不会进卖不动的书"后面的全删了。

　　"……他们不会进卖不动的书。"雅各布·加德纳最后读了一遍他的前任所写的笔记，然后关了手机屏幕，下了渡轮，步子迈得又大又坚定。雅各布二十七岁，有个非虚构写作硕士学位，这学位还算有点用。他不敢相信自己找到了这份工作。没错，薪水可以再高一点，但是他爱读书，一直爱读书，他相信书本挽救了他的生活。他甚至把C.S.刘易斯的一句名言文在手腕上。想想吧，居然成为那种谈论文学还有钱拿的那种人。他这样做不要钱都行，倒不是他想让他的出版人知道这一点。他需要钱，波士顿的生活费用不低，他只是做这份日间的工作来支持他在热情做着的事情：写一部同性恋歌舞演员的口述史。但这并没有改变雅各布·加德纳绝对是一位信徒的事实，他甚至走路都像是有使命在身的，有可能被人们误以为是一位传教士。事实上，他从小就是摩门教徒，但那是另外一个故事了。

来小岛书店是雅各布首次上门推销，他迫不及待想赶到店里。他迫不及待想告诉他们他在自己的奈特利出版社大手提袋里装着的了不起的书。那个袋子肯定都快五十磅重了，但是雅各布坚持锻炼身体，几乎没什么感觉。奈特利出版社今年的书单特别有分量，他有把握自己的工作会很容易。读者别无选择，只能爱上这些书。那位聘用了他的和气女人建议他从小岛书店开始。那位老板很喜欢犯罪文学小说，呃？好吧，书单上雅各布最喜欢的是一本处女作，内容是关于一个失踪的处于青春期的阿米什女孩。在雅各布看来，对于任何一个真正喜欢犯罪文学小说的人来说，这是必读书。

当雅各布走过那座紫色小屋的门槛时，风铃奏出熟悉的乐音，一个沙哑但并非不友好的声音说："欢迎光临。"

雅各布走过老旧的过道，把手伸向梯子上的一位中年人："兰比亚斯先生，我这儿有本书可真是太适合您了！"

致 谢

没有独角兽，也没有艾丽丝岛，A.J.费克里的阅读品位也并不总是等同于我的。

兰比亚斯和费克里第一任妻子有一句话变着说了很多遍："没有书店的小镇算不上个小镇。"可以肯定，他们都读过尼尔·盖曼①的《美国众神》。

凯西·波瑞斯编辑本书时不吝赐教，意见精当，无形之中改变了我整个人生。这就是优秀编辑的力量。感谢阿尔冈昆的所有人，尤其是克雷格·波普拉尔斯、埃玛·博耶、安妮·温斯洛、布伦森·胡尔、德布拉·林、洛朗·莫斯利、伊丽莎白·沙尔拉特、艾娜·斯特恩和裘德·格兰特。

我的经纪人道格拉斯·斯图尔特是个扑克牌高手，偶尔也会变个魔术。这些技巧在描写A.J.费克里的时候派上了用场。同样感谢他的同事玛德琳·克拉克、柯尔斯顿·哈茨，尤其感谢西尔

---

① 尼尔·盖曼（Neil Gaiman，1960–），移居美国的著名英国作家，斯蒂芬·金称赞他是一个"装满了故事的宝库"。

维亚·莫尔纳。还由于许多原因，同样感激克莱尔·史密斯、塔姆辛·贝里曼、让·费韦尔、斯图尔特·杰瓦格、安格斯·基利克、金·海兰、安贾莉·辛格、卡洛林·麦克勒和里奇·格林。

我的父亲，理查德·泽文，为我买了第一本有章节的图书《大森林里的小木屋》[①]；因为我喜欢这本书，后来父亲又买了约千本书，对我而言是一份快乐的礼物。我的母亲，埃兰·泽文，以前常利用工作时的午休时间开车带我去书店，所以我最喜欢的作者新书第一天开售，我便能入手。外公迈耶·萨斯曼和外婆阿黛尔·萨斯曼几乎每次见面都会送书给我。我读十一年级的时候，英语老师朱迪思·拜纳在我可塑性极强的年龄，介绍我读当代虚构文学。二十年来的大部分时间，汉斯·卡诺萨一直是我的第一位读者，也是最有耐心的读者。雅尼纳·奥马利、劳伦·魏因和乔纳森·伯纳姆为我编辑了之前的七本书。总之，这些事、这些人大概就是培养一位作家的秘方。

马克·盖茨是法勒–斯特劳斯和吉鲁出版社的销售代表，热爱结交朋友，现在已离我们而去，但在我2007年图书巡展的时候，他开车带我走遍了芝加哥。也许就在那时我开始了本书的构思。几年后，瓦妮莎·克罗宁亲切地回答了我关于销售电访和书目时间的问题。当然，本书若有错误，责任仍在我。

为免疏忽，我还要感谢许多书商、作家陪护、图书馆员、教

[①] 美国作家劳拉·英格斯·怀德（Laura Ingalls Wilder，1867–1957）的小木屋系列作品的第一部。

师、作家、图书节志愿者和各位出版业同仁，自我十年前出版第一部小说以来，他们举办了很多活动，与我交谈。小岛书店的出现正是基于这些交流。

最后，冒昧描写了罗得岛朴茨茅斯的格林动物造型园艺公园。有一点千真万确：公园冬季闭园，但在夏天，你真的能在那里找到独角兽。

马上扫描读客图书二维码，并回复"岛上书店"，就可以读到岛上书店老板A.J.费克里的私人书单，并第一时间抢先试读每月新书。更多有趣的赠书活动等你来参加！

全球文化，尽收眼底；顶级经典，尽入囊中！

请锁定"读客全球顶级畅销小说文库"。

我们不全是长篇小说，也不全是短篇故事

最后的最后，我们成为一部人生作品集

图书在版编目（CIP）数据

　　岛上书店 / (美) 泽文（Zevin,G.）著；孙仲旭，
李玉瑶译 . -- 南京 : 江苏凤凰文艺出版社，2015
　　（读客全球顶级畅销小说文库）
　　书名原文 : The storied life of A.J.Fikry
　　ISBN 978-7-5399-7181-0

　Ⅰ . ①岛… Ⅱ . ①泽… ②孙… ③李… Ⅲ . ①长篇小
说—美国—现代 Ⅳ . ① I712.45

　　中国版本图书馆 CIP 数据核字 (2015) 第 048094 号

THE STORIED LIFE OF A.J.FIKRY by Gabrielle Zevin
Copyright © 2014 by Gabrielle Zevin
Published in agreement with Sterling Lord Literistic, through The Grayhawk Agency.
Simplified Chinese translation copyright 2015 by Shanghai Dook Publishing Co., Ltd.
All rights reserved.

中文版权 ©2015 上海读客图书有限公司
经授权，上海读客图书有限公司拥有本书的中文（简体）版权
图字 : 10-2015-009 号

书　　　名　岛上书店

出　品　人　华　楠
著　　　者　（美）泽文 (Zevin,G.)
译　　　者　孙仲旭　李玉瑶
责 任 编 辑　丁小卉　姚　丽
特 约 编 辑　朱亦红　孟汇一
责 任 监 制　刘　巍　江伟明
策　　　划　读客图书
版　　　权　读客图书
封 面 设 计　读客图书　021-33608311
出 版 发 行　凤凰出版传媒股份有限公司
　　　　　　江苏凤凰文艺出版社
出版社地址　南京市中央路 165 号，邮编 : 210009
出版社网址　http://www.jswenyi.com
印　　　刷　北京正合鼎业印刷技术有限公司
开　　　本　890mm x 1270mm 1/32
印　　　张　9
字　　　数　167 千
版　　　次　2015 年 5 月第 1 版　2015 年 6 月第 2 次印刷
标 准 书 号　ISBN 978-7-5399-7181-0
定　　　价　35.00 元

如有印刷、装订质量问题，请致电 010-85866447（免费更换，邮寄到付）

版权所有，侵权必究